D0481403

Widows' Words

Widows' Words

WOMEN WRITE ON THE EXPERIENCE OF GRIEF, THE FIRST YEAR, THE LONG HAUL, AND EVERYTHING IN BETWEEN

Edited by Nan Bauer-Maglin

RUTGERS UNIVERSITY PRESS
New Brunswick, Camden, and Newark, New Jersey, and London

Library of Congress Cataloging-in-Publication Data

Names: Maglin, Nan Bauer, editor.
Title: Widows' words : women write on the experience of grief, the first year, the long haul, and everything in between / edited by Nan Bauer-Maglin.
Description: New Brunswick, New Jersey : Rutgers University Press, [2019] | Includes bibliographical references.
Identifiers: LCCN 2018031137 | ISBN 9780813599533 (cloth: alk. paper)
Subjects: LCSH: Widows. | Widows in literature. | Grief. | Bereavement.
Classification: LCC HQ1058 .W535 2019 | DDC 306.88/3—dc23
LC record available at https://lccn.loc.gov/2018031137

A British Cataloging-in-Publication record for this book is available from the British Library.

"Eye Triptych" artwork on Parts II, III, and IV by Tara Sabharwal.

⊜ The paper used in this publication meets the requirements of the American National Standard for Information Sciences—Permanence of Paper for Printed Library Materials, ANSI Z39.48-1992.

www.rutgersuniversitypress.org

Manufactured in the United States of America

In memory of Jon-Christian Suggs

CONTENTS

Widows' Words

Introduction

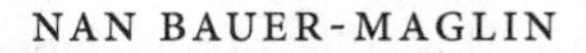

NAN BAUER-MAGLIN

You think that their
dying is the worst
thing that could happen.
Then they stay dead.

—**Donald Hall**, excerpt from "Distressed Haiku"*

This book is a collection of writings by and about widows, conceived out of personal loss and sadness. Death is at its center, along with grief, sorrow, and despair; but there is also energy, strength, hope, and even joy. The book spans perspectives—before grieving, the first year, the American way of grieving, experiencing no grief at all. There are different stories—a woman loses her female partner; a daughter lives with her mother's widowhood; a young widow faces parenthood alone. Widows try to find succor in religion, in bereavement groups, in creative activities; they build resilience and find pleasure.

Great thanks to Yael Ravin for reading and editing this introduction over and over again.

* Donald Hall, *The Painted Bed* (Boston: A Mariner Book, Houghton Mifflin Company, 2003), 31.

Widowhood is becoming more prevalent in the United States, as the size of the older population continues to grow.* And widows far outnumber widowers, not surprisingly, as women outlive men by about five years.† In 2016, for example, it was estimated that about 1,444,000 married people lost their spouse; 998,000 of them women.‡ According to the U.S. Census Bureau, there were over three million widowed men but close to twelve million widowed women in 2016.§ *Widows' Words* is a collection of writings by forty-three widows, creating a record of some of these voices.

The forty-three women who contributed to this collection vary in their circumstances—they differ in age, education, family, religion, and when in their life they lost their partner. Generally, though, these women in *Widows' Words* are more similar than different. All describe a private loss due to sickness or accident, not as a result of personal issues, such as suicide or drug addiction, nor because of a larger political, social, or natural calamity. Most are heterosexual (although three write about the loss of female partners, and one identifies as bisexual). This collection includes mostly white, middle-class women, although there are women of other races and a mix of ethnicities. Most of the contributors live in the United States, predominantly in New York State, but thirteen other states are represented, as well as England and Canada.

* The 2010 Census indicated that the older population (sixty-five and up) grew faster than any other since the previous census. In 2010 it was about 13 percent of the total. In 2017 it is estimated to be 15.63 percent. https://www.census.gov/newsroom/releases/archives/2010_census/cb11-cn192.html; https://en.wikipedia.org/wiki/Demography_of_the_United_States.

† https://www.cdc.gov/nchs/data/databriefs/db293.pdf. For males, life expectancy changed from 76.3 in 2015 to 76.1 in 2016—a decrease of 2.4 months. For females, life expectancy remained the same at 81.1.

‡ "Marriages Ending in Widowhood in the Last Year by Sex by Marital Status for the Population 15 Years and Over," U.S. Census Bureau, 2012–2016 American Community Survey 5-Year Estimates, https://factfinder.census.gov/faces/tableservices/jsf/pages/productview.xhtml?pid=ACS_16_5YR_B12502&prodType=table. It should be noted that this estimate excludes nonmarried heterosexual couples as well as gay and lesbian couples. On many widowhood sites and in many books, it is stated that every year, 800,000 people in the United States lose their partners; most of the newly widowed—700,000 of them—are women. This repeated number seems to be from 1999 and is inconsistent with the census numbers quoted above in the text; see, for example, http://peaceloveandgrief.com/?tag=widow-statistics.

§ 2012–2016 American Community Survey 5-Year Estimates, https://factfinder.census.gov/faces/tableservices/jsf/pages/productview.xhtml?pid=ACS_16_5YR_B12002&prodType=table. Of the 11,871,137 widows estimated in 2016, 1,580 are 15–17 years old; 1,655 are 18–19; 8,678 are 20–24; 23,013 are 25–29; 43,524 are 30–34; 73,181 are 35–39; 120,855 are 40–44; 224,616 are 45–49; 396,127 are 50–54; 663,323 are 55–59; 933,492 are 60–64; 2,904,700 are 65–74; 3,555,383 are 74–84; and 2,921,010 are 85 years and older.

Statistics indicate that a third of women who become widowed are younger than sixty, and half of all widows lose their partner by age sixty-five.* According to census data, U.S. widows have been alone, on average, for fourteen years, and, as the population lives longer, widows will be alone for more years. The ages of the widows writing here reflect this span—a few lost their partners in their twenties; most did so in their fifties and later.†

For many women around the world, widowhood and age often mean increased poverty. Out of an estimated 258 million widows, 15 percent live in poverty; and the number is even higher (25 percent) among blacks and Latinas. For women of ethnic and racial minorities, who may be less closely tied to the formal economy of wages and pensions, the financial strain of long-term widowhood can be more pronounced.‡ According to the U.S. Social Security Administration, women widowed at younger ages are at greater risk for economic hardship after widowhood, and their situation

* "Widowhood: Why Women Need to Talk about This Issue," http://www.wiserwomen.org/index.php?id=274.

† In terms of age, six of the writers, including myself, experienced the death of their partner in their seventies. One lost her husband when she was eighty-three. Three writers report on deaths of their partners while they were in their twenties, three while in their thirties, and four in their forties. Fourteen lost partners while in their fifties (including the cover artist) and nine in their sixties. I do not have the age of one of the widows, and one writer is writing about her mother's widowhood. In 2011, the U.S. Census Bureau reported that the median age of widowhood across all ethnicities was 59.4 for a first marriage and 60.3 for a second marriage. Some sites give 55 as the average age of loss. See, for example, https://www.huffingtonpost.com/entry/widow-myths-lies-other-fallacies_us_58e794aee4b06f8c18beead8.

‡ The countries with the highest number of widows in 2010 were China, with 43 million; India, with 42.4 million; the United States, with 13.6 million; Indonesia, with 9.4 million; Japan, with 7.4 million; Russia, with 7.1 million; Brazil, with 5.6 million; Germany, with 5.1 million; and Bangladesh and Vietnam, with about 4.7 million each. From "World Widow's Report," https://www.theguardian.com/commentisfree/2015/jun/21/international-widows-day-poverty-social-exclusion and "The Loomba Foundation's World Widow Report."

Of the 258 million widows across the world, more than 115 million live in poverty. "37 percent of single mothers are living in poverty. With widows, it's 15 percent—25 percent if you're black or Latina." From "World Widow's Report," The Loomba Foundation (theloombafoundation.org), as quoted by Sheryl Sandberg and Adam Grant, *Option B: Facing Adversity, Building Resilience, and Finding Joy* (London: WH Allen, 2017), 26. See also http://globalfundforwidows.org/epidemic-of-widowhood/; http://www.widowsforpeace.org/un-women-statement-international-widows-day-23-june/.

Beverly Rosa Williams, Patricia Sawyer, and Richard M. Allman, "Wearing the Garment of Widowhood: Variations in Time since Spousal Loss among Community-Dwelling Older Adults," *Journal of Women Aging*, 24, no. 2 (2012): 126–139; https://www.ncbi.nlm.nih.gov/pmc/articles/PMC3601770/.

deteriorates with the duration of widowhood. In addition, "poor women are more likely to become widowed at a young age, because of the relationship between mortality and socioeconomic status."* In this collection, by contrast, only a few indicate money as an issue.

When I called for contributions, I did not get much diversity in terms of class, race, and ethnicity. I worked hard to expand the voices in the book, but it is not surprising that most somewhat resemble my own demographics. Still, I would like for more diverse voices to be heard, and I believe that the sites and organizations that represent widows can help achieve that. I hope that many other widows will add to the stories of the forty-three in this book, by sharing their own story with one another—within their local writing groups, religious groups, support groups, or online—by writing their own story or being interviewed by a friend.†

Join with the women in *Widows' Words* and add your voice.

There are many possibilities for organizing or categorizing the experience of widowhood in a collection like this, and they all inevitably intersect and overlap. For this book, I chose a chronological order—starting in Part I with women who are about to become widows, followed by women who have recently become widows in Part II, and then those with long-time experience in Part III. In Part IV, I grouped contributions that were either unique takes on the subject or that dig deeper into a specific aspect. For the Part V, *Widows' Words* concludes with a piece that addresses "all the other widows in the world—past, present, and future."

The voices are not confined within their section; rather, they cross over, talking to and echoing each other. Readers may want to follow the widow's story from before the death through long-term widowhood, or they may want to dip in and out of the sections following common threads, such as younger widows; themes like grief or resilience; or particular issues, such as what to do with the deceased person's belongings.

This collection is not meant as a self-help book, but I believe that these stories will help the reader navigate the painful path of widowhood, providing empathy and instilling hope.

* Purvi Sevak, David R. Weir, and Robert J. Willis, "PERSPECTIVES: The Economic Consequences of a Husband's Death: Evidence from HRS and AHEAD," *Social Security Bulletin*, 65, no. 3 (2003/2004), https://www.ssa.gov/policy/docs/ssb/v65n3/v65n3p31.html.

† Searching for widow's groups online returns 1,910,00 such groups. https://www.google.com/search?q=widows+groups&rlz=1C1CHBF_enUS738US739&oq=wiows+groups&aqs=chrome.1.69i57j0l5.6563j0j7&sourceid=chrome&ie=UTF-8). There are 176,000 widow bereavement support groups listed: https://www.google.com/search?q=widow+bereavement+support+groups&rlz=1C1CHBF_enUS738US739&oq=widow+bereavement&aqs=chrome.0.0j69i57j0l4.14492j0j7&sourceid=chrome&ie=UTF-8).

I. Prologue: Expectant Widows

The first six pieces describe coming up on a partner's death—either abruptly or over an extended period. Dread and approaching grief echo through these pieces as does a kind of energy that crises often evoke. To think, write, and read about the loss of a partner is distressing for most people. Of all the pieces in *Widows' Words*, these six might be the most affecting.

This section could be represented by a description in the first pages of *A Widow's Story* by Joyce Carol Oates: "A wife who dreaded any thought of becoming a *widow*."* Or as Gerda Lerner describes in *A Death of One's Own*, the dying partner and the nondying partner begin to go down separate emotional and physical paths: "We battled on separate battlefields, each very much alone. Mine to prepare myself for his death, to help him die a good death. His: to live."† And when the partner dies, the widow begins a new journey.

Each story is unique. Alice Goode-Elman chronicles the last four months of her husband's life after he is diagnosed with heart disease and inoperable lung cancer. Kelli Dunham describes a conscious joint decision to assist Heather, her partner, who has ovarian cancer, in dying. Penelope Dugan describes the fifteen-month ordeal after Ingie, her partner, is diagnosed with a brain tumor. Melanie K. Finney does things together with her husband, diagnosed with pancreatic cancer, to help them process his upcoming death. In contrast, I had no time to say goodbye. My own story is about being deserted by my husband, twice, first for a young woman and then, fifteen years later, due to an unexpected diagnosis of cancer.

Ellen Schrecker provides a bridge from this section to the next stage, describing the stressful six-year deterioration of her husband and, reluctantly, toward the end, rehearsing the expectant first days of her role as widow: "the funeral home, the brain donation, the notice in the *New York Times*, even the catering for sitting shiva when people come over to the house after the funeral."

II. Recent Widows

Immediately after the loss, there is shock. My journal documents the first half-year, describing what many widows may experience, such as confusion over the use of pronouns and identity issues.

Grief is the most dominant aspect of a new widow's life, and, naturally, many of the pieces in this section describe grief. In an interview by Maxine

* Joyce Carol Oates, *A Widow's Story* (New York: Ecco, 2012), 8.

† Gerda Lerner, *A Death of One's Own* (Madison: University of Wisconsin Press, 1985), 49.

Marshall, Raquel Ramkhelawan describes the unbearable pain she experienced on the death of her husband of twenty-one years. Having gone through the first year, Lauren Vanett is disappointed when grief washes over her even more intensely in the second year. The cloak of love and support now feels threadbare. Alice Derry is comforted by the writing of C. S. Lewis on his grief over his wife's death. Michele Neff Hernandez, losing her husband at age thirty-five, knew no one with a similar experience who could tell her how long the searing pain in her chest would last.

Many of the women use abundant metaphors to describe the early times of widowhood: Christine Silverstein (in Part V) talks about facing death as entering a third world country. Hernandez describes grief as an ambivalent friend. The images by Tara Sabharwal throughout the book provide visual metaphors for her grief following her husband's unexpected death.

While grief is still the dominant emotion, women take small and big steps to deal with loss. Elisa Clark Wadham explores what to do with wedding rings. Other material belongings need to be taken care of. Deborah E. Kaplan sorts through her husband's files, which hold affective power over her. P. C. Moorehead plants and nurtures a garden, finding comfort there, as an almost sacred place. Mimi Schwartz describes her reluctance to participate in formal and public forms of remembrance, and yet she does.

In a very honest account, Anne Bernays chronicles a two-sided experience: grief but also pleasure in her new freedom from worry about her husband's health and safety.

III. Long-Time Widows

As time goes on, widows experience a struggle to define themselves after the death of a partner. What label to use? Edie Butler wonders if she can even claim the title of "widow" as she was never officially married to her partner. What does home mean now? How do you construct a life on your own? Both Sonia Jaffe Robbins and Barbara E. Marwell struggle with these questions after long-term relationships. Debby Mayer describes this struggle in a list of ten "scary things" she did after her husband died. Elsewhere the topic of taking up work is discussed—is work a distraction from pain, a comfort or a discomfort?

How much presence to accord to the partner's work and possessions is another common theme. Roni Sherman Ramos questions whether to invest her time in a health clinic she and her husband started together. Doris Friedensohn, who was married to an artist, chooses to dedicate some of her time to writing about and promoting her husband's work. It took years for Nancy H. Womack to clear her husband's office. As Deborah E. Kaplan says in Part II, a partner's things are "suffused with so much personal meaning." They stand in for the person who is lost; giving them away has emotional implications.

Grief persists over the years. This is especially the case if the environment stifles the grief process, as in the case of Maggie Madagame, who was widowed in a rural, conservative, Polish-Catholic, midwestern community, where she didn't feel she belonged. But for others too, it is an aspect of their life that they continue to experience. In her poetry, Joan Michelson has intermittently returned to the subjects of loss, her husband, and the eclipse of time for grief over the twenty years since his death. While diminished over the years, grief keeps circling back, taking many forms, sometimes becoming a source for creativity.

IV. Unique Takes or Digging Deeper

Five women—Tracy Milcendeau, Merle Froschl, Andrea Hirshman, Molly McEneny, and Heather Slawecki—compare their experiences along several dimensions central to the experience of widowhood, such as the first year, the role of work, and relations to friends and family—and note how the different times in their lives in which their loss occurred (early twenties to early sixties) impacted the particular journey each went through.

The experience of a young widow is recounted by Kathleen Fordyce, who lost her husband when she was twenty-six and a mother to a two-year-old. Patricia Life sheds light on a similar situation, from a daughter's point of view, watching her mother struggle to support her sister and herself in the 1950s and realizing what a "domino-chain" effect his death had on their lives.

The experience of a double loss is described by Nancy Shamban, who loses her partner to dementia over a ten-year period, and then to death. Susanne Braham writes about losing her husband after thirty years of marriage and then dealing with her own significant hearing loss.

Religious beliefs and cultural practices are a focus of several writers (in this and other sections of the book). Alice Radosh, a nonbeliever, asks what gives one strength to face the death of a spouse, without religion or a belief system that promises an afterlife. Madagame chooses to separate herself from her family's religion. Others (like Ramkhelawan, Schwartz, Mayer, and Life's mother) find support in specific beliefs and practices. And others deal with somewhat conflicting beliefs and practices—Parvin Hajizadeh asks what happens when one faces death away from the culture one was raised in, as she longs to express herself in the Iranian way. Jean Y. Leung straddles two different mourning traditions: her own, Chinese Lutheran, and that of her husband, who was a South African Jew.

A unique perspective on cultural expectations is voiced by Joan Gussow, who shocked many when she declared that she did not feel sad upon the death of her husband. In spite of being judged by others, she reminds us that grief need not continue to dominate, need not always take center stage. Kathryn Temple, likewise, observes that the widow will be scrutinized for her feelings—is she sad and distraught? Enough, or too much? She mentions the many things "they" do not tell "you"—the widow; for example, about feeling anxious, angry, not alive; about having visions; about how death does not provide immunity, and how every joy will be mixed.

Finally, two contributors suggest practices for cultivating resilience. Carrie L. West advocates action, declaring that "resilience is something you *do* rather than something that you *are*," and Lise Menn counsels widows to engage in the writing process to find relief.

Part V. Epilogue

Christine Silverstein ends the volume as she contemplates the vow "until death do us part." She notes that we do not give that vow a second thought; we put death out of mind. It is like "a third world country with a name we can't pronounce," but it is a country that everyone in this volume has been catapulted into.

Some topics are barely discussed in this collection. Of the losses written about, the loss of sexual intimacy, a grief that Alice Radosh labels as sexual bereavement, is not voiced,* except, perhaps, for Braham, who mentions an affair with a much younger man as "my addictive escape from the pain of loss." Similarly, no one except for Ramkhelawan mentions survivor's guilt.†

Other aspects of widowhood are discussed by several contributors and recur across the sections. Several women discuss friends and family. Some, like Dugan and Dunham, are grateful for the help and support through the dying process and in the days and years after the death, with everything from onerous paperwork to invitations for dinner. In contrast, Shamban counts the number of friends who disappear as her partner descends into dementia. The two younger widows in "Widow-to-Widow" found that being around certain friends (couples, friends having children) was difficult to bear.

* In "What Is 'Sexual Bereavement?'" Alice Radosh writes, "Gone was the appreciation and understanding of bodies that had aged together, the decades of shared humor and pillow talk that were intertwined with sexual enjoyment" (http://modernloss.com/what-is-sexual-bereavement/. October 13, 2017).

† "Survivor's guilt is a thief of joy—yet another secondary loss from death." *Option B*, 96–99.

The writers share a lot emotionally. Most seemed to have had a positive relationship, although a few do not shy away from describing difficult relationships or occasional difficult times within relationships as, for example, "when both of us behaved less well than we should have" (Wadham) or when there were some moments of "terrible disagreements, the shouting arguments which often tore us apart" (Derry). For Butler and her daughters, in those last days before her partner died, there were some "sweet moments." While "fleeting," they were moments of connection.

A few experience hard times financially (such as Life's mother and Madagame); Mayer invokes the widow's specter of scarcity; whereas Robbins feels lucky in a "first-world" kind of a way with sufficient economic stability. Nonetheless, with the death of her husband, she is "disoriented," "unbalanced." Financial needs require some women to return to work as soon as they can, but the question of when to return to work after the death of a partner, even if there is no financial need, is a topic that brings up differing viewpoints among the five women in "Widow-to-Widow." And, when one returns, common pitfalls that widows might experience in the workplace, such as lack of concentration or awkward colleagues, are evident.

Several women describe what they felt when they took a break from sadness. Slawecki, a young widow, feels judged when she finds a new partner. West recalls an incident when she felt "relief and then guilt" upon laughing at a story recalled during her husband's funeral. Some are relieved at their partner's death because the suffering is over, mainly for the dying but also for the caretaker. Butler admits she does not feel the expected "howling, devastating" grief; Bernays has a sense of new freedoms; and Gussow finds herself skipping down the sidewalk two weeks after her husband's death. These women learn to ignore people who judge their behavior.

A number have re-created themselves in new ways, finding new interests in gardening, painting, writing, or with new partners, although Marwell asks whether there can be another after a loving, long-term relationship. In fact, as an older person, does one even want another relationship?

Many have pushed beyond grief—or while still acknowledging grief, found a way to move outside it, through making changes, big and small—moving out of a shared home, taking off the wedding ring, disposing of the partner's clothes and papers, or going to the movies alone—all common experiences for widows, seeking as Fordyce puts it, a way to create a "clean slate." Mayer declares when she sells the house she and her husband shared for eighteen years: "If moving forward is a necessary betrayal, well, my solo exploration skills were honed."

Most (if only by writing for this book) demonstrate resiliency as in West's list. They have made, as is said, lemonade out of lemons (Menn), or as Moorehead puts it, by planting and tending to a garden in honor of her husband, mourning gradually turned into morning. From her grief, Sabharwal painted: "Gradually painting led to acceptance and healing." Of particular interest is Hernandez, who created Soaring Spirts International,* a community of and for widowed people, which changed her life and which she hopes will change others.

While this book records widows' words about the loss of their partners, their grief echoes that of other kinds of losses, described elsewhere. Kathryn Schulz, in the *New Yorker*, describes the emptiness upon the death of her father: "Grieving him is like holding one of those homemade tin-can telephones with no tin can on the other end of the string. His absence is total; where there was him, there is nothing."† With the death of his wife, Roger Angell, in the *New Yorker* as well, unwillingly goes on with his life, a life clogged with everyday details:

> What the dead don't know piles up, though we don't notice it at first. They don't know how we're getting along without them, of course, dealing with the hours and days that now accrue so quickly, and, unless they divined this somehow in advance, they don't know that we don't want this inexorable onslaught of breakfasts and phone calls and going to the bank, all this stepping along, because we don't want anything extraneous to get in the way of what we feel about them or the ways we want to hold them in mind. But they're in a hurry, too, or so it seems. Because nothing is happening with them, they are flying away, over that wall, while we are still chained and handcuffed to the weather and the iPhone, to the hurricane and the election and to the couple that's recently moved in downstairs, in Apartment 2-S, with a young daughter and a new baby girl, and we're flying off in the opposite direction at a million miles an hour. It would take many days now, just to fill Carol in.‡

Finally, in my research for this book, I found two descriptions that achingly capture the absences felt by the widows writing in this book: Patti Smith's plaintive plea to her dead husband Fred (in a book that is not at all about him) is set off while watching a movie on a plane trip. An actor

* Soaring Spirits International is a nonprofit organization offering peer support, events, groups and online programs for widowed people everywhere, http://www.soaringspirits.org/.

† Kathryn Schulz, "Losing Streak: Reflections on Two Seasons of Loss," *New Yorker* (February 13 and 20, 2017), 74. (Also titled "When Things Go Missing: . . .")

‡ Roger Angell, "Over the Wall: A Change of Plan," *New Yorker* (November 19, 2012), http://www.newyorker.com/magazine/2012/11/19/over-the-wall.

reminds her "so much of Fred that I watched it twice. Midflight I began to weep. Just come back, I was thinking. You've been gone long enough. Just come back. I will stop traveling; I will wash your clothes."* For those who have lost a partner, solitude overwhelms; what was once a dialogue has become a monologue, and we yearn for the dialogue that was the fabric of our lives. Elizabeth Alexander, who lost her husband when she was fifty, calls out: "I lost my husband. Where is he? I often wonder. As I set out on some small adventure, some new place, somewhere he does not know, I think, I must call him, think, I must tell him, think, . . ."†

While grief over the death of a partner is overwhelming, I have found that writing and reading about it has helped me.‡ The writing assignments

* *M Train* (New York: Vintage Books, 2016), 171.

† Elizabeth Alexander, *The Light of the World* (New York: Grand Central Publishing, 2016), 41.

‡ In terms of reading, there is so much out there to read and listen to on the death of a partner, from articles to books to podcasts and blogs, so I will just mention a very few. There are many memoirs recording a solitary author's loss, such as Alexander's *The Light of the World*, Joan Didion's *The Year of Magical Thinking* (New York: Alfred A. Knopf, 2005), and Sandra Gilbert's *Wrongful Death: A Memoir* (New York: W. W. Norton & Company, 1995). And there are many useful how-to books, giving the widow advice on how to deal with grief, especially in that hard first year, such as *Seven Choices: Finding Daylight After Loss Shatters Your World* by Elizabeth Harper Neeld (New York: Grand Central Publishing, 2003) or *Healing a Spouse's Grieving Heart:100 Practical Ideas after Your Husband or Wife Dies* by Alan D. Wolfelt (Chicago: Companion Press, 2003).

In the literary area, two novels I particularly like are *Praisesong for the Widow* by Paule Marshall (New York: G. P. Putnam's Sons, 1983) and *The Life-Writer* by David Constantine (Windsor, ON: Biblioasis, 2016). Among many short stories, see Bharati Mukjherjee's "The Management of Grief" in *The Middleman and Other Stories* (New York: Grove Press, 1988). For poetry see, for example, Jane Mayhall's *Sleeping Late on Judgment Day* (New York: Alfred A. Knopf, 2004). See also *The Widows' Handbook: Poetic Reflections on Grief and Survival*, edited by Jaqueline Lapidus and Lise Menn (Kent, OH: Kent State University Press, 2014). *The Art of Death: Writing the Final Story* by Edwidge Danticat (Minneapolis, MN: Graywolf Press, 2017) is an overview of literature on death plus Danticat's story of the death of her mother.

The subject is regularly covered in newspapers and magazines, for example, www.huffingtonpost.com/topic/widowhood. Sheryl Sandberg and Elizabeth Alexander "On Love, Loss and What Comes Next," *New York Times* May 14, 2017, Sunday Styles, and on that same date in the Metropolitan section, the humorous but serious question was posed: "When is it O.K. to Hit on the Widower?" Sandberg is getting a lot of coverage for her book with Adam Grant: *Option B: Facing Adversity, Building Resilience, and Finding Joy* (London: WH Allen, 2017). Note that Sheryl Sandberg in *Option B* takes umbrage with the titles of what she calls "grief books": to her they are negative downers. She writes, "all the grief books had dreadful titles: *Death Is of Vital Importance* or *Say Yes to It*" (8).

On the podcast "Death, Sex, & Money," I was interviewed about a breakup with my husband and then his death after our reunion of 13 years (https://www.wnycstudios.org/story/cut-loose-breakups-death-sex-money/). "What Grief Looks Like" narrates the at my bereavement group (funded by Medicare), were helpful: thanking the partner, telling the partner what has happened since his or her death, imagining what the deceased might want to tell you, listing positive and negative adjectives about the relationship.* Menn also counsels: “Writing about grief—what it’s like, how one lives with the unbearable—is, despite everything, lemonade: it’s doing something potentially useful with that overwhelming bleakness that has sucked all the joy out of your life.”† And it’s been noted by others as well—Alexander said, “my husband’s death ravaged me”; so, for her, writing became a “lifeboat”‡ as it did for Edwidge Danticat who has suffered many family losses. “We write about death to make sense of our losses, to become less haunted, to turn ghosts into words, to transform an absence into language.”§ In a review article, Judith Newman refers to Patrick O’Malley’s advice: “telling the story of how you loved and how you lost gives shape and meaning to what first seems to be a meaningless, uncontrollable event.”¶ In a book review about Ariel Levy’s loss of a baby, Leslie Jamison writes, “This need to specify the terms of grief—to make it legible—is deeply human and deeply moving. It’s not a bid for sympathy but an attempt to honor what happened. Levy has done that here, mapped the force of what happened—written an imperfect account of the imperfect

---

experience of a woman widowed at thirty-two (http://www.wnyc.org/story/rachel-ward-widow-death-sex-money). The podcast “Terrible, Thanks for Asking” (https://www.apmpodcasts.org/ttfa/) was reviewed in the *New York Times* (Amanda Hess, “The Art of Talk about Sex and Death,” Art, August 2, 2017, C1 and C5), https://www.nytimes.com/section/well.

* Dorothy R. Cotton, who has written the booklet, *Out of the Ark: Alone in a Coupled World after the Death of a Husband—A Manual for Widows of a Certain Age*, writes, “For the widowed who have not found this elusive thing called ‘closure,’ it is imperative to link with others who allow the truth. With them, the energy used to repress emotional authenticity is not needed. An effective support group enables a process of ‘un-feigning.’ A genuine trust that you will not be judged allows and even encourages pure, non-socialized responses to ‘How are you doing?’ As a widow you do not need—and hardly deserve—the added pain of secrecy and shame. In a support group, you can relax and speak the truth; when the stress of self-censure is replaced by honesty, safety, and acceptance, an enormous burden is lifted.” http://outoftheark.weebly.com/.

† Some researchers have found writing can make a difference in the functioning of our immune system, reports Elizabeth Harper Neeld in *Seven Choices*, 226.

‡ “Love, Loss and What Comes Next,” *New York Times*, May 14, 2017, Sunday Styles, C2.

§ Edwidge Danticat, *The Art of Death: Writing the Final Story* (Minneapolis, MN: Graywolf Press, 2017), 29.

¶ Judith Newman, “Books on How to Grieve, and How to Die from a Medium, a Psychologist, a Priest,” *New York Times Book Review*, June 18, 2017, 27, referring to Patrick O’Malley’s *Getting Grief Right: Finding Your Story of Love in the Sorrow of Loss* (Louisville, CO: Sounds True Publishing, 2017).

art of surviving loss."* Kathryn Temple astutely notes here that "in past eras, widows were marked by widows' weeds, wearing black, or in some cultures all white. Now we mark our status, meaning our loss, meaning our lost spouses, not by wearing black, but by writing memoirs."

Since starting to work on this book, I have heard from several people about how reading works by other widows has been helpful to them. It is my hope that the pieces in this collection will help readers feel less alone, just as writing their story for *Widows' Words* helped these forty-three women feel less alone.

* Leslie Jamison, "Motherhood Lost," *New York Times Book Review*, April 9, 2017, 10, about Ariel Levy's *The Rules Do Not Apply: A Memoir* (New York: Random House, 2017).

Part I

Prologue

Expectant Widows

What We Were Afraid Of

A Memoir

ALICE GOODE-ELMAN

September 7

St. Francis Hospital, 6 A.M. You wait for an angiogram, and the complication of a stroke or heart attack haunts me. Suddenly, I'm aware of the fourteen-year age difference between us. I hold your hand and lean my head against your shoulder. You were doing okay on the medication, but you didn't like what it was doing to your sex drive. "I don't want to live like this," you kept saying. I'm superstitious enough to think you'll be punished for complaining.

Later, I find you lying on a gurney in the outpatient area. Dr. Schloffnitz wants to speak to us, the nurse says. The doctor is boyish-looking; his face flushes easily. There's an air of distraction about him when he speaks about doing bypass surgery. Finally, he says, "There was a density on the chest X-ray they took earlier. I'd like you to have a CAT scan, which we can do right now. Before you leave."

"I don't want to do this now," you say, but the doctor is persistent. You ask for a short break.

A longer version of this memoir previously appeared in the *Notre Dame Review*, no. 12 (Summer 2001), 16–54.

Outside, you light a little cigar, fumbling with the match. Your eyes stare wide open as if you're looking into a nightmare. "He thinks I have cancer. I know it!"

September 12

You call me at work. Your voice is breathy as if you've been gulping air. "Bernstein has the results. He's going to call you right now."

"Is it what we were afraid of?" I can't say the word.

"Call me back as soon as he speaks to you." You hang up in your familiar abrupt way.

The phone rings, and Dr. Bernstein yells into my ear. "This is terrible Mrs. Elman. Terrible. Inoperable lung cancer. I'm very sorry. You know I've known your husband and you, your family, a long time, and I'm very very sorry. This is awful." I hang up feeling as if I've just been the recipient of a condolence call.

"I don't want you to tell anyone about this. I don't want Lila to know, or anyone," you say.

I'm surprised by your reserve. "I don't want to lie. Lila's not a baby; she'll need to know," I say. "And Margaret too."

"I'll talk to Lila. I don't want her to worry. And Margaret has her play to worry about. I'll talk to her when I'm ready. I don't want you to tell anyone."

I am oddly relieved by this conspiracy of silence. I expected you to ask your daughters for sympathy. But I know you need time to absorb this. So do I. Still, it seems possible that if we don't talk about it, it will go away.

September 13

Our dinner guests enjoy the wine and you are a charming host.

In the kitchen, we bicker over the tuna cooking under the broiler. You've marinated it, so you have a proprietary interest, and you accuse me of putting too many pieces on the broiler tray. I beg you to let me turn the tuna over because you are clumsy with a spatula. You relent, but even before you do I feel a sudden surge of happiness next to you in this tight kitchen space, knowing this is precious, this standing next to your large flailing form intent upon the tuna.

September 14

You stand in the shadow by the bookcase offering me Sandra Gilbert's new book of poems about her dead husband. I cannot see your face. "I thought you might like to have this." I know you mean it as something to console me, but you aren't a memory yet, and I don't want it. I want to say something to cheer you up, but what can I possibly say?

"Look at it this way. At least *your* troubles will be over. *Mine* will just be beginning." That shut you up.

September 16

Lem is at the table going over the proofs of your literary memoir, complaining that he keeps finding mistakes no matter how meticulous he is. We say nothing about the real anxiety. You may not live to see the book in print.

September 18

You went to see Dr. Yen, your cardiologist. On my night table a letter addressed to me in your handwriting reads "Alice Elman/ urgent." I fear additional nightmarish news. Finally, I read:

Even dying men need to fuck.
The mortally threatened have a schmuck
they must appease and provide some ease
to their lovers, however they can.
Sick as I am I'm still a man
and with a scrotum full of Norvasc
I still yearn for you, O gosh,
and I love you very much,
and I revel in your touch.
See you after Dr. Yen, love Richie.

I am furious with you for terrifying me, my eyes brimming over as I laugh and cry at the same time.

September 19

"What have you told Lila?"

"I told her I have cancer and that I need more tests." Lila comes into the bedroom while we're discussing tomorrow's doctor's appointment. "I want you to tell me what the doctor says," she says. She seems angry, suspicious.

"You do what you need to do for yourself, and I'll do what I need to do," you tell her.

"Promise you'll tell me." We reassure her, and she seems relieved. I am grateful that she's able to concentrate on schoolwork.

October 6

In Manhattan we decide to see Dr. Bruckner at Mt. Sinai, the oncologist who treated my therapist. He is overweight and overworked in a crumpled white shirt. Propped up against the wall on a bookshelf are the stained-glass Hebrew letters for the word "Ch'ai"—Life. When I see them I am startled into feeling the hope we have come for.

"Look at him," Bruckner addresses me, noting how you are swallowing air. I realize this is the first time a doctor has taken the time to observe how you are feeling.

October 8

Lila is reviewing her college application to Brown. It is wonderful, and she has written it herself. I point to a place where I feel she needs one more sentence. You hear my voice and emerge from the bedroom. "Leave it alone," you snort. "Leave it alone." Your voice is menacing.

"I know about too many cooks," I say. "Still, I have a right to tell her what I think." Lila says nothing, her lips tight with resolve.

"You'll spoil it," you boom.

I hate your bullying. "It's Lila's essay, goddamn it. She'll be the one to decide. Not you." Under her gaze, you turn quiet and retreat to the bedroom.

October 9

"This stuff is poison," you say, reading, *The Facts about Chemotherapy.*

"It won't help you to think of it that way."

Trying to fight the paranoia that is your natural response to life when you're stressed, you don't disagree.

October 10

Hooked up to the chemo dripping into your veins, you shout: "I'm GEMZAR-MAN! I'M GEMZAR-MAN, yes siree," and I smile as you transform your fear of being poisoned into this superhuman infusion of power.

October 25

An old man in his eighties, a Hasid with a white beard, sidelocks, and a large black hat sits opposite you. A prayer book is in the hand that is not hooked up to the chemo IV.

I sit by your side grading papers. We are all quiet, until the old man speaks to you in Yiddish. "Tochter?" he asks. The word for "daughter" is one of a handful I recognize from my youth.

"No," you tell him, I am your wife. Then the Hasid says: "It's good to have a young wife."

October 29

At a party for the Flanagans, you are in good spirits even though your hand is burned from the chemo backing up into the IV.

You relate that your doctor is an orthodox Jew and regale Tom Flanagan with the description of Hasidim in long black caftans.

Marlo says something about the importance of faith for healing.

You hold up your wine glass. Tipping it in my direction you say, "I believe in love."

October 30

The neurologist examines you and sees your balance is off. He says the brain scan you had shows an obstruction. The cancer may have spread to your brain. You need a high-contrast MRI. Soon.

November 3

I have the pictures of your brain to show Dr. Bruckner. I wait with a woman who is pale faced and ill. Her daughter is a girl with long, thick braids doing her homework next to her. I wish the mother could be well for her daughter.

Bruckner holds the large films up against the fluorescent light, shaking his head in disappointment. In the silence, I know it is not good, even as I wish he would say something hopeful. "Here, and here," he points to a gray area and a few white specks. "The cancer has spread to a number of places."

November 5

I don't cancel my classes yet. In the lecture hall the students seem far away. I make eye contact with the woman who has multiple sclerosis, and the widower who's auditing. Do they recognize their suffering in my face?

"Aphrodite, the goddess of love, cannot stop death. Death is part of the natural world, a beast, the wild boar she warns Adonis against confronting. When he is slain, the power of her grieving love transforms his body into new life, an anemone." I look down and read: "Yet the flower is of brief enjoyment for the winds blow upon it—with difficulty it clings to life and falls under the blasts and buffeting."* Somehow, the awful beauty of this language consoles me.

November 12

On the opening night of Margaret's play, you agree to use the cane I got for you because it is shaped like a ski pole and makes you look athletic. In the theater lobby you open the program, read the dedication, and tears stream down your cheeks.

November 18

I hear your voice calling me out of a heavy sleep. You are naked on the bathroom floor, your underwear pulled down above your knees. There is blood on the white tile floor and all over your stomach.

"I'm all right," you say. "I can't get up. Help me up."

Your voice seems clear and calm in spite of all the blood.

December 13

There is a letter for Lila from Brown University. I am tempted to open it, and I hold the envelope up to the light.

"I got into Brown! I can't believe it!" Lila screams.

You laugh your slap-happy laugh. "Why of course they accepted you! I knew it!" you say. "I knew they don't get any better than Lila."

I love the confidence you have in our child.

December 15

I wake and find your side of the bed empty. This is the third night this week that I've found you eating ice cream or pancake batter at 3 A.M. "Don't lose weight," the doctor said when you were first diagnosed. Don't worry about cholesterol."

December 16

I walk past the stairs and see you struggling, your body sprawled over the steps. You slide backwards. "You can't do this! Do you want to crack your

* Ovid, *Metamorphoses* 10. 731–739, quoted in *Classical Mythology*, 10th ed., ed. Mark Morford, Robert J. Lenardon, and Michael Sham (New York: Oxford University Press, 2014), 202.

skull?" You manage to reach the top, and when you can't stand up you turn over on your back, your knees bending toward your chest, huge and helpless, howling.

December 17

The veins in your arms are shot, and at Mt. Sinai they will put a port-a-cath in your chest for you to receive the chemo. My brother will meet us there. He's a physician, and he is a little hurt that we hadn't consulted him sooner.

While you are in the operating room, my brother asks me, "Is he incontinent yet?"

"No. Does that happen?" He looks at me as if he is not sure how much is good for me to know.

"You'll have to start distancing yourself," he adds. This is the last thing I want to hear.

December 25

"Help me, Help me," you call, "I'm dying." The clock flashes 2 A.M. I turn on the light. You don't call my name or say anything more, don't complain about pain or being unable to breathe. "Why is Herbert poisoning me?" you say about your dear physician friend who lives in Boston. Could you be talking in your sleep?

"It's 2 o'clock in the morning. Go back to sleep." My voice seems to calm you, though you are still restless, and over the next four hours you wake me numerous times, trying to get out of bed.

December 26

"I don't care how you get him here, Mrs. Elman, so long as you bring him in," Dr. Fiorelli says when I call ahead about our appointment. I don't want to call an ambulance. That would mean this is an emergency and you are in worse shape than I want to admit. I help you dress. There is a plastic bottle on your night table and I help you urinate into it. Then I make you stand up and walk. "I can't," you say. "Yes you can," I insist. I telephone Lem, and he agrees to come over and help me get you into the car.

At the emergency room Dr. Fiorelli explains that you don't show a temperature because you are taking steroids, which mask the symptoms. "You have an infection, Mr. Elman, we need to get you on antibiotics right away."

Dr. Fiorelli takes me aside. He looks me in the eye and says, "Mrs. Elman, you know that your husband is a very sick man. I need to make some things very clear to you. Have you discussed with your husband what he wants to do if he begins to fail?"

"We would like everything to be done to save him," I tell him. "I know there is no cure for his disease at this point, but the tumors are shrinking and we have reason to hope for remission." I can't believe I am speaking so calmly about the decision to keep you alive.

You must remove your rings for a CAT scan. The turquoise one on your index finger comes off easily now. In the past, it was impossible to remove. You give me your marriage band and the other large Zuni ring on your right finger. You never remove these rings. I hold them in my hand and want to cry.

A Dr. Sugarman takes over for Fiorelli. I wish I didn't have to meet another strange doctor. Sugarman is in his early forties with thick black hair and a broad chest like a quarterback's. He takes my hand and I am strangely unnerved by his warmth.

You are transferred to a private room on the intensive care unit where you are hooked up to oxygen, IVs filled with antibiotics, and a catheter to catch your urine. It is close to eight at night, and you seem to be resting comfortably.

I feel punch drunk. We've been indoors for so long, the chairs in the room are backbreaking, and the nurses say there are no reclining chairs to be had. A gnawing in my gut is hunger. I decide that Margaret and Lila and I should go and get a bite. You are dismayed. Margaret offers to come back after dinner and asks if there is anything you'd like us to bring you from home. A radio, you answer.

"Thank you for coming back," you say, when we return to the hospital and set up the radio.

December 27

In the hall Dr. Sugarman says, "These infections often take a turn for the better or worse in the first 48 hours." I am relieved your care is no longer my responsibility.

You watch me sipping coffee. There is a small oxygen mask over your nose and mouth. You push it away clumsily with your left hand. "I'm hungry," you say.

"You're getting everything you need intravenously, Mr. Elman. You need the oxygen, please don't push it away." You ignore the nurse and look at me biting into a bagel.

"I'm hungry goddamn it," your voice is loud though muffled through the mask.

"Mrs. Elman, maybe you shouldn't eat in the room," the nurse says softly.

"Can't he have something? What about Jell-O?"

I arrange your glasses over the oxygen and give you the newspaper. You sit with the book review open in front of you. Your brother Leonard walks in while you are propped up in this healthy-looking, familiar pose.

The nurse has brought in Jell-O and you want to eat it. "He needs to keep the oxygen on as much as possible," she says.

"When I say ready, you take the mask from your mouth and then put it back as soon as you take a mouthful, okay?"

You nod, and together we coordinate the feeding of Jell-O. "Go," I say, and you move the mask and open your mouth. As soon as you close your mouth, you move the mask back again until I am ready with the next spoonful. You open your mouth wide like a child or a baby bird eager to be filled with nourishment, and I am so gratified to be feeding you. "Go," I say and together we are happy, lulled by the repetition—spoon, mask, go, spoon.

December 28

"Where the hell were you?" You are clean-shaven with an oxygen tube in your nostrils and your voice is strong, your anger familiar. I feel guilty, then angry, but decide to forgo an explanation.

"That's a nice hello." I lean over and kiss your cheek. It is smooth, and I am relieved that you are visibly comforted by my touch. I put the newspaper and some mail down on your tray.

"Where is she?" The nurse says as she smiles at me. "Where **is** she?" "That's all he's been saying, all morning long."

I smile back. She is not reproaching me, I realize. She is telling me how much you missed me.

December 29

1 A.M. The voice on the phone calls me up from the depths of the sea.

"Mrs. Elman we are going to have to intubate your husband."

"Please telephone Richard's friend Dr. Herbert Krohn about the situation."

"I have been given the orders Mrs. Elman, I have to intubate your husband regardless of what Dr. Krohn will say."

At the hospital the elevator takes forever, and they've already begun by the time I get there. I see the resident holding a plastic tube near your mouth. Instinctively, you move your head away to avoid the tube, and even though I know you must be sedated, I can't help but feel you panic. The doctor sees me watching, and someone draws the curtain. I turn away and stuff my fist into my mouth. Sobbing, I walk to the exit doors, certain I'll never see you conscious again.

December 30

Bloated, pumped up with fluids, the tube comes out of your mouth and the respirator is breathing for you. Dr. Sugarman looks at the monitors above your bed. "Don't give up yet," he tells me.

I ask about your mental state. Is it like sleep? He says you are heavily sedated but sound of some kind may filter through to you.

I want to encourage you, even subliminally. "Come on Richie," I say, wrapping your stocking feet in my arms close to my chest.

Later, Lila looks at you and talks to you in a little girl's voice. "Hi Daddy." I suggest we read some of your poetry to you. "That should make him want to stay around," I joke. Lila has never read some of these poems before. She reads: "In the Woods," which is dedicated to Margaret.

The little black pig
ran out from under the oak leaf caves
and dropped his snout
when he heard my footfall
and spun about
and ran the other way again,
causing this piece of the forest
to shake its cabbage palms
down at me, and then
a deer loped sideways through the underbrush
with a cow and her two veal.
She was orange
and she stared laconically
and wiped the air
between that deer and her babies,
her tail bright with flies.*

The sound of your words comforts me. Lila says, "I don't know. I feel terrible. I'm having such a good time reading these poems."

* "In the Woods," Richard Elman, *The Man Who Ate New York* (Moorhead, MN: New Rivers Press, 1975), quoted in *Complete Poems of Richard Elman (1955–1997)*, ed. Alice Goode-Elman (New York: Junction Press, 2017), 34.

December 31

"We've done all the tests we can do to determine why your father can't breathe on his own. It's not his heart, and it's not the infection. It's the cancer. We've done everything we can. There is nothing more we can do. I'm sorry."

I look at Margaret, hoping she will take charge.

"Well that's not my father," Margaret says.

I am confused. Why does she disown you? Then I realize, she means that you are no longer yourself. I look at your body, huge with fluids, the tubes distorting your face. This is who you are now.

"He said he didn't want to be kept like this," I say.

"No, of course he wouldn't," Margaret says.

Lila says nothing. She is tight-lipped and doesn't look at me.

I am afraid to be alone with you. You will know I have told them to pull the plug. You will think I gave up too easily.

In semidarkness I play your favorite Chet Baker on the radio tape deck: "Time after time / I tell myself that I'm / So lucky to be loved by you."* Outside, the sky is black. Before we seemed in a rush. This is how we will be together from now on. You in my head, inside of me.

In the most tender voice, a nurse I've never seen before introduces herself to me. She adjusts some of your tubes, then leaves. The resident comes in and tells me he will remove the breathing tube from your throat. I walk outside into the hallway. A young woman, one of the interns I've seen over the last few days, comes up to me. "I just want you to know what an unusual family you have. I've seen many people here, and you just don't see the kind of love you express."

"Why thank you." I feel oddly shy.

Lila and Margaret return, and I share what the intern said.

Small breathy sounds come from your throat. Now your dying is audible. I stand embracing your feet. I'm sorry Richie. I'm so sorry. I listen until you are quiet.

Margaret and Lila leave the room. The nurse with sad eyes speaks to me. "Mrs. Elman, they're going to ask you if you will want an autopsy performed." The thought of their cutting you open is unbearable. "No. No autopsy." When she asks if there is anything else she can do I tell her I want every attachment removed from your body.

In the hallway interns gather for morning rounds.

* "Time After Time," *Chet Baker Sings*. Pacific Jazz Records, 1954.

You look more familiar without tubes and tape. Your arms rest over the sheet. "I'm sorry." I feel as if I'm abandoning you. I close the heavy metal door behind me. The sound is loud in my ears and stays with me.

November 1

Postscript from your laptop

If I survive this cancer I may still be an invalid. I may be able to walk around in the world, exchange breath, possibly be helpful to some people in some ways, but my writing days of concentrated time may disappear entirely. Can I sustain even the briefest thoughts? And when time seems foreshortened and limited is not the time to be making plans of a creative nature, it would seem.

I am not trying to be alarmist or self-pitying. I want to get well. But how well can that be from now on?

The Queen Has Spoken

KELLI DUNHAM

As I prepared the anti-nausea drugs that my partner Heather would need to keep down the powerful dose of sedatives that would end her life, I was grateful for my nursing experience. Years of practice guided me through the multistep process, even as my hands and voice were shaking. I administered the clear medication, watching as it made its way through the IV tubing and disappeared into the central line in Heather's chest.

I tried to hum the theme from the Peanuts cartoons—a song we both considered music for happier times—but Heather interrupted me.

"You know you're doing that for yourself, right?" she said. "You know I'm okay?"

"Okay" seemed like a bit of an overstatement, but from her own words I knew she was "tired and done" from her six-year fight with ovarian cancer.

And while I wasn't precisely okay with that strange moment when I was called on to help end the life of the person I loved most in the world, at least none of this had been sprung on me last minute.

In fact, a few years before she died, Heather made sure I was on board. During my last visit before I moved from Philadelphia to Oregon to close the distance in our long-distance relationship, she had taken my hand while we sat in a friend's garden.

"Here's the plan Stan," she said, tapping my shoulder playfully. The tone of her voice was what you'd use if you were involved in a good-natured faux argument about which variety of carryout pizza was best. Then she frowned and sighed.

"Okay, so if you come out here and we make a go of this, I need you to understand, I don't know how long I have. If it gets to the point where the pain or the nausea is too bad, I'm going to take my own life. I want control of this. I need to know the people closest to me aren't going to oppose me."

If you spent more than twenty-seven seconds with Heather, you became acutely aware that she was a person who knew what she wanted. I lovingly called her "my Queen." She was such an imposing force, so clearly The Boss, that even her oncologist referenced her as such to me. It was as if the Oregon State Health System paperwork had added a new relationship category she could check, and they would understand: Beloved Person In Charge.

So it wasn't surprising to me that my Queen would want the final say in her final hours. And after an eight-week stint of unremitting nausea the previous fall, she knew she didn't want to suffer like that if there was no hope she could get better.

I tried to sound confident in response to her announcement. She certainly sounded confident.

"Yup, my Queen, I got it."

We never legally married (it wasn't legal then, and as Heather loved to say, "we really much prefer living in sin"), but that moment solidified our partners status. We had both had our share of heartache in each of our thirty-eight years, but with this mutual act of trust, we knew we were both definitely in.

There had been more than a year of relatively good living wedged in between the date of that conversation and the point at which Heather made the decision to go off chemo because it was no longer working and was making her miserable. She started on hospice just before Christmas, and we were granted what felt like a reprieve. We decorated our tree with hand-strung popcorn, made cookies, and had friends in for hot chocolate.

"It's like something from Norman Fucking Rockwell," Heather observed.

I'm grateful for those moments, pockets of time when she could step aside from cancer and treatment and I could step aside from my fear of hurtling toward widowhood. In our four years together cancer had always been at least a shadow on our future. Now that it played such a central part, every breath felt precious.

The weeks that followed, however, grew steadily more difficult for Heather. She had unremitting pain that continued, even when we were giving her IV phenobarbital, even after she was put on an IV pump and given pain medicine around the clock. She had also been essentially unable to eat, and many nights we were up until sunrise, sometimes with the hospice nurse present, trying to get her symptoms under control.

In Oregon, physician-assisted suicide is legal, although it requires filling out many forms, meeting with several clinicians, and finding a pharmacy willing to fill the prescription. Heather had already begun the paperwork to obtain the meds to help her hasten her death "just in case."

One night in early February, I was sleeping curled up beside her when I heard her talking on the phone.

"Yeah, you better get here as quick as you can. I've had enough. I'm doing it tomorrow." I waited until she finished the phone call and then tapped her on the back.

"Pardon me, my Queen, but when a person decides they are going to use assisted suicide to hasten their death, they're supposed to tell the person sleeping beside them before they start telling the world."

"Oh, right," she said, almost mocking me, "I'm sorry. I forgot for a moment the proper procedure."

Heather was overambitious in her proclamation that she would "do it" by the next day. Whether you're updating your address at the DMV or filing an application to end your life, bureaucracy can be rushed only so much.

It took until the following Tuesday at 7:30 A.M., but everything was put in place. Heather wanted to die surrounded by the people who loved her. It felt like half of Portland was at our house; a bright yellow, barely converted Hare Krishna temple. Joining us were Heather's best friends, one of whom had flown in from Michigan, another wearing thigh-high boots for the occasion; a half dozen ex-lovers/current friends; Heather's massage therapist, a '70s-era lesbian who talked about organic kale and asked if our cat wanted energy work. A group of radical faeries visited and left the house smelling like patchouli and body odor. Heather's biological sisters had traveled to join us, and they completed the circle. It felt good—if a little surreal—to have us all acting together as family.

We had been lucky enough to find an assisted-suicide liaison at the hospital where Heather had been receiving treatment—a generous assisted-suicide liaison who came to our house to finish the last of the paperwork. She made conversation with our gathered tribe, legs crossed in her Ann Taylor suit. She looked as if this was all very customary and that, in fact, this was the fourth barely converted Hare Krishna temple she had been to that day.

The gathered family of friends all alternately kept it together and lost it. The potheads smoked some, well, a lot, of pot. I consumed my own weight in Diet Mountain Dew. At some point we ate takeout chicken. Heather drank a soda, cuddled with each of us in turn, and, when she was craving a cigarette and was headed outside to the porch, stopped and thought for a moment.

"Wait I don't smoke inside because I don't want to get my clothes and stuff smelly. I'm not going to have to worry about that anymore."

The Queen smoked her last cigarette sitting on the couch.

There's surprisingly little to say about our goodbyes, perhaps because at that point it was as if Heather was waving back over her shoulder at us. Like she was already gone.

As the moment got closer, she seemed almost delighted in her final act of self-determination after so many months of intractable pain and nausea as well as being held captive to the whims and torments of the health care system.

Heather's best friend's partner had bravely offered to mix up the lethal dose of medication that Heather had been prescribed. The instructions said to open two capsules and mix the contents into water or applesauce.

"The last taste in my mouth will absolutely not be applesauce" said the Queen. And so the white powder was swirled into Heather's requested medium, Kozy Shack chocolate pudding.

Heather ate the pudding.

She died.

It was awful.

Some friends said it was less awful than watching her suffer. I longed for the compassion (or perhaps, the distance) to feel less ambivalent. I wanted more time with her, even if it wasn't great time.

Why didn't I beg Heather for this?

Because I knew it would be ethically wrong?

Because who wants to be that kind of jerk?

Because the Queen Had Already Spoken, and a no would have added another layer of devastation?

I would hope it was the first of these choices, but most likely my motivation was a mixture of all three.

Heather didn't want to die, but she didn't want to suffer, and she especially didn't want to be out of control. Assisted suicide wouldn't have been my choice, but it was not my choice to make.

My participation—ambivalent though it was—was the last gift I could give her, and it was made possible only by her gift: absolute resolution, crystal clear intention, and surprising verbal frankness about her illness and death.

It was most certainly devastating, and I am most certainly proud of the choice.

Living a Life

PENELOPE DUGAN

We had always said we could face anything as long as we were together. In our twelve years as a couple, we had gone through each of us being fired by the New Jersey college where we taught, a lawsuit seeking my reinstatement, commuting every weekend to be with each other, and eventually getting jobs at the same upstate New York university. Ingie wrote then, "Be of good cheer, my plucky Penel. Our love has been strengthened by struggle."

Our last struggle was Ingie's brain tumor, an inoperable anaplastic astrocytoma grade three in her parietal and temporal lobes. I could remain at Ingie's side throughout her treatment if I appeared calm and kept silent. I remember holding Ingie's hand during the stereotactic biopsy as neurosurgeons screwed the Browning ring into her head. She looked like Jesus with his crown of thorns. Blood trickled down her forehead. Ingie, doing her yogic breathing, appeared serene. When the doctors asked me to leave to go to the waiting room, Ingie kissed the air and said, "Ommmmm." I heard her chuckling as I shut the door. She was not the suffering Christ but the laughing Buddha.

I knew I couldn't do anything about Ingie's diagnosis, but I thought if I found her the best doctors I could buy her more time. My own adrenaline speeded me up while the phenobarbital Ingie took to prevent seizures slowed her down. She avoided my growing file of articles and computer printouts. I thought then she was in denial. Two days after Ingie's death, her secretary gave me the diary Ingie had kept on her office computer. The first entry read: "It's been a little more than two weeks since my seizure, and my universe has totally turned around. So many conversations about doctors and medicines, which even though they affect me I still find boring. I must force myself to read up on the materials on cancer. I must find a middle ground between passive acceptance and frantic efforts. I'm not into finding miracle cures, I just wish to develop a helpful regimen, and find technically the best clinics and physicians and have them do what they can."

To Ingie, my library searches, calls to the National Cancer Institute and National Institutes of Health, and attempts to follow up all leads must have seemed frantic. While I mailed sets of Ingie's MRIs to radiologists throughout the Northeast, she sent faxes to members of Congress demanding an end to the Bosnian arms embargo. I accused her of being more interested in Bosnia than her own brain. She said her brain was her favorite organ, but she knew more about Bosnia.

Two weeks after her first diary entry, Ingie wrote: "There may not be much time—one day, one month, one year—but I must strive gently to make it precious, and have Penny to make it precious with. Suddenly I was shifted from planning and scheming programs at the college, teaching, and research to the face of death and I have not come to grips with it yet (and may never) other than appreciating the simple things—the good life—or as some might call it the saintly life—reconciliation, love of oneself, others, and of the universe, with bemused detachment, not fearing to engage."

Ingie continued to write and to speak about Bosnia until six weeks before her death. Then she refused invitations for lectures and interviews. She asked me not to get her the *New York Times* anymore. "It's too late," she said.

Ingie lived fifteen months after diagnosis. She followed every direction given her by doctors, underwent each treatment they suggested. She had daily radiation for six weeks in hopes of being a candidate for stereotactic radial surgery at Boston's Brigham and Women's Hospital. She wasn't. The radiation had reduced the mass of her tumor but not the area. She endured months of chemotherapy, which sickened and weakened her. After ten months of the protocol, the doctor at Sloan-Kettering suggested Ingie stop treatment and concentrate on her quality of life.

I hated the expression "quality of life" and its cousin "quality time." What did it mean? The purpose of life is life itself, I thought. In the middle of the night, while in the hospital, Ingie woke me up to ask if she were a fox or a hedgehog. A fox, definitely, I answered. I got her reference. But I'm still not sure I gave her the right answer.

Ingie worked throughout her illness. Even when she broke her ankle, which never properly healed and confined her to a wheelchair, she went in to her office. "If I stop working," she told me, "I'm just a person with cancer. I will be invisible. I need my title, I need my big desk, I need my secretary who loves me and makes lousy coffee." And I think Ingie needed to be apart from me for some of the day. One night a week, I taught an evening class. I would come home to the smell of marijuana and a mellow Ingie. Neighbors told me the house shook with Mahler symphonies.

The keeper of notes, the maker of appointments, I was a silent presence at each meeting with doctors. While the doctors examined Ingie or talked with her, I looked into the eyes of their young female assistants. Their looks told me how hopeless the situation was. I struggled to contain my rage. I couldn't drive people away. We needed their help, and gregarious Ingie needed their recognition, their laughter, their approval, their love. Whenever she was hospitalized, she soon had a group of residents and interns who dropped in on her during their off time. She couldn't stop team building, inspiring, gathering people to her and sending them off with a sense of purpose and gladness. When she taught, Ingie had ended classes with, "Do good and fight evil."

Only in the "We Can Cope" support group for family members at the local cancer treatment center could I admit to my rage. Five husbands and I huddled together in a hospital courtyard, so we could smoke and get away from the social worker facilitator. With each other we didn't have to be upbeat or even good tempered. We talked about the unfairness of it all, the things we had wanted to do and now never would, the stupidity of doctors, and the kindness of some of the oncology nurses. We hated that we smoked—though none of us did at home—and said we didn't care if we got cancer too. At first the recurring question was, "Why her and not me?"

Why Me? was one of the many self-help books friends sent to Ingie after her cancer diagnosis. It made her smile. "Why not me?" she asked. Bernie Siegel's *Love, Medicine, & Miracles* arrived in hardback, paperback, and video tape. "So how is it?" I asked. "Siegel is for people who haven't read the Stoic philosophers. Epictetus could have sued him," Ingie said. I know the book bothered her. At first, Ingie blamed herself for her cancer. She obsessed about what she had done wrong until an acquaintance said, "Look, cancer is a molecular accident." I don't know why she could hear this but she did. Ingie became calmer than I had ever known her to be. Granted she was on phenobarbital, but I also think she was making a tremendous effort to live well. I was stunned to find a Post-it note on Ingie's desk reading, "Ask Penny what she has to do each day, what she is afraid of and hopes for." Prediagnosis, this had been my role with Ingie. I took to calling her Mahatma but waited for the other shoe to drop. I feared when her rage came it would sear us both.

The last entry in Ingie's diary, written five months before her death, reads "It's clear I won't have the energy to write everyday, so I'll keep the diary weekly. The point of writing this down is to work on anger and obsession. How can I assure that my anger will not explode? I strive for eternal calm vigilance, making a joke of it, making light of it. There are more important things to focus on, both the beauty of creation and the true horrors and injustices in the world. In other words, laughter and forgetting and detachment and perspective."

At my urging, Ingie had a session with a psychologist. Apparently, the woman's first question to Ingie was, "How do you feel about having a terminal illness?" Taken aback, Ingie said she spent the rest of the session telling witty stories, trying to cheer the shrink up. "What help can she give me? The talking cure won't work. Besides, I'm losing words."

And she was. Nouns and names started to disappear. Instead of "lobster," Ingie would call it a red fish with claws. Some nouns were referred to by their function—the thing you drain spaghetti with—some by their appearance. We laughed about it and said middle age would be one long game of charades. Ingie's first language was German, so I began to wonder if her functional descriptions of objects were really translations of their German names. I worried about losing the ability to communicate with this most verbal of women. When Ingie was dying, I had German-speaking friends with her, whom she talked to in German, but she continued to talk to me in English until she couldn't talk.

In what seemed a parallel universe to the world of Ingie's illness, I won my lawsuit against the college in New Jersey. I was to be reinstated with back pay. But it felt like the entire upstate New York town and state university were participating in Ingie's care. How could I return to New Jersey? I put my house there on the market. I did not want to live in it without Ingie. The house sold within a week.

On a beautiful August day, I loaded Ingie's wheelchair into the trunk and we headed thirty miles down the Northway to Willsboro, New York. Ingie had once given a talk in the tiny village library, and she remembered the warmth of the people there. She thought we were having one of our "rejoice in the beauty of creation" drives. With the sale of my house and the prospect of more money than I had ever seen, I was intent on buying Ingie her house on the lake.

Driving down Willsboro Point Road, we saw a For Sale sign at the bottom of a long dirt road heading up a hill into woods. We turned up the dirt road and drove through the woods where a red house and a smaller gray one stood in a clearing. Sunlight filtered through tall pine trees. "We're Hansel and Gretel," Ingie said. A six-foot-tall woman in her seventies came out of the red house and greeted us. "Was that your sign at the end of the road?" I asked. "We're the only ones around, so I guess it is," the woman joked. She told us her name was Ruth, and she and her husband, Bert, were getting too old for the place. The Realtor had just left, and the sign had been up for less than an hour. We were the first to see it. I asked who lived in the gray house, and Ruth told me it was their guest cottage. My mind reeled. A separate house for guests. This would be perfect for Ingie's boisterous eastern European friends who traveled in packs, drank and danced all night, and argued all day.

Ingie stayed in the car, since she couldn't manage the three steps leading down to the red house, while Ruth took me inside. I looked at the flow of the rooms, the view of Lake Champlain and the Green Mountains from each room, the width of the doorways, the huge master bedroom with adjoining handicapped-equipped bathroom. Bert, Ruth told me, had suffered a stroke shortly after they bought the summer house six years ago. She fitted out the house to care for him there. Ruth saved the bus room for last. She told me that Mildred and Sidney Tripp, the first owners, had driven an Albany city bus onto this land in the 1920s and literally built the house around the bus. Mildred had cared for Sidney in this house until his death in 1981.

I was on board. I was transported. I was buying this house. I didn't even look at the gardens planned and planted over sixty years by Mrs. Tripp. I didn't walk down to the rocky beach dotted with purple loosestrife. I told Ruth I would be back the next day with her Realtor. Two women before me had cared for their mates in this house. I would be the third.

The Realtor knew how to maneuver a wheelchair down steps. Ingie rolled into the living room and spun her chair around a few times. She rolled down the hall into the master bedroom. "This is it," she said. I arranged to give Ruth and Bert every cent I had as down payment and signed a ten-year mortgage, which they would hold.

"What would you like to call the place?" I asked.

"Camp Ingie, of course," Ingie replied.

It was a golden time for Ingie. She occupied center stage at the camp where friends came to visit her. She sat by the fireplace in a reclining chair—her command post she called it—with her binoculars at hand. I situated the chipmunk and bird feeders so she could see them from the bedroom, living room, and dining room windows. She claimed to have identified fourteen different chipmunks and would call out, "Here come Irving, Moishe, Seymour, and the rest of the mischpoche." Ingie said that the chipmunks were like me, scurrying back and forth, storing up nuts against an uncertain future.

When Ingie was alive, I did not look at the view or watch the birds and chipmunks. I would not stay in bed to enjoy the sunrise that woke us and outlined the Green Mountains across the lake in purple, orange, and golden light. I got up saying, "It's time to feed the livestock" and went to the terrace to put out peanuts and sunflower seeds. Ingie would wave to me from the bedroom window, and I would make a sweeping gesture toward the lake and mountains as if presenting them to her. And that's what I was trying to do. I wanted the beauty to be hers alone. I wanted her to have as much of it as she could in the time she had left. I felt that if I looked too, there wouldn't be enough for her.

In April, Ingie was back in the hospital. She was dehydrated and her sense of balance was getting worse. We returned to Sloan Kettering, where they suggested Ingie stop chemotherapy. It wasn't retarding the growth of the tumor, and Ingie was growing weaker. I used the return to the camp as an incentive to get Ingie to eat, to get her to undergo a platelet transfusion. "I won't live in your dream house without you," I said.

Ingie and I could never discuss her death. She called death "the great unmentionable." I asked Ingie if she wanted to be hospitalized at the end. "Do what's easiest," she said. When I talked about the possibility of having her doctor authorize hospice care, Ingie refused, "That would mean I have six months to live."

In May, we moved back into Camp Ingie. Doctors had warned me that the tumor was moving toward Ingie's brain stem and that over the months she would lose her ability to see, to talk, or to move her arms and legs. It happened in a period of days. On Memorial Day, the anniversary of our twelve years together, Ingie could not get out of bed and had difficulty forming words. I called High Peaks Hospice, and friends, who called other friends. Friends came from thirty miles away and five hundred miles away. I didn't know what to ask of them. It was like teaching a book that I had never read before.

The house and guest cottage held the dozen friends who gave Ingie round-the-clock care in the week of her dying. We kept a fire going day and night in the living room fireplace to comfort the comforters. My sister and two of our friends went to daily mass in the village. They told me that after mass one day, the priest asked how the other sisters on the hill were doing. We laughed to realize the only way he could construe vigorous middle-aged women without makeup and without men was as nuns. Camp Ingie was both hospital and convent.

High Peaks Hospice gave me the confidence I needed to care for Ingie at the end, but it was our friends who made it possible. They cooked, they cleaned, they dealt with the outside world. My world was Ingie. Changing her, feeding her, sitting with her alone through the night—I could not do anything for her other than what I was doing. I was finally at peace.

I read to Ingie from Adrienne Rich's *An Atlas of the Difficult World*. She had asked for the book when she was first hospitalized. It remained at her bedside for the next fifteen months going with her to hospitals as her world contracted. Over and over, I recited Rich's words, "your spirit's gaze informing your body, impatient to mark what's / possible, impatient to mark / what's lost, deliberately destroyed, can never be / returned, / your back arched against all icons, simulations, dead letters / your woman's hands."

Two nights before Ingie died, she told me she was going on "her journey." Too tired to think, I asked where she was going. "I don't know," she said. The next morning the hospice nurse came and took Ingie's vital signs. They were strong, she said. I could hear friends laughing and talking in the living room. Ingie opened her eyes and said, "It's not as easy as you think to go snip, snip." I went into the living room to ask people to be quiet, saying that Ingie could never leave a party.

Later in the morning, Ingie was agitated and said that she wanted to go for a walk. I held her hand and watched her face relax as I talked us through a walk of our shared memories. I described the silver birches, the bluebells on the path, and the sunlight on the lake. When Ingie squeezed my hand, I made the description more detailed to include the wetness of the grass on our bare ankles, the mayflies circling us, the size of the stick our dog, Seamus, carried in his mouth.

Ingie died two hours before sunset, six days after her fifty-second birthday. She took two quick breaths as if she were going to dive and was gone. Gradually the gray pallor of her last day was replaced by a translucent glow. The six women still in the house—Rosemary, Kathy, Lil, Susann, Di, and my sister, Phil, went into our bedroom one at a time to sit alone with Ingie's body before we bathed and dressed it. The hospice nurse came to certify the death; the funeral director came to remove the body. Ingie was gone.

Four days after her death, Ingie's ashes were given to me. She had joked over the years that she wanted me to scatter her ashes in St. Petersburg, Paris, and Dubrovnic, the only way she figured we would ever travel together to the cities she loved. She laughed with friends about a happy wanderer like herself joining up with a determined nester like me. I couldn't scatter Ingie's remains. I needed to know where they were. I wanted to go off by myself to bury Ingie's ashes, but I knew she would want a party—friends telling stories about her and laughing. My sister and I dug a circular rose bed on the hillside outside Ingie's and my bedroom window, overlooking Lake Champlain. We planted white and pink tea roses and dug a small hole in the middle of the garden to bury Ingie's ashes when friends arrived the next day.

Hap Wheeler played his guitar softly while friends circled the rose garden. His wife said that when a person's body is cremated it becomes part of the atmosphere. We would see her in every sunrise and sunset. I knew Ingie would have groaned at the suggestion she was now atmospheric pollution.

Liz recounted the signs and wonders of Ingie's last week—the disabled crow that appeared outside the door, the colorful air balloons we could see over the lake from Ingie's bedroom window, the hummingbirds that hovered outside the window for the days of Ingie's dying and vanished when she died, the cry of the loon on the night of Ingie's death.

Ingie would have laughed at this talk. She would have said that a crow is a crow, a hummingbird is a hummingbird, and a loon is a loon. They aren't signs for anything beyond themselves. The wonder is that fifteen women dropped what they were doing to drive hundreds of miles to nurse a dying friend. Celebrate human actions of solidarity she would say.

I told the story of Ingie's visit to Beth Israel hospital for a PET scan. While Ingie was inside the machine being scanned, one of the doctors said to me, "Is she your mother?" Not wanting to go into any explanations, I said yes. From the depths of the PET scan, we heard, "BITCH!"

The state university held a memorial service for Ingie at the Newman Center. She would have enjoyed the celebration, especially since the word "dyke" was used frequently from the pulpit. Ingie's mother, whom Ingie had not wanted at her deathbed, flew in from California. She contested Ingie's will. This was in the days before marriage equality. When everything was settled, I thought I had done whatever Ingie wanted and now I could kill myself. I think I didn't do it because I was too depressed to figure out how. I worried about who would clean up after me, who would take care of Ingie's grave, what would happen to Camp Ingie. I went to see a shrink with these questions as my presenting problem. He prescribed Zoloft. In a few weeks, the world went from gray to colors and it had other people in it.

I started to attend a hospice-sponsored grief group. There I had intimations of what it must be like to be black in a white world. At every session, people would say something like, "Now, Ingie was your close friend, right?" Before they could accept and share my grief, they had to figure out who I was, what I was. But I continued to go to meetings because I needed to know how to keep on living.

On the night of her diagnosis, after I had pushed a hospital bed next to hers, Ingie held me close and said, "When I die, do what the boys do. Find yourself a juicy, young nurse to take care of you in your old age." A year after Ingie's death, I did. My lover gave me back my body, my need to touch and cherish. We parted after six years and remain friends. I am grateful for my friends and for the life I live.

Preparing for the Journey through Grief

MELANIE K. FINNEY

June 26, 2012

Cottage Outside Ardara, County Donegal, Republic of Ireland

After a quiet evening that included only one pint at the local pub, we walked back to our rental cottage outside Ardara, in the northwestern part of Ireland. For the last few days, my husband, Jerry, to whom I had been married ten years, told me he had a nagging lower backache, which we attributed to spending too much time in the small rental car we drove around rural Ireland. He was never one to take medications, but I convinced him to take a couple of ibuprofen to see if he could find some relief. Shortly after we arrived at our cottage, for the first time in many years, Jerry vomited. The next few days, he felt a bit out of sorts, and didn't feel much like eating lunch or visiting sites, something we regularly did on our trips to Ireland. Eventually, he seemed to feel better, but these were the first symptoms my husband had and that eventually led him to the doctor six weeks later. After months of tests, in October, he was diagnosed with stage IV pancreatic cancer.

A previously healthy sixty-five-year old man was suddenly facing a terminal illness with a poor prognosis. Without treatment, we were told he had three to six months. With treatment, if successful, six to nine months.

Only 6 percent of people diagnosed with stage IV pancreatic cancer live beyond five years. We were devastated. The day the spots on his liver and pancreas were detected on a CT scan, he apologized to me—as if any of this was his fault. One week later, biopsies confirmed it was indeed adenocarcinoma of the pancreas with metastases in the liver and abdomen. That evening as we tried to wrap our heads around how to proceed, he told me, "I'll fight, but I will not be a martyr." Aggressive chemotherapy began two weeks later, and we began a journey we'd never before considered.

Professionally, I had studied coping with grief and loss from both social psychological and communicative perspectives in a variety of populations for over twenty-five years and was well acquainted with this literature. And personally, I knew about loss. I had survived a difficult divorce many years before and the loss of grandparents and both parents. I knew that some of my personal losses required extensive periods of coping, while others seemed to be somewhat easier to reconcile and integrate into my overall life experience.

I knew that various kinds of loss affected people differently. While there is no hierarchy of loss, not all losses are equal. Some losses, such as the loss of a home or a career, can certainly affect a person's sense of security and safety, and in most cases, even cause feelings of inadequacy or loss of self-esteem as one's identity, as well as finances, takes a hit. But these losses, while challenging, can often provide new opportunities for change, growth, or relocation. Difficult yes, and in some cases they significantly affect how people exist in the world, but they are not necessarily permanent types of loss. Loss of physical mobility or activity, such as what results from an illness or accident—perhaps a broken leg or arm, or a stroke that causes loss of speech or movement, or onset of debilitating arthritis can also occur, and while unpleasant, accommodations can frequently be made that allow those who have been afflicted to still have positive life experiences. The death of dearly loved ones, however, generally creates serious, prolonged periods of grieving that can adversely affect people's mental, emotional, as well as physical well-being for a long time.

Additionally, the manner in which women become widowed also affects how they grieve and cope with the loss of their partners. I only have experience with the type of loss that comes from knowing that death will come in a short period of time. I have never lost anyone close to me in an unexpected or traumatic way. I know that when one is widowed unexpectedly, there is no possibility of engaging in pre-death griefwork. There are so many other kinds of issues survivors of those who have been violently killed or who have died accidently or even of natural causes face, and some of the things I describe here may not be relevant to those individuals.

So while I *knew* all these things, I realized there was so much I would have to experience on my own terms, in my own way, concerning the illness and eventual death of my husband. My goal here is to explain some of the things we did together, and what I did individually, that I believe helped me in my grief journey following his death ten months after diagnosis. I offer these, not necessarily as hard "how-to" pieces of advice, but as examples of the intentional ways we moved toward his passing, in hopes that I would develop appropriate coping skills once I became widowed. Everyone is different, and I tend to be both pragmatic and sentimental, and many of the things I did reflect both of these personality traits. Additionally, the suggestions that follow fall into these general categories as well: pragmatic and practical aspects one should consider prior to widowhood and then the sentimental, relationship-specific ideas that may make coping a bit easier. I realize that my husband and I were both very open in talking about what he was facing, but not everyone feels comfortable doing so. Take what makes sense or seems to fit how you experience your world, and discard the others.

Dealing with the Practical—Important Conversations

If you've not already done so, it is important to discuss issues such as who will be the designee to make health care decisions and then complete legal instruments, such as a living will, health care power of attorney, and advance directives. While the wording of such documents varies based on where one lives, you have several options for making these arrangements. Of course, attorneys have necessary forms, but you can also get information from your local hospital, public library, and community hospice or palliative care organizations. Once the forms are completed, keep in mind that it may be necessary to have them signed in front of a notary public in order for them to be legally binding.

It is important that everyone understand what kinds of decisions are desired, even if they are difficult to enact later. A few weeks before my husband died, he passed out as I was walking with him in our home, and it took several minutes for him to regain consciousness. Later, I told him I had almost called for medical assistance, and he gently reminded me that he had requested a DNR (do not resuscitate) order. I was disappointed that had slipped my mind in the moment, but we discussed again what procedures should be followed. When I told him I wasn't sure if I was brave enough to follow this decision, he told me, "Do the best you can." It is difficult, but important, to honor your loved one's wishes.

We also had the difficult conversation about what he wanted to do once he became very ill, and he decided he wanted to pass at home using hospice services. Together we discussed what his final arrangements were to be and considered such things as burial, cremation, or donating his body to a medical school. Jerry wanted to make the funeral arrangements himself to prevent disagreements with other family members, so I planned for a person from the funeral home to come to our house so we could make the prearrangements together. We also made plans for funeral services and whether and where to hold a visitation, wake, or other gathering. Jerry selected the readings he wanted for his service and asked one of ours sons to deliver the eulogy. About a month before his death, I wrote his obituary and the program for the wake, and selected the container to hold his cremains. He approved and made suggestions about these decisions. While these were difficult conversations to have, once we did, we both felt better knowing what was in place. Afterward, we agreed that now that we had addressed his death, we would not revisit this topic, and we could spend the rest of our time focusing on living life. It was one of the best things we did because it allowed us to confront his death together, and I think he was reassured knowing that I wouldn't have to face these difficult decisions by myself.

We also discussed financial issues, and I assembled necessary information concerning life insurance policies, bank accounts, pensions, investments, and the like. We reviewed his beneficiaries and disposition of possessions. Given that we now live in a digital age, I knew I would need access to various online accounts after he died, so I created a file with his account user names and passwords. Realize that it is not important to have all of these discussions at once. Sometimes dealing with these kinds of practical matters becomes overwhelming, and we didn't address everything immediately, but eventually, we were able to put these details out of our minds.

It would also be helpful to know where important documents, such as birth certificates, marriage license, passport and driver's license, and Social Security card are located. These may be necessary later when it is time to file for any insurance, pension, or Social Security benefits.

Finally, on a very practical note, once Jerry became more ill, I didn't feel comfortable leaving him alone, yet there were times I needed to shop. Friends were helpful in picking up groceries, but they could not shop for me for clothes, so I resorted to online shopping. After several packages had arrived, he asked what I was getting in the mail. I was a little embarrassed to admit that I was shopping for dresses to wear for the funeral. He asked me to model them for him and he told me which he liked best. It was a bit awkward, but he handled it gracefully and even thanked me for "respecting me and wanting to look nice for me." Honestly, I went into the bedroom and cried as I changed back into my regular clothes. Having to face these very pragmatic things made our situation much more tangible, and sad.

Making Memories for the Future

I've always been an empathic, sentimental person. I experience emotions deeply, both for myself and for those close to me. As we faced the reality that he had less than a year to live, we consciously decided to make as many memories as we could. The first thing we did was go to a nearby park to have professional pictures made of just the two of us, "while he still looked healthy." While it was emotionally difficult, those photographs are some of my most treasured possessions. The day after we took the photos, he had the biopsy performed that confirmed cancer.

During Jerry's illness, I also created two different photo albums of pictures that I had taken. The first album was of our last trip to Ireland. As an amateur photographer, I have thousands of images stored electronically, and since I had previously made albums from our other trips, it was important that I create this last one as well so we could share it together. At the time of our trip that preceding summer, we didn't know it was to be our last major trip together, yet somehow I had taken dozens of pictures of Jerry. Sadly, there were only two pictures of the two of us together on that trip. I crafted a second album, devoted specifically to Jerry, and included photos of him with our children and grandchildren, our pets, and of course, us. This second album, simply titled, "Jerry's Book," was displayed at the wake, in addition to a large print of my favorite photo of him. The act of making the albums was very healing for me as I sorted through the hundreds of images on my computer and we were able to talk about those memories together. I'll always remember him looking at the albums and saying, "we've had a really good life together." The visual images seemed to bring clarity to our memories, both during the selection process and especially after he was gone.

A love of music was also something we shared. Years earlier, Jerry made me a CD of our special songs, and I found it and we played it frequently. Having this was a wonderful comfort to me after he had died. You may wish to select your favorite songs together and create a playlist or a CD to store these audible memories. Additionally, he asked me to make a CD for each of our sons, with a single special song, and to give it to them after he had died. I also helped him write short personal letters to each of them, and gave them the letter and CD a few months after his death.

Even though we all know death is inevitable for every single person, when we are faced with its immediacy, we try to find things to hold onto. We may even search for tangible objects that will outlast the person who is dying. If you have the opportunity, finding or creating these special objects may provide comfort after the person is gone. We chose to have something made for our sons and me that had a truly personal touch. There are businesses that will provide material to make a mold of either a thumb or fingerprint, and in the case of pets, even a paw or nose print. The mold is then returned to the artist, who can then create a piece of jewelry with the print. We did this about two months before he died, and ordered a type of heart-shaped pendant for me, and oval discs for our sons, that arrived shortly before he died. He fully participated in this and chose what he wanted engraved on the backside of our pendants. Later, being able to touch the silver ridges of his raised fingerprint, brought me tremendous comfort after he was gone, as I felt I could literally feel his touch.

Plants also live long after a person has died. Shortly after he was diagnosed, we selected two trees and planted them in our yard, as well as rose bushes and lilies. What we selected had specific significance to us, so these choices can also be incredibly personal, and seeing them come back to life after the winter cold always touches my heart. My point here is not to suggest that you should make jewelry or plant trees or flowers or make photo albums to remember your loved one. Instead, I want you to consider that just as each relationship is distinctive, symbols that are meaningful to you can be selected or designed. These reminders can provide comfort and will smooth the sharp edges of grief and despair later. Frequently, when we are consumed with the business, the "busy-ness" of illness and dying, we don't consider what will happen once our partner is gone. I encourage you to try to think consciously about what may bring you comfort later, and do what feels appropriate for you.

As much as I tried to anticipate my needs following bereavement, one thing I neglected to do was to have audio or video recordings of my husband's voice. His health was seriously declining when I finally thought of purchasing a small, handheld voice recorder, but he felt awkward simply talking into it, so he didn't use it. Later, he agreed that if I talked with him, we could record him, but he wanted to wait until he felt better and his voice wasn't "shaky." Unfortunately, we never got around to doing that. I thought it would have been lovely for him to tell stories about how he grew up, or share some of his favorite memories as a father, or other stories or lessons he wanted to later pass on to his grandchildren. While I regret that we didn't accomplish this, if the person who is terminally ill feels comfortable doing so, I think it would be a tremendous gift to have. I lament the fact that I don't have any audio recordings of his voice.

Similarly, it would be helpful to write down as much information as possible about the family genealogy, including where people lived. For example, on his first birthday after he died, I drove to Jerry's hometown and tried to find the house where he had grown up, where he had gone to school, and where his parents were buried. While we had never done that, at least I had his address and similar information so I could go see those places that had been a part of his life.

Finally, I found it helpful to keep a written record. I found I was unable to remember even important things as my cognitive abilities seemed pushed to the limit with doctor's appointments, treatments, medications, diet, and the like. And I was still working! I did not want to forget the big and small things that friends and loved ones did for us, so I began keeping a file on my computer titled, "Intentional Acts of Kindness." Later, as Jerry's illness progressed, I began writing brief notes about how he was feeling and the things we did. This record became a treasure for me as I read it after he had died and I saw all the things that people had done for us, as well as the things that we had done together or for one another. Additionally, beginning this journal of sorts helped me to continue writing after he passed, and helped me find my way back to myself over many, many months.

I'm not sure there is anything we can do to actually prepare us for the death of a loved one. But as we worked through our emotions, both individually and as a couple, we talked. We talked a lot, both about the future and our past. We talked about regular everyday things too, like home repairs, St. Louis Cardinals baseball, and our favorite books and television shows. And then, four days before he died, as we sat together in our living room, we agreed that we had had the privilege of saying everything we needed to say to each other. That evening, Jerry tenderly whispered, "we'll just let our hearts do the talking now."

August 14, 2013

Our Home, Indiana, USA

After an emotional but surprisingly quiet day, I sat by his bed, holding his hand. Over the last year, we had traveled far from home to a remote location in northwestern Ireland and had returned home again. Just a few short months later, we had completed another journey together. I now had come as far as I could with him. That evening, as I whispered words to him about an enchanted place in County Sligo, he slipped away, and I began a new journey without him, but one for which we had prepared as much as we possibly could. We had loved well together, we had grieved together, but now, it was time for me to begin my own, single journey into widowhood.

Deserted/Dumped for a Second Time

NAN BAUER-MAGLIN

August 2016

Written over three days while watching my husband die

Not again, not again. I cannot live through this again.

When I was sixty, my husband, Chris, who was sixty-one, left me for a twenty-five-year-old student of his. At that point we had been together and married for twenty years, with children from our previous marriages. He has three and I have one. We both have adopted kids, his African American and mine Colombian. (His two other kids are biological.) And we are accumulating a lot of grandchildren: ten so far, with one more expected by September and another in February. So it has been a big, complex rainbow family.

When he left me in 2002, he declaimed pretty loudly that he had been unhappy in the marriage for some time and had found someone who was more from his class (working class), less controlling and judgmental and clearly more adoring. She was Korean; I am white, culturally Jewish from an upper-middle-class family. The age difference was most salient, I believe. The story of our split is complicated: surely my narrative and his differ.

When he left the first time, I was devastated. I took anti-anxiety pills, drank Sleepy Time tea to put me to bed, and hardly ate. So I did look pretty good in tight jeans as I had lost a chunk of weight. He moved in with her and I stayed in our apartment in Manhattan, which we had just moved into from Brooklyn. It was supposed to be our retirement apartment (we had both retired from college teaching). There were many effects of being dumped at my age. One of them was that this city, which was supposed to be our magical new adventure site, became a hostile one for me; I would imagine the two of them around every corner, sitting and sipping espresso in every café I passed. This rejection set alarm bells off over my sense of myself as a woman, an older woman, a woman with gray hair, a woman who would probably never meet another man. I felt unattractive, invisible, and vulnerable. One, and maybe the only, positive result of this cataclysmic event was that I have come to truly value my friends and depend on them. Also our children were busy, taking care of their own kids and carrying on being an architect, a prosecutor, a restaurateur, a preschool owner. His three were in contact, but I think they were somewhat embarrassed by their father. My daughter was especially attentive and called me almost every day. But loneliness is loneliness.

After about two years (and some false starts), we got back together. He says he looked in the mirror and saw an aging man with a young girl. And I had looked into my own mirror, gone into therapy, and learned to withhold some of my nagging, my criticisms, my excessive desire for lists and schedules and control. We have been back together for about thirteen years now. We have always been intellectually and politically well matched; now I think we are happier, easier partners.

An aside: As I watched Hillary at the convention and watched Bill celebrate her nomination, I felt like a sister to her. Not everyone can understand why we return to or remain with our partners who have hurt us so much, but some of us do, and often the relationship is better afterward, even if the pain does not entirely disappear.

In the spring of 2016, Chris developed a cough, started getting weak and dizzy, and had some pain around his midriff. We thought he pulled a muscle from all that coughing. We canceled a July trip to France (we were packed to go for an evening flight, but I was afraid to be alone in France if Chris became seriously ill) and started making the rounds with doctors, in search for a diagnosis. His tentative diagnosis came on July 28, after two CAT scans and lots of blood tests: stage four pancreatic and liver cancer.

In the last weeks he has descended into sleep much of the time, not able to walk because of dizziness and weakness. People who have been caretakers to the dying know that every day is about loss: for the sick person, loss of appetite, loss of strength, loss of focus. For the caretaker, it is mostly about exhaustion and despair. I have spoken to an acquaintance at the American Cancer Society. I have talked to a social worker at End of Life Choices New

York. I have read with both excitement and some skepticism the latest articles in the *New York Times* about immunology therapy. I have followed up on suggestions about what to feed him, how to support him, and how to keep our spirits up.

I have just interrupted the writing of this to bring him some water. He told me that he has a police procedural playing in his head; he wasn't sure if he saw it once or was writing it. I said maybe he had an internal subscription to Acorn TV.

As difficult as these last weeks have been, part of me does not want him to die. As long as he is here, I have a job to do. I am not alone. I am not lonely. I am exhausted and teary, but my life is full: from making him smoothies to holding him up as he makes his way from the living room couch to the bathroom to reading to him from the daily newspaper. Lots of overwhelming decisions to make, big weighty ones and small practical ones: treatment, no treatment, palliative and hospice care, what is covered by Medicare and what is not. And lots of things to do: ordering a hospital bed, paying the bills, and buying ingredients for raspberry banana smoothies. But the other part of me does want him to die a quick death, even if it means deserting me. It is too hard to see him diminish, disappear in front of me, too hard to see that brilliant mind shrink. He said to me that he is used to holding disparate information in his head and then trying to synthesize it all into something bigger, richer. That is what the profession of literary critic, literature teacher, writer about law and literature and African American literature does, he said. He can no longer do that.

On August 2, we opted for home hospice instead of a treatment regimen. We were urged by many people to fight it, to look for a clinical trial, but he is too weak, too tired. Also, surprisingly to me, he is pretty clear (at the moments when he is clear now) that he has had a good life and is accepting of the next step.

So many people have written and called to send their love, their prayers. As Chris gets weaker and weaker, his voice squeaking while he dictates email replies to me, he has not lost his sense of humor: "Looks like the prayers are not working!" Most touching are his PhD students and his undergraduate students, one of whom, an African American man who is now an associate professor, calls him Poppa: "Poppa! What can I do?" Chris texted back: "Just hang in there for right now, Son." He replies: "Rest up Poppa." Other people write "this sucks," "I am gutted," "my heart is heavy." Many of his colleagues at John Jay College CUNY write about how he hired them and encouraged them. Many of his intellectual colleagues around the country write of the importance of his writing, especially on African American literature and the law. Three days ago he declared that he wants to find students who can pick up the various projects he has been working on: one is on searching the Russian archives from the thirties, unearthing letters and manuscripts from American writers. He wants to give some of his book collections to two New York City scholarly libraries. With two other men, Chris has been dedicated to building *More Than A Mapp*, a smartphone application that allows users to locate, experience, and create African American history right from the palm of their hand. He talks about giving some money to *MAPP* so the effort can continue.

Unfortunately, the disease is progressing so rapidly he can only state his wishes; he cannot pursue all of them to their conclusion. That is left to me and others to sort out. These texts, emails, and letters give me comfort; they acknowledge his life's work, his dedication and importance. When I am low I can reread these tributes; when he is gone I can revive his memory by holding on (literally) to these missives. And the four children and their partners and the grandchildren have been there for us both in person and in texts. I feel embraced, . . . but loss is loss. Death is desertion, a desertion I cannot rewrite. A desertion I cannot rewind—unlike the first time.

From Pre-Widow to Merry Widow

ELLEN SCHRECKER

For several years before Marvin died, I thought of myself as a pre-widow. My husband was there, but he was not the man I had been married to for thirty years. He suffered from an unusual form of Alzheimer's—although we didn't know it until we got the autopsy report. The plaques and tangles that destroyed his mind were there, all right, but they were located almost entirely in the areas of his brain that controlled speech and behavior. As a result, he displayed the symptoms of a different disease—frontotemporal dementia, or FTD—which shrinks the brain, rather than clogging it up. Still dementia is dementia and Marv certainly had it. Confusion, anger, incoherence—and, later, incontinence and a loss of mobility. No memory problems though, Marv recognized people. He just couldn't converse with them; his disease had deprived him of language.

He had words, but they rarely made sense; and it was never clear how much he understood what was being said to him. It must have felt as if he was living in a foreign movie without subtitles. He did have a few conventional phrases that he employed at appropriate moments: "Good to see you," "Thank you," "I love you." He often used words randomly or made them up. He couldn't hold a conversation; but, like a two-year-old who hasn't quite learned to talk, he could usually make his needs known. When he couldn't, and when his inability to communicate became too frustrating, he lashed out like a two-year-old with a tantrum.

But a scary one. He was a well-preserved eighty-year-old, a former athlete who was bigger than me and much, much stronger. But that was the ticket I bought at the raffle, the price I paid for three decades of a very good marriage. And since I wasn't about to dump him into an institution, I tried to provide him with the best quality of life possible for someone in his condition.

In any event, it made no difference whether he had FTD or Alzheimer's. There is no cure. The people who suffer from either disease die from it, unless they succumb to something else sooner. At best, there are medications that control the symptoms. But the course of the disease is unpredictable. Even his doctor had no idea how quickly and in what ways Marvin would deteriorate. His behavior went first. Then his language. Physical symptoms appeared toward the end, tremors and then an awkward gait and pitched-forward posture that his neurologist called "Parkinsonism." He became incontinent and sometimes could neither dress nor feed himself. But he was able to walk and interact with people until four days before he died and so was spared ending his life as a vegetable.

His death was peaceful. He was in home hospice and just slipped away under the care of a compassionate aide. But his last six years had been stressful. Deprived of language and increasingly unable to perform what are called the "activities of daily living," his moods and capabilities fluctuated from day to day, sometimes from minute to minute. Occasionally, there were traces of the loving and energetic man I had married, but all too often he would turn against me. Toward the end of his life, when he could no longer speak, he would shake me when he was upset. It never really hurt, but for several months my upper arms were ringed with bruises.

It all began in the summer of 2010 when Marv was diagnosed as having a "mild cognitive impairment"—a medical euphemism for a condition that could be the early stages of Alzheimer's. It had been obvious for a while that he had trouble expressing himself, but the loss was so gradual we let it pass. His daughter, visiting from California, found the deterioration more striking. She made us see a physician. Dr. M., a highly recommended colleague of my neurologist brother-in-law, administered some cognitive tests, ordered an MRI, and prescribed a mild memory-enhancing drug that she did not think would make much of a difference.

Marv took the diagnosis well. Though he had been a political activist and prolific author who had produced the first important book about the Vietnam War, he dropped his teaching and writing. Still, he maintained his other daily routines—bike rides in Riverside Park, concerts and operas at

Lincoln Center, and classes at the Art Students League of New York. But his behavior began to change. He had always had a bad temper. It got worse. He also began to lose touch with reality.

A gifted amateur artist, as his disease took hold he developed a grandiose idea of his talent. "I'm not as great as Michelangelo or Leonardo da Vinci," he would explain. "Probably on a par with Picasso." He spent hours every day at the Art Students League until he was kicked out when his erratic behavior in a print-making studio full of chemicals and sharp tools endangered himself and everyone else. His output was prodigious, large canvases and huge drawings of the League's nude models that began to cover the walls and fill the closets in our apartment. He was spending hundreds of dollars each month on art supplies, even more on frames—a symptom, I later learned, of the uncontrolled spending common to some people with dementia. He was also hanging out in the cafeteria of the Museum of Modern Art hoping to meet up with a curator who would mount his one-man show.

At the same time, he was looking for women. Our marriage was over, he announced. He was going to find a girlfriend who would join him in an artists' colony in upstate New York. That the place existed only in Marv's imagination was irrelevant. I didn't put up a fuss. By then I was so desperate to get his behavior under control that I played along with that fantasy. I did, however, suggest that we consult a psychiatrist to see if our marriage could be saved. This was a ruse. It seemed the only way to get him a behavior-modification drug that would keep him under control. Modern medicine, it turns out, is so specialized that the neurologists who treat people with dementia do not know the appropriate drugs for controlling their aberrant behavior. That was the province of psychiatrists.

We saw three. Even though they knew Marv had Alzheimer's, they never came up with the wonder drug of my dreams. And they cost a lot of money, since it was hard to find a psychiatrist in New York City who took Medicare. The first one we saw, Dr. S., homed in on our marital problems. He assumed that some kind of sexual dysfunction was involved. He did admit that Alzheimer's could be an issue, but seemed to agree with Marv on the therapeutic value of his artwork. Hobbies, he explained, were a perfect outlet for older people like us. "Why, I myself," he told us, "benefited enormously from taking up the classical guitar." After several sessions of talk about music lessons and sexual techniques—and no prescription for a behavior modification drug—even Marvin felt it was time to sever our relationship with Dr. S.

Our next psychiatrist, Dr. A., did supply a medication. "Seroquel, a marvelous drug. It has worked with dozens of my patients and you can increase the dose without any side effects." Turned out that you could increase the dose without any effects at all. Marv and I met separately as well as together with her. I had no idea what she and Marv discussed—that is, when he didn't cancel his sessions. At mine, we talked about how to arrange placements in psychiatric hospitals. After a few months, it had become clear that the Seroquel was having no impact whatsoever on my husband's deteriorating mind and aberrant behavior, but Dr. A. kept on upping the dose. At one of our joint sessions, when Marv was berating me for my lack of enthusiasm about his artistic career, she ventured that our real problem was that we needed to learn to communicate better with each other. I kept silent, though I wanted to yell, "Lady, can't you see this man's brain is turning into mush?" We never went back.

Our last psychiatrist, Dr. R., at least took Medicare. He was particularly interested in our multinuclear family and wanted to see its members. Admittedly, the dynamics of our extended household were untidy. I had one ex-husband and two sons, while Marv had two ex-wives, two sons, and two daughters. But, as we worked through the multipage questionnaire he gave us and arranged to find dates for sessions that would accommodate at least some of the children, it was hard to see how exploring Marvin's parenting practices was going to calm him down. Perhaps Dr. R. might have given Marv a new prescription, but we only saw him three times before what I came to call the "911 moment" arrived.

In the nearly eighteen months since the original Alzheimer's diagnosis, Marv's condition had seriously deteriorated. He would blow up without any warning, accusing me of mistreating him and "putting him down." Once he even slapped me in front of my granddaughters, an incident that terrified them and ensured that they would avoid his company whenever they could. Proud of his identity as a "street fighter from the Bronx," he also picked fights with strangers when he thought they were dissing him. It was only a matter of time until he got himself hurt, or, worse, hurt someone else. His language was failing as well. He could still make sense most of the time, but became increasingly upset when he found himself unable to communicate.

Meanwhile, I was scheming to get the situation under control. Though Marv had handed his driver's license over to Dr. M., he had no intention of surrendering his keys. So, the car got "stolen." I drove it to my son's house in Brooklyn, then pretended to call the police. Marv never caught on. Medicating him successfully was more problematic. Even if he were to get the right pills, there was no guarantee he would take them. He would have to be compelled to do so. That meant putting him into a psychiatric hospital until the drug or drugs took effect. But, according to the law that all of us good civil libertarians naturally support, people can only be committed involuntarily to such an institution if they are "a danger to themselves or others." Marv, out-of-control though he was, was neither suicidal nor genuinely dangerous. So, I waited, hoping, dare I say it, for him to do something outrageous enough to ensure that the police would not laugh in my face but take him to a nearby psychiatric ward.

Finally, in early November 2011, that "911 moment" arrived. An old friend was staying with us, making Marv more truculent than usual. When he walked into the kitchen, cursing me while waving a chisel in my direction, I knew the time had come. Not only did I have a witness, but he had a sharp tool in his hand. Though I knew he wouldn't use it against me, the incident would pass the 911 test. I went outside and placed the call. Marv had already begun to calm down by the time four of New York City's finest arrived. He believed that they had come to help him with the "stolen" car and willingly went along with them.

When I saw him next in the Mt. Sinai geriatric psychiatric ward, he was dopey from a heavy anti-psychotic drug—and furious. "Why did you put me in prison?" That refrain never went away during the nearly three weeks that he was in the hospital. I couldn't blame him. The ward was chaotic, with a few patients walking around screaming epithets at nothing in particular while others simply sat. Marv drew portraits of most of them and claimed that he had made friends and had found a girlfriend. Even so, he was miserable and desperate to get out.

But where could he go? Both the chief psychiatrist in the unit and its head resident admitted that Marv probably couldn't be stabilized enough to come home. Whatever medications the hospital staff had been giving him, they had not diminished his antagonism to me, his wife, the "put-down queen," who had "called the cops and put me in prison." I was afraid to bring him back to the apartment by myself.

To begin with, it was not clear that the drugs he was getting at Mt. Sinai were working. Sometimes he was as agitated as ever, ranting about my treachery and fantasizing about moving to the upstate artists' colony with his new woman. At other times it seemed as if he had been way oversedated. He would sleep for hours during the day, then shuffle around the ward in a barely conscious zombie-like state. He was to remain pretty out of it throughout much of his time in the hospital and was dopey when he was finally released.

Moreover, there was no guarantee that he would take the medications once he left the hospital. Even there, where he was supposedly being supervised, he only sporadically took his pills. I certainly wouldn't be able to make him take them, and it would be insane to believe that he would do so on his own. He had been telling his daughter and other visitors that, once he got out of Mt. Sinai, he would no longer take any medications because he was not sick and didn't need to be "tired and crazy."

Obviously he would have to be released into some kind of residential facility. Easier said than done, since there were few such places that would accept someone in Marvin's condition and keep him safe. And even fewer that had an opening. Finally, I found one across the Hudson River in suburban Rockland County, about twenty-five minutes away. It was a locked Alzheimer's unit in a special wing of an assisted living facility. The building resembled an upscale airport hotel, but it was pleasant enough. Marv would have a private room, with ice cream available 24/7. Admittedly, the other occupants looked much older; most sat dozing in wheelchairs in the activity room or watching nature videos with the sound turned off. When I explained to the staff that Marv was still quite vigorous and would need more stimulation, they cleverly proposed to offer him a "job" as director of their art program. He would give art lessons to the other residents.

The paperwork took awhile, but finally Marv made the transfer. He seemed to be placated by the assurance that the facility was a temporary place to stay until he could move to his new home in the upstate artists' colony. After all, almost anything was better than the geriatric psychiatric ward at Mt. Sinai. I visited several times a week, usually to take him out for lunch or go for a walk or see a movie at a nearby mall. At first he was content. He claimed to be making friends and had begun to paint. The program director assured me that she was about to set up the art classes for him to teach.

But it soon became clear that his "job" was not going to materialize, nor did a promised trip to a nearby swimming pool. The facility was simply not set up to deal with someone as physically active and independent as Marv. Though he was calm and actually glad to see me when I visited, the failure to provide him with enough stimulation was affecting his mood. Within a few weeks, he had begun to demand to be released. At one point, he told a staff member that he would kill himself if he couldn't get out. Following protocol, she immediately called an ambulance and sent him to the nearest hospital where he was put on a suicide watch. It took two days to get him released.

Meanwhile, there was a hitch in the paperwork. Although Marv's stay would be covered by our long-term health care insurance, it wouldn't kick in until the facility sent in a few additional documents. And, despite repeated requests, the documents never appeared. Since there was no way we could pay for Marv's accommodations without reimbursement from the insurance company, I began to search for an alternative.

I had been able to bring Marv home with an aide from the facility for a day at the end of December. He enjoyed being back in our neighborhood. Though he was still preoccupied by his artistic career, he was no longer angry at me. It might be possible that he could move back into our apartment with a full-time aide. And, after making contact with a company that supplied such people, I decided to take that risk.

I also took Marv to see Dr. Huey, his new neurologist. He gave him the same set of cognitive tests that Dr. M. had a year and a half before. The results were discouraging. Where Marv could once identify common objects like a stapler or a watch, he now stumbled and finally gave up. His behavior, however, had improved. He was docile. The anti-psychotic medication that the Mt. Sinai doctors had prescribed was finally working. Huey thought Marvin probably had FTD, but explained that there could be no definitive diagnosis until there was an autopsy. And when that would occur, he had no more idea than I did. "Could be two years, could be ten."

So Marv came home. Though it was a difficult decision, it proved to be the right one. For the next five years, Marv remained at home in our large Upper West Side apartment, where, with a series of full-time aides, he was able to have as satisfactory a quality of life as it was possible to give him. He did have occasional rages and had given up painting. But most of the time he was content with the few pleasures he could still enjoy: food, music, and the companionship of his friends and family.

His main aide in the beginning, Lindsay Spence, was an experienced caregiver in her early thirties. A calm, gentle woman, she was genuinely interested in Marv and soon figured out how to handle him. The two of them bonded, enjoying walks in Riverside Park, visiting Marv's young granddaughter every Wednesday, and going out for pizza and frozen yogurt on Broadway. Even after she found another full-time job, Lindsay was so fond of Marv that she still came in one day a week until the end of his life.

It was harder to find someone to fill in for Lindsay on the weekends. The first aide worked out well. Marv and I both liked her, but she became pregnant and left after a few months. What then followed was a succession of older, somewhat sedentary women, less willing to take Marv for walks and more set in their ways. Though he was no longer the monster he had been before his hospitalization, he still got frustrated and angry when he couldn't make himself understood. And these aides, accustomed to dealing with frailer, less independent patients, were unable to handle Marvin. Instead of trying to figure out what he wanted from them, which Lindsay managed to do, they got into unwinnable power struggles and eventually left.

Finally, after about six months of these battles, Maurice Yapp arrived. Like Lindsay, he was in his early thirties, experienced, and flexible enough to let Marv set the agenda. He readily accompanied Marv on his rambles through Riverside Park. And, when Lindsay left, Maurice took over. Again we shuffled through a number of weekend replacements before the agency sent the somewhat older, but equally warm and intelligent, Musa Tunkara. He was with Marv when he died.

None of them, or I, had an easy time of it. Marv would still lash out when he got frustrated. There were physical struggles as well, especially when he became incontinent and had to wear diapers. In the beginning, he refused to put them on, pushing us away and flinging the paper underpants across the room. Lindsay, Maurice, Musa, and I learned to wait him out. Showers were even worse. Like a child, he hated having water on his face. He refused to use the bath chair we got for him and would occasionally slip and bang himself up. We all tended to postpone the ordeal until he got too gamy.

Food was less of a problem. Until the last few weeks, he could feed himself. But he did have his fetishes. He liked pizza, but he really liked chicken pot pies. For several years he would eat one every day for lunch. And then—inexplicably—he turned against them. No more chicken pot pies. It was corn on the cob and grilled cheese sandwiches. And, until he couldn't cope with the mess, it was chocolate covered Klondike ice cream bars. An entire six-pack a day.

Our cultural life picked up. We could no longer go to movies because Marv couldn't understand the dialogue. But he loved music and since we lived near Lincoln Center, we had ready access to concerts, opera, and dance. Music, it turned out, reached a different part of the brain from the one that controlled speech and behavior. Marvin responded to it in much the same way I did, even if he didn't have the words to explain it.

He was particularly fond of opera. He actually sat through all five hours of Wagner's *Parsifal*. I never knew whether he could understand the subtitles, but he was certainly getting the plot in some way. That became clear the evening near the end of his life when we saw *Rigoletto*. It is hard to imagine a sillier libretto. Rigoletto, the evil, hunchbacked courtier who works for the libertine Duke of Mantua, finds out that his boss has seduced his innocent daughter, Gilda, and hires an assassin to kill him. Gilda discovers the arrangement and, still in love with the duke, lets herself be killed in his stead. The denouement comes when the assassin hands Rigoletto a sack that he thinks contains the duke's body but actually holds that of his dying daughter. At that point, Marv, unable to restrain himself, shouted at the top of his lungs, "Jesus Christ!"

His other outbursts were not always so benign. For some reason, he had developed an antipathy to the elderly Orthodox Jewish men who lived in our neighborhood. Whenever he saw any of these bearded gentlemen, he would head straight for them and give them a shove. It was a little scary, since Marv could have easily hurt some of the more fragile-looking ones. It was embarrassing as well, since I didn't want to say that he had targeted them specifically because of their rabbinic appearance. So I would mumble something about dementia, then drag Marvin quickly away.

A year and a half before he died, Marv developed a new friendship. Maurice had gotten married the previous year and had brought his bride, Carmel, into the household. Connor was born a few months later. From the first, Marv, who had always loved children, adored the baby. He would sit on his favorite couch, clasping the beautiful little boy to his breast, a beatific smile on his face. As Connor grew, he reciprocated the love. The two "boys" became playmates and "partners in crime," in Maurice's words. Neither had language. Connor's vocabulary consisted of "Mommy," "Daddy," and "Wow!" Marv's was only slightly larger. But they understood each other perfectly.

Once he could get around on his own, Connor would creep into the study where Marv would be dozing slumped over on his favorite couch and rest his head on my husband's knee. Roused from semiconsciousness, Marv would open his eyes, straighten up, and smile. Then the two boys would play together, babbling happily, if incoherently, as they kicked a ball around the room or looked at picture books together on the couch. Sometimes, they even sang—tuneless, wordless songs. Maurice recalls the day when Connor toddled over to Marv, pulled at his arm, and led him into the bedroom. Once there, he somehow managed to get Marv to lift him up so he could play with the digital clock that he was not allowed to touch.

Meanwhile Marv began to lose it physically. His tremors worsened. They frightened me, but didn't seem to bother him. Then he began to fall. Again, nothing serious. But he was banging himself up, with new scratches and bruises appearing daily. He still took walks—especially in the morning when he would often go into a rage for no apparent reason. The medical literature talks about "sun-downing," the aggressive behavior that many Alzheimer's patients display in the late afternoon. Marv was a "sun-dawner." If I didn't get him out of the house before 7 or 8, he would become physically abusive, get into fights with the toaster, or throw his breakfast on the floor. But the walks became shorter. Marv tired easily and, unless someone was holding onto him, would pitch forward onto his face. He became incontinent as well. Sometimes he could make it to the toilet in time. Sometimes not. Then his aides and I would find puddles on the floor and small deposits of shit in wastebaskets or on bookshelves.

But it wasn't all bad. On his good days, Marv could still be loving and cuddly. We slept together until the last few days of his life. There was no sex. It had stopped a few years before he died. By that point, I recall thinking every time we made love that it might well be the last time we would be doing that. And then it was. But it wasn't so much the sex I was missing as it was the intimacy. The dailiness of having someone at the breakfast table to share the morning's *New York Times*, of having someone help me decide which of the dresses I bought for my stepson's wedding I should keep.

So, it was a relief when he finally died. I had been rehearsing the moment for years: the funeral home, the brain donation, the notice in the *New York Times*, even the catering for sitting shiva when people come over to the house after the funeral. Sure, there were unforeseen problems like a lost will that I feared he had disposed of when he had furiously tried to "straighten up" the house. The kindness of acquaintances was a pleasant surprise. I had so many dinner invitations that all I wanted was a quiet evening at home to do my laundry.

Eventually the invitations tapered off. I began to operate within the parameters of my new life. The goal was to avoid loneliness. I had been practicing during the last few years of Marv's life, making it a point to have at least one face-to-face interaction with another human being besides the aides at least once a day. But I missed having a man in my life. Because I knew that I was doing all I could for Marv, I felt no guilt about looking for his successor. I needed my girlfriends—but relationships with them just weren't the same. They lacked the frisson of allowing myself to be vulnerable to another person who was not like me. At one point, I even toyed with the idea of subscribing to some kind of Internet dating service, but realized that the recently bereaved, left-wing intellectual of a certain age that I sought would probably not turn up on Match.com. And, in any event, I was so computer-challenged that the logistics of the website would have defeated me.

I was, therefore, quite prepared to remain alone. It was certainly better than living with a demented husband. I would soldier on through the later stages of my life as a single woman, depending on my friends and family for companionship and emotional support. Then, suddenly, there was Mark. It wasn't totally unexpected. I realized that if I were to find a compatible person, it would probably be through my work. And it was. Still, it was amazing, at nearly eighty, to be experiencing the pleasures and insecurities of an early relationship. But much more calmly. It may well be that once you live through hell, contentment comes more easily.

Part II

Recent Widows

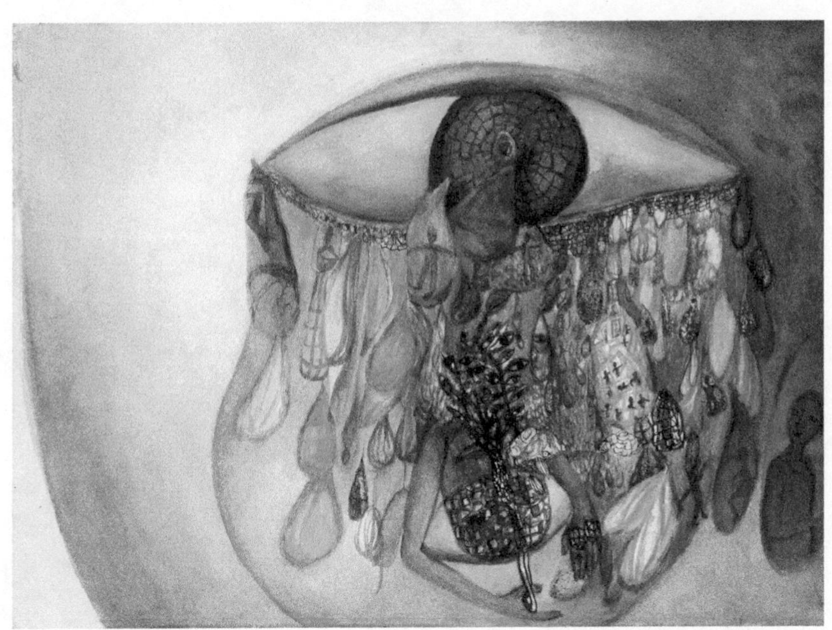

A Widow's Notes

The First Six Months

NAN BAUER-MAGLIN

My husband, Jon-Christian Suggs, was diagnosed with terminal pancreatic cancer on Friday, July 29, 2016; a week later on Friday, August 5, he died. He was seventy-five; we were married for thirty-five years. I started this journal the day after he died and continued for six months (with a break of over three months).

8/6 He Dies

Josh, our son, sat up with Chris all night and into the morning of 8/5. I joined him at five in the morning. Chris was quite restless, clearly disturbed. In tears, I kept telling him it was all right to die, that I would be okay—even if I did not believe it. At 7 A.M. Josh, because it is Manhattan, went out to move his car so he would not get a ticket. Chris died while he was gone.

I informed the hospice, and they called a local funeral home. Two burly guys came to get the body for cremation. They said they would wrap him in the sheet on the hospital bed. My immediate (and typical) reaction was to say no; I had put a good sheet on the bed. They should use their own sheet. They replied that they did not have a sheet; they did have a body bag but always used a sheet first. "For $2000 you do not bring your own sheet?"

Thanks to Florence Tager for editing suggestions.

I asked in disbelief and annoyance. So I gave them one of my older sheets. A dark funny moment in the face of death.

8/8 House Grieving?

Water coming from the floor above through my ceiling, soaking my front room floor. Later a number of the lights go out and the toilet breaks. Is the house grieving?

8/10 Money

I immediately begin the arduous process of getting his retirement money from TIAA, stopping his Social Security, trying to get back the $2,000 we spent on airline tickets for a trip to France, canceled because of his developing weakness mid-July, and an upcoming trip to Mexico for January 2017. Social Security gives a one-time check of $255 for a death benefit—that might have covered a funeral in the 1930s.

8/15 Pronouns and Tenses

Do I say "I" or "we"? Do I use past or present? We live in Greenwich Village? I live in Greenwich Village? We lived in Greenwich Village?

Am I an "I" if I am not part of a "we"? I am wondering about my feminism as I do not feel like a full person without a partner, without someone to affirm and recognize me.

8/26 Despair

In the middle of the movie I felt like crying and giving up. . . . keeping going is hard. I email a friend. She writes back: "Yes, but you DO keep going, and you're inundated with friends and family, and your life is so multidimensional! Really, you're exemplary. And in my opinion, feeling like crying—or actually crying—is nowhere close to giving up. Two very different emotional states."

8/27 Deleting

The other day I began deleting his emails off his phone and his computer—his gmail account and his John Jay College account. And I began to go through and discard the big stack of business cards he had saved over the years—lawyers, academics, boxing rings, agents and publishers, journalists, business owners. It feels as if I am deleting him. He is disappearing; our relationship is disappearing. Did he ever exist? Did we ever exist?

8/28 Empty Home Syndrome

Coming home is hard—it is not only the emptiness but also that I know I have to face all the problems and chores alone. A single friend wrote me: "I do think it is particularly hard coming home to an empty house! I always feel it after my long travels with different people. I am sure it is twice as hard for you as it is not only about loneliness as in my case but also about loss in your case and it makes loss more apparent."

8/29 Photo of His Last Day

Text from our daughter Quin: "I want to be honest with you. Last night when I had your phone for Waze, I opened your photos and saw the photos of him in the hospital bed at home the day before he died. I quickly looked and closed it because I couldn't believe what I saw. I shouldn't have done that because I had a different vision from my last vision of saying good-bye to him the last day I saw him. I broke down and cried because I shouldn't have looked and because that's not the man I knew and loved so much. He looked so defeated; it broke my heart."

NAN: I am crying.
QUIN: I am crying too. I know there was a reason you didn't show me those photos. I should never have looked.
NAN: Looking is important.

8/30 Disappearing

Slowly his things are disappearing: I put away his coffee pot as I only make one cup a day; I gave all his black and white collarless shirts to son-in-law Anthony. His shoes are tucked away in a closet. (I think about Joan Didion's book *The Year of Magical Thinking* about the death of her husband; she left her husband's shoes out for him to wear when/if he reappears). In the bathroom the hooks hold only one bath towel instead of two. A slow disappearing act: my husband and his things are vanishing.

His books: I know Chris wanted to give some of his African American early literature to the Schomburg* and his working-class literature to the

* The Schomburg Center for Research in Black Culture, New York Public Library.

Tamiment.* He would also have liked some of his PhD students to have some of his prized books. But I do not know if I can live with a lot of empty spaces in the bookcases. I also have to clean out his offices and deal with all his unfinished research and writings.

9/1 The Double Bed

Last night I stretched out to his side of the bed. Up until now I had stayed on my side as if he were still going to sleep on his side.

9/3 Charge Card

I went online to check charges as I am increasingly nervous that I am not managing our/my money, as Social Security and TIAA have cut off a lot of my income. I notice a 9/1 $70 charge from our cleaners. Odd—I have not taken anything to the cleaners for a long time. So I go to investigate. I am told that in the late spring Chris brought two pairs of wool slacks to have taken in as he had lost weight. Apparently they had just done the adjustments and had sent them on to storage. It was too late to cancel the order. It was not the money that bothered me, but the ghostlike appearance of Chris.

9/5 A Month

A month has passed. I was particularly teary as it turned midnight; it must be that I am marking this month milestone emotionally.

9/7 Vanishing

An email from a friend: "Well, the memorial is upon us. In less than twenty-four hours it will be finished and everyone will no doubt be feeling very glad to have been there, albeit extremely sad and even puzzled at Chris's having vanished so swiftly from their lives. . . . See you a little before six tomorrow."

9/8 Memorial

The memorial was so powerful and touching. The program had a jaunty picture of Chris in his brown felt hat with printed scarf up against a

* The Tamiment Institute Library is a center for scholarly research on labor history and the history of socialist, anarchist, communist, and other radical political movements.

self-portrait of Edward Hopper in a similar hat—the last picture taken of him before his rapid decline. Brittany (daughter-in-law) sang "Like I'm Gonna Lose You" while our young grandchildren Lola and Layla ran around and climbed up on her; Zane (grandson) accompanied on the viola. A number of Chris's African American male students (now all educators in their own right) spoke about how he was like their "poppa," seeing them through the tough road of a PhD. But why is Chris not here to hear all this appreciation?

9/15 Clothes

His felt hats—gray one to Jim and brown one to no one yet. So glad some of his best clothes will be worn by Zane, one of our grandsons.

9/16 Birth of Baby

A son born to Quin today. He is named after his two grandfathers. Domenick, paternal grandfather, died August 2015; Jon-Christian (Chris), maternal grandfather, died August 2016. A baby for a death. A baby and a death. A baby and two deaths. A welcoming and still long goodbyes. . . .

12/28 Your Birthday

Gathering to see a slide show and to listen to his last thoughts on what would have been his seventy-sixth birthday. Pictures of all the places we traveled to: drinking, laughing, hiking, exploring. We will never travel again. This is a horrible realization.

See you talk in the video we made when we made our will: we laughed about how the children and grandchildren will watch this if we are dead. That is no longer funny. You are dead. But it was good to see Chris as grandfather, professor—funny and smart, advising the grandkids to take risks and to give back in some way.

The four kids, their four partners, the eleven grandchildren plan to converge at our upstate house on the first anniversary of his death and spread the ashes among the flowers (a large patch of black-eyed Susans that he planted for me on my seventieth birthday).

2/2/2017 Six Months

I stopped writing for a number of months. Taking care of everything (getting his retirement payments, getting refunds from two airlines, handling all the bills, changing the car into my name, changing all automatic payments onto my new credit card, dealing with college funds for all the grandchildren, etc., etc.) has taken all my energy. Also, since I could not face the days alone, I booked up my time so that I was hardly at home, hardly had time to think, much less to write. I was so grateful to have so many, mostly women, friends to eat with and go to the movies and museums with.

It is now almost six months—a half year since Chris's death. Is it easier? Yes, much of the paperwork has been conquered and money distribution settled. So I have more space in my life, but that means a recognition that he is not here, that my space is empty. Do I cry as much? No, but I tear up often, especially when I encounter something that reminds me of us. When people are loving to me, I also tear up because, I think, I miss having someone who cares about me, who cares for me. It makes me aware of what I no longer have. Am I less depressed? I think so, yet I carry around such a heavy weight inside me, such a deep sadness.

To date, the bereavement group funded by Medicare met once at the end of January. Of the seven, all but one man (and me), still have their wedding rings on their left hands. I have moved mine to the right hand. Listening to their tales of heartbreak and despair, I certainly feel stronger than most. I think it is because I have a large and devoted support group, I have children, but more important I am active and still in the world. Despite our differences within the group (for example, three depend on religion to get them through), loss is loss and that is what we all have experienced. We talked about whether it is "better" to have the death happen quickly, or over a period of time. While quickly is good so the dying person does not suffer for a prolonged period and the caretaker is not exhausted by a seemingly unending process, with Chris, it was too quick. We had no time to say goodbye. I have no loving words to hold onto as I go forward.

One last thing: The election of Trump makes this difficult experience of the death of my partner of thirty-six years so much harder. Depression heaped upon depression—how to untangle and be free of this suffocating bind? Start with the million women's march and go forward!

2/8 Fading

Last night I listen to a *Modern Love* podcast ("Seeing The World through My Wife's Eyes") about a man who over time was losing his sight. He worked on memorizing how his wife looked so when he fully lost his sight he would have that picture in his head. But he says as time goes by he cannot hold onto the picture of his wife; it got hazy, blurry, lost. While I can see pictures of Chris, I feel memories retreating, stories getting vague, and the fact that I had a marriage, a loving caring relationship, is almost a fantasy.

2/14 Valentine's Day

Listened to the McGarrigle sisters sing "Talk to Me of Mendocino." That was the song we played thirty-five years ago in the red VW, our first weekend away when I was still married to my first husband. For the first time since his death, I made scrambled eggs (he usually made them on special occasions). I cried a lot today.

My Other Half

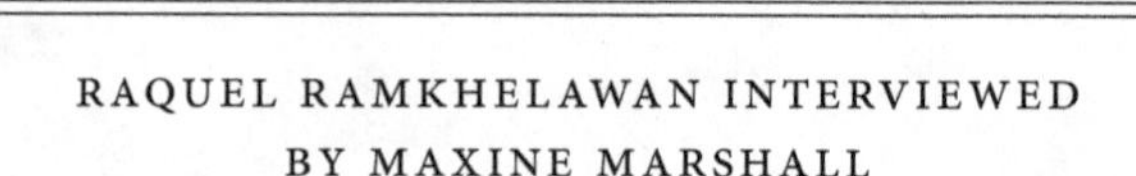

RAQUEL RAMKHELAWAN INTERVIEWED BY MAXINE MARSHALL

Via a series of emails and phone exchanges I interviewed my husband's niece, Raquel, about the unexpected death of her husband, David. This interview was conducted two years after his death. At the time of his death they had been married for twenty years. Raquel was forty-eight and David was forty-six. They had three children. One grandchild was born a few days after the anniversary of David's death. Raquel and David were both born in London, where they met and lived among a community of mostly white, middle-class friends and neighbors. Raquel is of Afro-Caribbean descent, and David was of Indo-Caribbean descent. She works for the National Health Service (NHS) as a pharmacy systems manager, and David was an IT project manager for Camden Council. Raquel and my husband grew up together and would spend summers and Christmas holidays in Luton, England, with the family, but they are now separated by an ocean.

Maxine Marshall

MAXINE: How did you learn of David's death?

RAQUEL: Thursday November 12, 2015, I got up to go to work for NHS as usual. Thursday was not my workday, but my colleague was leaving and handing her work over to me so I had to go in. David got up early to take our daughter to school, as she had to go to school early. I remembered him brushing his teeth by the bathroom door so clearly as I said good-bye to him. He mumbled good-bye with a smile and I started to make my way out, but for some reason I paused for a split-second, thinking maybe he should take the day off, and I will too, so that he could rest as he was so exhausted the night before. However he seemed vibrant that morning so I shut that thought out of my head—now it sticks.

At 9:30 A.M., while my colleague went for a bathroom break, I reached for my phone to call him. But I thought he might be rushing to a meeting, and I didn't want to disturb him, so I thought I would just expect his call after the meeting. About 1 P.M. the head of my department entered the meeting room my colleague and I were in accompanied by two policemen. I instantly thought something had happened to my son, that someone had gotten him into trouble. From my heart beating to thinking "it can't be that bad," I was told I may want to sit down. At that point, my mind went blank. The only words I heard was, "I'm sorry to say . . . your husband . . ." I didn't hear the other words. I refused to hear them. I went silent and told them to take me home.

MAXINE: What was the cause of David's death?

RAQUEL: My husband had a massive heart attack on the train at West Finchley Station, two stops after dropping off our daughter. They had to shut down the station while they tried to perform CPR on him for over an hour. He wasn't ill, or so I thought. He was tired, but not ill. I wasn't allowed to see him until the following day in the mortuary. All I wanted to do was see him, touch him, and choose the last words I wanted to say to him, if not for one last time. I felt robbed, cheated. I still do.

MAXINE: Tell me a little about your relationship.

RAQUEL: He was literally "my other half." We worked near each other for fifteen years. We went on holiday together every year. Called or texted each other at least five times a day. We went to events and parties together. We had arguments, complaints, and hardship together.

MAXINE: What were some special things you did together?

RAQUEL: Going shopping together late at night with the kids. Once they grew up it was our regular shopping date. We would shop in Asda (a British supermarket) for up to four hours. Going on holidays with the children every year. Then spa hotel weekends. Talking on the phone about work and all sorts of things. Meeting up for lunch every week. Watching *Star Trek* and sci-fi programs.

MAXINE: What was a particular challenge for you and David?

RAQUEL: Communication was our main challenge. I, being an extrovert and coming from a large and noisy background, and he, being an introvert and coming from a small and quiet family background.

MAXINE: What was your initial reaction to his death?

RAQUEL: The pain was unbearable, like someone ripped out my insides and mocked me, except it wasn't physical. I wanted to hurt myself so that I could cancel out this "nonphysical" pain. I wanted the ground to swallow me up. I wanted to die there and then so that this unbearable, indescribable pain would stop. I'm ashamed to say suicide was briefly an option.

MAXINE: Who and what supported you during the first year?

RAQUEL: My faith saved me. It's not allowed. God wouldn't give me more than I could bear. . . . was it a lie? I couldn't bear it. I screamed until my throat bled. I banged my fists on the wall, the floor. I knocked my head on the wall. It wasn't real. My faith saved me. I couldn't and wouldn't blame God. I remembered Job. He went through worse. God wouldn't give me more than I could bear. My unfortunate experience quickly taught me how easily a sane and strong mind could turn to a disturbed and weak one. I am so grateful for choosing to trust in God over hurting myself. I'm eternally grateful that I had my family, my friends, and the church community to help get me through the first year. I soon learned that whatever feelings I was experiencing at that moment, however bad, negative, good, or positive, it was okay for me to feel that way so long as I didn't dwell on it if it were bad or negative. How long it took depended on me. My family and friends have also been great. There's always someone there when I need them. My manager, George, was great. I don't think I would still be working if it hadn't been for my manager. He has since retired. My sister, Juliet, has been my rock. My children have been amazing, considering the circumstances and being in the middle of A-level and GCSE exams (British exams for students leaving high school). I have the children's partners, particularly my eldest daughter and her partner, to thank. My younger children's friends were there for them as well, which helped me a lot. I forced myself to encourage us to talk about their Dad. It was hard at first, but it got easier, especially when we found we could laugh together at the funny things we used to do with him, or when we remembered his nonhumorous jokes.

MAXINE: What else did you do to get through the first year?

RAQUEL: I found talking kept me sane, and I didn't find counseling helped me much—it's a bit too clinical for me—so I attended a course called The Bereavement Listening Course. It was a branch of a Bereavement Support Service Organization to help the bereaved. Some of the people who attended decided to set up a Bereavement Listening drop-in group as there wasn't any such local group. People like myself just wanted to talk and have someone listen. Family and friends are great, and counseling is great for some people. But for some people like me who felt they were being a burden on others, they could just turn up at this group and talk, and there would be listeners there at hand to just listen. I found the group helped me on both sides of the coin. Listening helped me understand what others were going through, such unique experiences. Talking helped me to let it out without feeling guilty or shy. The group is open to talking not only about losing a loved one through death but also through divorce, or losing a pet, losing a friend, moving far away, having an estranged parent, losing custody of your children, and the like.

MAXINE: How have you handled it over time? What were the various emotions you experienced? Did you take time off from work? What things did you do to get through this time?

RAQUEL: I went through the motions thereafter, I just existed. I had lost a soul mate, friend, lover, and companion, someone I could scream at and love. He was always there for the children and me.

It helped to start up a bereavement listening drop-in group after just fifteen months. I was told they recommend at least two years of grieving before going on the Bereavement Listening course. But I was desperate. Desperate to find a purpose, a reason to fill that black hole inside of me, consuming me, a feeling I never want to experience again. I battled with my feelings and how society perceived me to feel. At times when I felt okay I felt guilty, and when I was low I felt guilty. Sometimes when I looked at David's pictures and I felt okay, I felt guilty because I was alive and he wasn't. Also, some people, unintentionally, made me feel that I should still be feeling low as proof that I really loved him, or would compare me to someone who grieved for years and would say "she must have really loved him because she's been grieving for more than eight years now."

I have since learned to ignore things people say when those things don't help me. I now take great comfort in the words, "But we do not want you to be uninformed, brothers, about those who are asleep, that you may not grieve as others do who have no hope" (1Thessalonians 4:13). For I have hope, that I intend to live and live one day at a time. But from listening and talking to others about their experiences I'm learning to manage my feelings positively, that it wasn't just about how I was feeling inside but also how I responded to other people's reactions toward me.

MAXINE: Are you part of an organization or is it informal?

RAQUEL: It's informal. Just a group of local neighboring members. But the group provides on-hand information for seeking professional guidance and professional groups and other drop-in listening groups.

MAXINE: What are some of the specific things that people said to you that may have been unintentionally offensive?

RAQUEL: "These things happen"; "Just need to get on with it"; "Time is a healer"; "You should have made him go to the doctors"; "Are you working?"; "I know what you're going through"; "You've got your family." These sayings are true, but said in the wrong manner they can make you feel ungrateful or guilty. If someone said something that I found offensive or upsetting I would tell myself they meant well. They were not deliberately being malicious.

MAXINE: How has this experience affected or influenced you?

RAQUEL: It may have been the most painful experience I've ever had to endure, but I have turned it into a rewarding experience. I'm using the experience to help others, as I'm now passionate about helping those who don't have family or friends to talk to and share their grief and problems with, especially those who are depressed or suicidal. This is playing a great part in helping me to adapt to this great change.

MAXINE: How are you helping others who may be depressed or suicidal?

RAQUEL: Listening to others with sincere empathy. I could never tell them I know what they're going through. Quite frankly no one knows what someone else is going through, no matter how similar the circumstances. But more importantly, without force, gently suggest that they seek professional guidance from a counselor, doctor, or religious leaders. If someone seems suicidal to you or tells you that they are, you should tell them that you intend to alert someone to retain their trust. Someone depressed or suicidal may not know or admit they are. Most importantly, from this experience, I can truly testify that God Almighty continues to help me become whole again, by sending me opportunities to talk and listen to people about their experiences, which in turn numbs my grief.

He also turned a great sadness right around to a great joy. I now have a beautiful granddaughter who was born five days after the first anniversary of my husband's passing. I can honestly say I'm now at the "letting go" and "adaptation" part of this great change in my life's journey and becoming whole again through the help of the Holy Spirit.

MAXINE: How do you feel about sharing your story?

RAQUEL: Twenty months on I didn't realize it would still be difficult to write about my husband's passing, especially since I freely talk about him and my experience quite often. I hastily agreed to write this short summary about my experiences hoping it may help others. I'm not ashamed to say that as I'm typing this sentence tears are rolling down my face. Yes, it still hurts. But that's okay.

The Cloak

LAUREN VANETT

My husband, Alex Forman, died on July 9, 2009, at age sixty-two from chronic lymphocytic leukemia. We'd been together for thirty years. I spent the first year after his death going to work, teaching positive psychology (ironic, I know), being with friends, spending time alone, trying to sleep (often unsuccessfully), seeing a grief counselor, journaling like mad, hiking and dancing to release all the pent-up energy running through me, and committed to grieving as best I could. Because his death felt so radically different from any other loss I'd experienced, I did my best to listen inwardly for what I needed to do. When I wasn't a wreck, I began to notice the way grief worked inside me. I found it fascinating. I recognized that I didn't have to make it happen, that grief would slam or flow through me just fine on its own if I could only keep out of its way. The journey was daunting and devastating on a daily basis and yet, I had moments of joy and insight and even a sense of progress now and then.

Early on I learned to appreciate the wildness of grief, its whispers, its rages, and everything in between, realizing that it was, in fact, a forceful companion. Even though I sometimes felt possessed by this alien energy moving within me, I came to understand how brutal it would be to be without it, to feel only a vast emptiness, where my relationship to my husband had been. Better to have something alive and pulsing within me to grapple with alongside my endless sorrow. So, when it took hold of me and grabbed my heart, despite the pain, I accepted this new and unpredictable partner.

By August 2010, I felt like I'd crossed a threshold. I'd gotten through that first year. Then September rolled around and all bets were off. Everything I'd previously come to rely on didn't seem to help. I was physically and emotionally undone. If you had mentioned anything to me about the significance of a cloak back then, I would have had no idea what you were talking about.

What follows are excerpts from my journal. Beginning the night after Alex died through December 2011, I wrote almost daily. It was how I got myself into bed at night. With journal and pen in hand, I felt a little less alone and a little more anchored than I surely would have been had I not used writing to chronicle my feelings and make sense of my experience. This was especially true on days when the oscillations of grief came forth with an overwhelming relentlessness, which was exactly what happened during the month of September 2010.

September 1, 2010

Deep grief is back. It's not only my birthday later this week that's bringing up all these feelings, but it will also soon be a year since the celebration of Alex's life. I hadn't considered that this, too, would be a gut-wrenching anniversary.

September 2

Uncontrollable sadness keeps cropping up. At this point, when I tell people about it, they often don't know what to say. Hell, I don't know what to say. It's more than a year since Alex died, and I sense that some friends either want to reframe it and make it better, or tell me that it will change and I should just move on. I understand I may have worn them out. But the truth is, I don't want what's happening to be reframed or made different. I just want to be accepted as I am right now.

September 5

I celebrate the day before my birthday with a group of dear friends. We go out to Limantour Beach and find a great spot in the dunes where we picnic and talk on this crystal clear day. It is so lovely to be with all of them, these friends whom I've known for over twenty-five years.

At one point, as we laughed and chatted, I had a vision of Alex walking up the beach and surprising us. Just the thought of him showing up, with his beautiful smile, shook me to my bones. Though I could see him vividly, I dared not linger here. That would be more pain than I could handle. All of us miss him.

In bed tonight, I keep breaking down. Yet my sadness is how I carry Alex inside me. It hurts, and at the same time, it is my way of integrating him more within me, making a different kind of internal space from the way I held him when he was alive. Despite how uneasy it makes me feel, I tell myself it is a show of my love for Alex, for us as a couple and even for myself to not run from these difficult places. I do not pretend everything was perfect with him. To grieve fully, I understand I have to feel the unresolved pieces as much as what was beautiful and complete.

September 6

My birthday today and I wake up with a grueling spasm in my back. Maybe I slept in a weird position. Am spending the day with a friend. Out of desperation, I take a muscle relaxant and hope for the best.

Back home, I appreciate my time with M., sharing in deep conversation and laughing, but not too hard, since the pain in my back never let up. I am not sure how I will manage going to work tomorrow.

September 7

Went into work late in the hope that I could make it through teaching this evening. Tonight's subject: optimism. How many times do I need to teach this stuff while I am under duress? I pulled it off without too much fumbling, and, as usual when I teach, I felt better psychologically if not physically.

Spoke again with the friend who has been feeling impatient with me, and I understand she can no longer offer me emotional support. She is ready for me to move on, regardless of where I am. She thinks I'm stuck. I feel like I'm riding the waves of my experience in the best possible way that I can. Here is where relationships change. Losing Alex was hard enough, and now I see that I may lose others as well.

September 8

I can't believe I am still being tossed around like seaweed in a wave. Maybe I shouldn't be surprised at the intensity of what I'm feeling, but I am. I feel shaken and a little scared at the depth of emotion that keeps coming up. Maybe the reality that I am alone is hitting me at another level still, and the force of that is intense. Plus, my back, though a little better, still hurts.

September 10

I went to an acupuncture appointment today, but my back actually feels worse. And I keep struggling with blindingly raw and endlessly present emotions. Tears come out of nowhere and I can't stop them. This morning I looked at something—I don't even recall what it was—and felt a pain so unmasked and visceral, I thought I might throw up. That emotional pain and its physical reverberation, however, were not the actual problem. Rather, the truth of my life without Alex felt so coldly real it nearly knocked me off my feet.

I understand why people say the second year after a death is harder than the first. The shocking unknown of such deep loss is no longer a blind mystery. It feels frighteningly knowable. It is now me up against me. I suppose this is both preparation for my own death as well as the rest of my life. If I can make it through this, perhaps when my time comes, I will feel braver than I otherwise might. Bottom line . . . I have to create a life without Alex, and I haven't had to do that for over thirty years.

September 11

My muscle spasm has still not abated, even after another acupuncture treatment, which my acupuncturist generously gave me for free. Not sure what to do next. Someone suggested I try homeopathy, though I don't know if I truly believe in it. Feeling desperate.

Another thought on year two of grieving. I realize that it is not unlike the second year of an illness. When Alex first got diagnosed, he was healthy and in a good shape. But being sick takes something out of you, and his ability to fight back wasn't as strong in year two. Likewise with grief, I don't have the same emotional stamina I did a year ago, and I still keep getting hit with huge feelings. I'm also not as fascinated as I was by the mysterious nature of this process. I feel weighted down and stressed out by it instead. I miss Alex in whole new ways that I can't even begin to explain. And I don't understand this flood of emotion that won't cease.

September 12

Rough day. I felt the deafening silence of being here alone. I was so overwrought that it was hard to handle. A year ago today was the celebration of Alex's life. Three hundred people came to this gathering filled with enormous energy and love. Now I feel emotionally desolate, I can't move very well, and the future feels unimaginable. Am devastated all over again.

Made it out to Trader Joe's and ran into a woman I met at a gathering, where we'd all shared some writing. She quoted a line of my own poem back to me, which she'd said has helped her in difficult times. "Look back at your old life in awe," I'd written. "Dare to look at your new life the same way." I thanked her for reminding me of my words, though I don't seem to be doing such a good job of applying them right now.

Some relief tonight—went to a movie with V. I shared with him how all the grieving I've done up to now, which I'd felt so strong and good about, seems to have gone by the wayside. It's as if I'm starting from scratch and know nothing about how to do this, like I've been dropped off on a different planet, where the rules or belief in my process no longer apply. Clearly, whatever I'd been doing up to this point felt authentic and right at the time, but in this moment, none of it seems to matter, like I've been walking in a big circle while my mind seemed to think I was getting somewhere.

Of course, grief isn't linear. Of course, I'm spiraling around, back to some early place but even more raw and unguarded, if that's possible. I need to remember I have not gone through this last year in vain. I am not back at square one, though it sure feels like it. It's just hard to know how to proceed.

September 13

My back still hurts despite my attempts to relax it. I talked to my grief counselor, and she said it was okay to be totally out of control, to take a Valium if I need it, that grief is wild and unwieldy, and at some point, everything I know won't work. Not surprisingly, she said feeling badly about feeling so out of control was a setup. She basically gave me permission to fall apart and take care of myself.

Between my emotional meltdowns and physical pain, however, I'm barely keeping it together. I definitely have some fear about the physical pain becoming intractable or chronic. I haven't been able to exercise, and I probably still won't be able to go to dance on Saturday either.

And yet, something is beginning to dawn on me. The severity of what I've been feeling has a real poignancy to it. I haven't put words to it before, but it's as if I'm now knowingly feeling what Alex felt, or at least my projection of what that was, as he realized he was dying. It's like I've been seeing the world through his eyes as we went places for the last time, and it is agonizing. Maybe this is because I never heard him tell me outright that he was at peace with dying. I know on some level, by the end, he was ready to leave this life, but we didn't have the conversation explicitly. I wonder if that's what's happening inside me.

Here's what I know right now:

I am way more emotional than I've been in a while.
I have been in chronic back pain for going on a week.
I want to escape my feelings, not go into them; they feel like a vortex that could take me down, not like something useful to go through.
It's even harder to ask for support; I feel like I've used up all my chits with some of my friends.
I neither feel like I have any answers, nor that my process is trustworthy, the way I did up until recently.

Tomorrow, I teach a class on resilience. Ha!

September 14

I had a dream last night about being in Germany with one of my oldest friends. We are walking down a cobblestone street, go into a store and come out the other side to discover we are in Poland and that Auschwitz is nearby. We had no idea we could get to Poland this way. We find ourselves on another cobblestone street lined with shops. I see what I think is a bank machine with the acronym "DAC" on it, which I assume means something in Polish. I decide not to get out any cash despite needing money since it won't be in Euros.

Later, I look up "DAC" on the Internet. Its definition: "Descent Assisted Control," to be used when putting on the breaks in Ford trucks. Descent Assisted Control? Yeah, I'll take some of that—anything to ease the hurtling downward spiral I seem to be in.

I tell a friend at work about the intensity of the emotions I've been experiencing and about the dream. She suggests making an altar to my ancestors and asking for help. Hmmm . . . not exactly my style, but I'm ready to try anything. The reference to Auschwitz in the dream, however, makes me think of my ancestors in the broader sense, and I wonder if this avalanche of tears has somehow moved beyond me and opened the possibility that I am grieving for someone or something much bigger than my own personal loss—not that it doesn't merit such huge feelings—but this whole process has felt so counter to the way I have felt my grief up to now; before, I wanted to feel it all, and now I am trying to protect and distract myself from it.

Took my third teaspoon of the homeopathic remedy I'd been given, and I am feeling better, less emotionally volatile and on the verge of overflowing with tears. Maybe this is working, placebo or not.

My class went well tonight. The group is responding to the materials, and I felt present and with them. It seems I do know something about resilience after all.

September 15

Had dinner with my adopted brother/body worker, D., tonight. Awhile back, I told him if I could have had a brother in this lifetime, it would be him. He felt the same way toward me so we mutually adopted each other then and there! When I told him about my latest saga with back pain and endless crying, he said I'd likely popped a rib from all that sobbing, that it probably happened gradually, which is why I might not have attributed the spasm to movement of a bone. I have an appointment with him on Friday.

September 17

Went and picked some exquisitely sweet tomatoes from my neighbor's garden this morning and by 11:30, I could barely move my back. What was I thinking? I saw D. this afternoon, and he's pretty convinced I did pop a rib. In addition to giving me some exercises, he adjusted my neck and ribs, but the muscles in my upper back are stiff in a way I've never felt before. Perhaps a night of longed-for sleep will help.

Tonight, soaking in the bathtub, candles lit and the gentle chanting of Deva Premal playing in the background, I reflect on all the times Alex and I took baths together, or how, sometimes, I'd hop in first, and when the water would cool down, he'd get in for the second shift. Bursting into tears, I understand that I've spent the last fourteen months mourning Alex, the person, in all his many facets. Suddenly, I realize the obvious, that I not only have to mourn him, but also my life with him. I'm sure I've thought of this before or talked about it with others, but it was still a concept as I was so immersed in grieving Alex and all that he was to me. Now, at a gut level, I realize I have to mourn life as I knew it, and it hit me in the tub, remembering all our bathtub experiences—from the baths we used to take in Brighton, England, back in the 1980s when we were visiting friends to here at home in the old, mauve-colored tub we inherited when we bought this house. Such a strange trigger, though of course, anything can trigger anything where grief is concerned.

It astounds me how there is layer after layer of grief that reveals itself on its own timetable, how I get an intimation of something physically or intuitively and then sometimes weeks, or even months later, I'll suddenly understand it in a new way.

I was ready to be done with this whole process. My mind and being had had enough, but I think the urge to get out of it coupled with such severe emotion was in anticipation of this next underpinning of loss and the enormity of it. I've gone beyond the feeling of losing Alex in a very concentrated way into this diffuse, expansive past I knew as my life.

Up till now, I haven't ventured too heavily into memories. I couldn't go there—too hard. And now memories have been finding me, first in the sense of seeing the end of Alex's life through his eyes and the sorrow he must have felt at having to leave before he was ready. This was followed by shifting into my own sequence of memories, starting out with taking baths, and then, like falling through a cylindrical beam of light, I watched memory upon memory open up before me.

So now I understand that I am grieving my whole life with Alex—the beauty, the pleasure, the pain, and the profound love and depth of connection we shared. It's like my grief about him just got amplified exponentially. No wonder I can barely move my back.

September 20

I think this is the longest stretch of feeling awful I've gone through so far. Maybe I'm just coming up against the most lost side of myself—I don't know—but I feel caught in a new way that I can't seem to get over.

Came home from work and felt like bursting out of here. Went up to the ridge and walked. Beautiful—almost a full moon, wind rustling through the trees, sunset sky. I realized something about grief—that sharing a life for so long with another person and then suddenly being alone requires a massive kind of shape shifting. I don't know how to do it exactly, but I get that it's about allowing the internal molecules to be rearranged just as profoundly as the external ones have been, that something enormous and dynamic is happening inside me that is mirroring the dramatic disappearance of Alex's physical and emotional presence in the outside world.

In the meantime, I have to tolerate being in my own uncomfortable skin, and it's getting increasingly difficult. I have to be present in the unknown when all the tricks for finding comfort don't work. One minute I feel like I'm on the other side of a total crash—crazy scared but on the other side, and the next I feel I'm back in it. Not very much is reliable, and that's a hard place to be.

September 21

Had another good class tonight. My students are wonderful, and I'll miss them when the course is over. One woman gave her final presentation on gratitude, and I felt the sadness well up in me. I so desperately want to tell Alex how grateful I am to him—for his intelligence, for all the singing and sweet sounds of his guitar, for his lifelong commitment to social justice and caring for the planet, for his humor and generosity, for his awesome laugh, for his love.

I think I am feeling my own edges more. Alex and I were pretty merged in ways that weren't always clear. It's like we each wore an invisible cloak that integrated the other, and mine has fallen off. I carry him inside me, yet that outer protection, that extra layer of warmth and comfort, has disintegrated, and now all I feel is the pointed edge of my own dislodged bones. Maybe this disintegration of the part of him that held me, anchored me in the world in some way, is what has been so torturous this last month. I still don't fully know what that two-week descent into pure sorrow was. I feel it now. As I write, tears are streaming.

September 22

Still reflecting on these last weeks, how I kept feeling like I was seeing Alex's death through his eyes, not mine. The image of his face would come up, so thin and quiet, and I felt him silently working with himself in this realization that he was letting go of his life. This broke my heart more than anything—all that vitality, curiosity, humor, heart and love, all that vast intelligence getting shut down. I think that's why I couldn't stop crying. I think that's why I popped my rib. I think this sadness, his sadness, which largely went unspoken, was too big for me. After all, I wasn't dying! But, I absorbed his sadness because we were so close, maybe too close in some ways. I couldn't see I was taking it in because I'd been so preoccupied with my own feelings about losing him. And now that I've released so much of my own grief, I think, perhaps, I've had the space to experience some of his, because it, too, was inside me.

And when I finally got to the other side of that, I became aware of the cloak—invisible yet permeable—that we unconsciously wove around each other's shoulders, that field that close couples create and refresh day after day, that soft protection you take with you when you leave each other in the morning and renew again each night. That cloak, thirty years in the making, so strong that it stayed with me a full fourteen months after Alex died, had finally started to fall apart. It became threadbare, got holes in it, and then, just like that, it fell off because Alex has not been here to infuse it with new energy, to sustain it, fluff it up and keep it light.

Likewise, the unconscious energy I continued to send out to him during this subliminal exchange would leave me and dissipate for lack of its recipient. This was the energy of loving and being loved, and it had been in a steady two-way flow for a long time. In the same way that, aware or not, I had continued to feel that flow from him, I was also still sending it out, this purposeful expression of my love, and off it would go, looking for the scent it knew, and when it couldn't find it, it, too, disintegrated in confusion.

So, now I stand here with bones exposed, and it is cold. Whatever remained of Alex's energy outside of me is gone. I need to let my bones settle back into my body, get used to the new temperature of my skin. I need to feel the truth of my separateness from Alex, and of my own mortality, for that matter. I need to learn to live without the cloak, that extraordinary, invisible garment that I'd never even known I'd had, not till I'd lost it for good.

"The Most Precious Fit"

A Dialogue with C. S. Lewis's *A Grief Observed*

ALICE DERRY

I wrote the following passage in my journal days or weeks later:

> *In the space, I was quietly cooking dinner. I felt at peace in my kitchen as I bent to my domestic task. Your last gift to me. That morning we had talked of a new book you wanted to read. Our best times. By all appearances, you went about your preparations for sawing and splitting firewood across the road. In the backseat of your car you had laid out clothes, water, notebook, chocolate. You had set your hat and glasses on the log pile and put your ear protection on, this time for a sound you couldn't anticipate. A door opened, and you stepped through.*
>
> *What I found was only the light shell left behind on the ground, nothing solid except your flesh, gone hard and cold, all the suppleness released. So small, so bird-bone light, hollow, your face grizzled. With my flashlight I picked you out of the April dark, brimming with promise. I could hardly come to you, touch you. Medics, squad cars, flashing lights, officials, and I was shuffled off to make a recording, do this, do that, hardly allowed to be at your side.*
>
> *No, No, No, I cried, kneeling beside you until they took you away. Then the long night ahead, lying on our bed with my clothes on, all the lights of our house blazing to keep darkness over there, across the road.*

I was still floundering in the shock of my husband's death when my youngest brother sent me some passages from C. S. Lewis:

> No one ever told me that grief felt so like fear. I am not afraid, but the sensation is like being afraid. The same fluttering in the stomach, the same restlessness, the yawning. I keep on swallowing.
>
> At other times it feels like being mildly drunk, or concussed. There is a sort of invisible blanket between the world and me. I find it hard to take in what anyone says. Or perhaps, hard to want to take it in. It is so uninteresting. Yet I want the others to be about me. I dread the moments when the house is empty. If only they would talk to one another and not to me.*

A poet all my life, I couldn't read poetry when I lost my husband, Bruce. Until, some months later, my brother gave me the slim volume that contained the quotes, *A Grief Observed*, I was medicating myself on nineteenth-century novels—the far, harmless past. Lewis's truth provided my first comfort. I am an atheist, but I was raised in a strict Protestant household, my childhood imbued with the Bible. I could let Lewis understand my grief, while not worrying about his religious arguments. I knew those already.

Lewis tells the familiar story of the man whose leg is amputated. If he doesn't die from the operation, he can still feel his absent leg as he recovers. Gradually, that too fades. "He has 'got over it'" (53). However, Lewis goes on,

> His whole way of life will be changed. All sorts of pleasures and activities that he once took for granted will have to be simply written off. Duties too. At present I am learning to get about on crutches. Perhaps I shall presently be given a wooden leg. But I shall never be a biped again (53).

At the time, just struggling to right myself, Lewis's last sentence freed me. I could quit trying to return to the person I had been.

In thinking about the path of my grief, which still winds forward, over three years later, I want to draw on those comforting passages from Lewis and show how they mirrored my experiences, which I recorded in a journal I kept for more than two years.

When I asked a friend—so gentle with my grief, although she had lost her husband fifteen years before—what she missed most, her answer was immediate: "I miss having someone to tell the daily to, the minutia which

* C. S. Lewis, *A Grief Observed* (New York: HarperCollins, 1994), 3.

means nothing to anyone else, but which, by its being witnessed, makes your own life real." This is the heart of companionship, your partner listening to how impossible a teaching colleague is, that a poem was published, that you can't find a good winter coat, that tomatoes are actually ripening in the garden, our daughter has fallen for another boy, needs new shoes, got an A on that hard test. Then you talk it out: don't let that colleague get to you, we'll take our daughter out this weekend, I can look for a good coat for you. Then his troubles: the tax office and his tender stories of clients with their risky, difficult lives, living on the edge of no money. We joked that when we met people in town, either I knew their grades or he knew their income, even though we couldn't remember their names. Our worries held exclusively between the two of us, we supported each other.

Or heading to Eastern Washington together—visiting my parents or friends, or our family of three going camping—we carried the unspoken understanding that we loved our rainy Olympics but had both lived childhoods in sagebrush country and cherished its openness. Thirty-three years and 365 days in each—the other knows immediately how to counteract disappointment, support a project, and, for me so important, be on my side, even when we both knew my side was unreasonable. Lewis writes: "The most precious fit that marriage gave me was this constant impact of something very close and intimate, yet all the time unmistakably other, resistant—in a word real" (19).

What about the terrible disagreements, the shouting arguments which often tore us apart? They were destructive, no way to ameliorate that, but the bond held underneath, the bedrock values and common understanding. I wrote in my journal: *The inner core of our beings joined wordlessly, dream-like, but impressed like words into stone, decades of wearing at them before they could be erased.* Husband comes originally from an Old English word meaning *to dwell, to inhabit.*

I taught all my adult life, married Bruce, raised our daughter with him, published books of poems. Every day was packed full, no real time to contemplate the meaning of life; it was in full bloom all around me, as Lisel Mueller so movingly pictures in her poem, "Curriculum Vitae."* When I did ask, the answers were easy: I'm helping the least among us get a degree, I'm raising someone who will be a good citizen. I have my domestic peace—husband and family.

I describe in my journal a night I came home from a concert, not long after Bruce died: *Then it's home alone, not to tell you how animated and joyful Maeve was, singing in her choir, not to lamplight and your sitting by it, reading, raising your eyes to me, glad I've stepped in the door. Now I open to*

* Lisel Mueller, *Alive Together* (Baton Rouge: LSU Press, 1997), 5.

a house empty and the chaos of what is undefined. Directionless just as you are now—nowhere—the house creaking through the long nights, nothing ghostly about it. Lewis summarizes my feelings: "The old life, the jokes, the drinks, the arguments, the lovemaking, the tiny, heartbreaking commonplace. . . . All that is gone" (24–25). "The act of living," he describes, "is different all through. Her absence is like the sky, spread over everything" (11).

The nights are lonely, and I worry I'm going crazy. As if the world moves on without me, I write, trying to describe my loneliness after I lost Bruce and a good share of myself. I was alone much of our married life, writing, teaching, traveling when he didn't want to go along, seeing my women friends. I never felt alone; I felt free. Almost every evening brought us together for dinner and talk. Every morning he was beside me. Our loved independence worked within an aura of belonging.

Dinner has become the worst time of day. I often cooked while we watched the news and talked. Then we ate and talked and watched more news and argued back and forth. The day ended in companionship. In the earlier years, we often had guests over, and the conversation was supreme. Now I sit glued to any reading that makes me forget I am eating dinner. I cook seldom and eat the same things again and again. When I have guests over, I am looking for Bruce, for his confirmation. Out with friends or by myself in a crowd, I panic at my invisibility, my nothingness. Everyone seems to be in a couple. I go to my best friend's house for dinner and she's there with her husband, as is my daughter, Lisel, with her husband; I'm alone among four people who love me.

No one cares whether I get up, whether I go on a walk or write poems, eat lunch or visit a friend. Of course, in reality, that's not true. Lisel is in loving contact more than once a day; I visit her often. My five brothers care if I carry on—after my husband's death, one called me every day of the first year. My friends have given generously of their time and support—as they go on with their full domestic lives. Sometimes, though, I get a feeling these actions are not because they want my companionship or value me. They might be checking up—I might not be socializing enough, I might be falling apart, I might get suicidal, I might be weighing on them.

Sheltered most of my mature life by a husband, I hadn't realized how much men still determine women's images of themselves—at least in my generation. Recent revelations of the "Me too" campaign reinforce my thoughts. As a married woman, I was fairly visible to my male colleagues. Men in the community's business world could hear me. My own air of confidence made the difference: I belong intimately to someone, so I belong. Widowhood makes me an undefined person, a has-been, maybe even a dangerous person. I feel worthless.

I write in my journal: *It's horrible to be alone again—just like the fall I moved to Port Angeles, before I met Bruce. As if all the years together weren't in between. They were.* I have to make that statement emphatically. Lewis reinforces my feelings: "What pitiable cant to say, 'She will live forever in my memory!' Live? That's exactly what she won't do. . . . What's left? A corpse, a memory, and (in some versions) a ghost. All mockeries or horrors" (20).

All mockeries or horrors—that Lewis phrase describes the grief I know. Grief begins its mockery by visiting in waves. One day I am aching and weeping, Bruce almost as close as he was when we could touch. The next, my heart feels like stone. As Lewis writes: "But the times when I'm not [thinking of his wife] are perhaps my worst. For then, though I have forgotten the reason, there is spread over everything a vague sense of wrongness, of something amiss" (35). A few days of calm, the slow drag of the sea farther and farther out after an earthquake, then the tsunami wall of grief rushes back. Lewis describes this experience as a bomber slowly circling and at intervals dropping yet another bomb (41).

My journal offers this description: *So another day. They are on one side the frenzy of activity to settle intestate affairs and on the other, the days of dullness and "the Hour of Lead" Emily Dickinson speaks eloquently to, indifference, deep (but not really available to me) sadness.* No visible pain, just the slow gripping into my body, so the missing is visceral and undefined, stomachache and exhaustion. My mind, seemingly fine, circles around my problems, my body grows its ache. Forward and resistance: slump. Then comes the fresh blood of weeping, and the memories of weeping over ways in which I lost him when he was alive. What is shocking—that I would keep on losing him. A certain scabbing over. I beat at the surface but when it falls, just new bright impenetrable skin underneath. That sack holding us together if we are to go on.*

This acute pain could determine entire days. *My mind knows you are dead, but my body looks for you everywhere. Up the mountainside to Deer Lake, past a whole field of bleeding hearts getting ready to bloom, the buds heavy and dark purple, all up that mountain, I worried and worried about the hours you lay before I found you. The horror of your lightly unshaven face caught in my flashlight, your eyes so decently closed, and your flesh, earth already, but still I wanted to kiss it, as I will kneel close to the dirt when I can, plump it around lobelia it is going to shelter all summer.* "Sorrow," writes Lewis,

* Emily Dickinson, *The Poems of Emily Dickinson*, ed. R. W. Franklin (Cambridge: Harvard University Press, 1999), Poem 372.

> needs not a map but a history, and if I don't stop writing that history at some quite arbitrary point, there's no reason why I should ever stop. There is something to be chronicled every day. Grief is like a long valley, a winding valley where any bend may reveal a totally new landscape. (60)

Metaphorically, I write about the crowding of grief: *Imagination, filling all the space you left, departing, imagination beating wings to set itself free of grief, and for me, no way forward. Now that the house is empty of you, I find you at every turn. I am with nothing, and nothing has hollowed out a place for itself.*

"How often," Lewis questions "will the vast emptiness astonish me like a complete novelty and make me say, 'I never realized my loss till this moment'? The same leg is cut off time after time. The first plunge of the knife into the flesh is felt again and again" (57).

I was in my late sixties when Bruce died; I knew what and whom I cared about—my passions—all connected to him. After his death, nothing seemed important; I didn't want to do or be anything. The excitement I had felt traveling, visiting museums, theater, dance, was gone. "And grief still feels like fear," Lewis writes, "Or like waiting. . . . it gives life a permanently provisional feeling" (33). Three and a-half years later, I am beginning to regain my interest in things, start them, even finish them, but a great nothingness—the power of death—lies behind them. I am back to writing again, but my ambition to be an important poet is gone forever. Why would it be important? What is important, I express in my journal: *Yet the path I'm on is leading me to understand not-thereness, to wrap myself in the rich garments of your nonbeing to learn it. What remains interior erasing the outside world. "What will you do now?" people keep asking me, but my hours are crowded with your lessons.*

I want to bury myself in benign books, I write in another place. *I want to eat a hundred pounds of chocolate. I hate everyone. A poem seems a cruel substitute, but words slather me, you, smother us both as they insist. There is no specialness in grief. Everyone is doing it. All of it outside me, where no one can help. "Sorry for your loss," and they take up their lives, happy to be free of contagion.*

I will just go on, I resolve in another place, *running through me, an undercurrent, always there, always in the background, weighing things down. Hearing the doctor tell me today I need no more pap smears because I won't be sexually active. The silence got to me last night. I could be in silence forever when Bruce was alive. But I can't be with people too much either. They are on a different track, where their lives still have meaning.*

At least, at least, I'll sometimes see him in dreams, Bruce as himself. But for months, I had no dreams about Bruce. A few dreams of reunion floated away, then began the bad and distorted dreams. After that, the great silence, death itself. In a rare good dream, I put my arms around Bruce and hold him to me: *He was all just air really, because he was dead, but he was friendly and nice, his old self who loved me.* I dreaded the next dreams, coming with such scary frequency, I begged never to see Bruce again. Many of them centered around our house, which Bruce started but never finished. We argued plenty about still living on rough flooring, the windows staring out from their gray frames, wrapped in Tyvek. Ironically, feeling the most homeless since I met him, I was able to get help with finish work after Bruce died. In the dream, Bruce walks into the house. "I thought you were dead," I say. "No, I'm not," he replies. And he begins to rearrange everything. I am worried and ashamed that I have made all these changes without him. When I woke up, I was saddened that my first remark had not been: "Oh, gosh, it's so great to see you again."

Then nightmares galloped over me. In one, Lisel and I were covered with a fine red dust, which burst into flames, burning us. I was trying to brush the dust off, but it clung persistently. However horrible the dreaming, the waking was a comfort in the same way Lewis comforts me: grief will burn again and again. The issues we had in life, portrayed in an extreme form, are merely the symbol for the extreme that did happen: he died. In my journal I lament: *How this dream world presents itself, real and terrible, but so ephemeral, so closed to memory, so slippery we can't remember. Even written down, dreams often slip away. They imitate death, building a world consciousness can't enter.*

Now that I've lost Bruce, I have nothing to hold him to me but my grief, no matter how painful. If grief fades, it will be as if he never were. Bruce died in April. In May, I write in my journal: *The valley has changed out of its white-green. The great flurry of the spring flowering in the maples ends. That means the leaves are taking over—their pointed tents of breezy summer and their umbrella shade. The Peninsula stands still to breathe deeply of warmth and return.* The seasons make their familiar round; I am reluctantly pulled along.

More than a year later, I write: *What a terrible beginning. Couldn't sleep. Took melatonin. Slept too late. Couldn't get up. Had trouble with my woodstove and the furnace. Fur scattered below my deck means something was killed. What is it? Where is it? Couldn't get printer and computer to work. Lisel having a hard day. I'm having a terrible day. Fighting with insurance company. Can't manage the house. Every step forward opens up more trouble.* Nothing is working because, deep down, I don't want it to work. I don't want to manage. I don't want anything to keep me from the still moments of grief.

"Time itself is one more name for death," writes Lewis. "It [his married life] is a part of the past" (24–25). Most people around the griever are looking at the future. He writes of a woman who has lost her child. This Christian woman has not lost the hope that her child is with God or that she herself will eventually be with God. Lewis continues: "A comfort to the God-aimed, eternal spirit within her. But not to her motherhood. Never, in any place or time, will she have her son on her knees" (26–27). And since she will never be able to bathe him again, or tell him a story, I add to Lewis's comments, she doesn't want to leave that place where these things once happened. Neither does he: "For this fate would seem to me the worst of all. . . . my years of love and marriage should appear in retrospect a charming episode. Thus H. would die to me a second time. . . . Anything but that" (61). Grief is deep and overwhelming and of a different world. It makes me listless; hunger is stilled. Then, having forced me deep into its world, it lessens, leaving me again bereft.

The birth of our daughter added a great richness to my life. I was thirty-nine, almost too old: she was the miracle. Besides getting to be with her, I felt transformed. I was falling in love again, with its attendant excitement and tenderness. These qualities deepened the poems I wrote; I became a kinder, more compassionate, more relaxed teacher. I was flexible and open, looking forward to over half my life.

When my husband died twenty-eight years later, I was retired, I had made my contributions, and I wanted a leisurely walk to the end without big changes, him by my side. His death, a loss, not a gain as Lisel was, catapulted me helter-skelter, unwilling, unhappy, into the territory of making a new self again. Suddenly I was responsible for everything: car, house, property, our daughter, daily decisions, buying and stacking firewood for winter heat. The difference—I didn't want to learn the necessary new skills—all without the person I needed to give me counsel.

Embraced, the new self forms quickly; resisted, it comes along haltingly. I fight it the whole way. Lisel's behavior as a child explained much of my past to me and relieved me of its pain; I understood my new self. All I know about this new self is that I am someone other than I was. Disorientation is still my major feeling, culture shock: *Coming home last night, tired, missing and missing Bruce, missing connection, missing who I am. Drugging myself with lives in the fiction I read, because I know nothing about my own life. That's still it. I don't know who I am. Say all you want about finding yourself as you go along, something supreme is missing, and I feel totally disoriented. I make the days, I go on, but not out of any source, any sense of history behind me, making me who I am.*

Hiking in Olympic National Park and its environs—almost in our backyard—was an important bond between Bruce and me. We loved being out in the wild. Paradoxically, when he died, hiking may have saved me. The wild is itself totally alone, totally indifferent, it makes no judgment, and if handled according to its rules, is pretty safe. I could go out alone, even if only a few miles, and not feel weird or out of place. The trees felt neutral about the fact that I was hiking without companions. I didn't have to worry about appearances, about being old, about seeming odd to others because I was alone so much: none of these things made any difference to the mountains. I didn't have to worry about all the tragedies happening in the larger world: that I was doing nothing to help. My poems didn't haunt me. I could just be, as my surroundings were, fully in the present. After the long exertion of a hike into the mountains, my self seemed to disappear and join my surroundings. Nothing really otherworldly, but peace, wonderful peace.

Another new self is grandmother. Ronan was born close to Bruce's birthday, two years after his death. He has been an unmitigated joy in my life, allowing me to fall in love once again. As in the mountains, life with a sweet baby is fully in the present. Nothing else intrudes. However, all he is and who I am with him seem to run parallel to my grief, not erasing or changing it.

Lewis writes:

> Bereavement is a universal and integral part of our experience of love. . . . We are "taken out of ourselves" by the loved one while she is here. Then comes the tragic figure of the dance in which we must learn to be still taken out of ourselves though the bodily presence is withdrawn . . . and not fall back [on] our sorrow. (50)

Lewis set a high bar for himself. I'm certainly not there. Most recently, I attended a poetry reading with a friend. In the small auditorium, I was surrounded by more friends, many of them widows. When the reading was over, however, what most affected me was the men helping the women slip into their coats, a gesture so practiced, it makes the bond between them visual. I couldn't stand the thought of a possible twenty more years of life without a partner. I write: *Ached for Bruce all day yesterday. What am I aching for? The day at the cove watching otters, that's what. Our wordless companionship. What hovers is the almost reaching. Then the "I can never be with him again, not once," the force of it being the days, one after another.*

Ironically, poetry, which I wanted to dismiss, poured out of me when Bruce died, the practiced way I knew to my feelings. A poem has its own being, beyond the writer's intent. I could follow the way a poem pointed and reach new understanding. In a poem about a solo campout on Washington's wilderness beach, I write: *The wild rose up in me, as it does when you go into it, expecting nothing. . . . It's not letting you or refusing you.* Sleeping alone in my tent, I realized: *Losing doesn't allow itself to be pure and unatoned. . . . We know the living and dead are entwined, but where / I am never without the tide's sound of losing and finding, / that the twining should be so finally unknowable, so final knowable.* I imagined the oneness I had when Bruce lived and what I have now: *Like Rilke's lovers, we lay here that first time, all the wildness loose in us, thinking of ourselves / as one, thinking no further than one.*

Outwardly, now that the initial shock has passed, I probably seem much the same to others: I have a new book of poems appearing; I see my friends; I loved being Peninsula College's 17th Writer in Residence last spring; I volunteer. I visit Lisel and her family; I delight in my grandson. Life offers two choices: going on or dying. Treasuring much of what life has to offer, I've chosen the former. Deep inside runs the stream of my grief. I am still exploring where it is taking me.

On Grief

MICHELE NEFF HERNANDEZ

Phillip Hernandez asked me to marry him on Valentine's Day of the year 2000. We'd been dating for one month. My friends and family were shocked when we married six months to the day after our first date. As things turned out, my decision to marry so quickly allowed us more precious days as husband and wife; our time together would span only five brief years. On August 31, 2005, Phil died after being hit by a car while out for his evening bicycle ride.

At the age of thirty-five the word "widow" suddenly applied to me. My mind, my heart, and my body wrestled daily with the reality that Phil was never walking through the door of our home again. I desperately wanted to know how long I should wear my wedding ring, whether or not I should give away his clothes, and how long the searing pain in my chest would last, but I didn't know anyone who outlived their spouse or partner to ask, and I felt sure that only another widowed person could answer my questions.

These questions, and many others, led me on a search for a community and eventually to living rooms, coffee shops, and kitchen tables of widowed people from all walks of life who shared their personal stories with me. I discovered that we all answered the questions I posed differently, but what really mattered wasn't that we shared the same opinions or handled the challenges presented by grief the same way, but that we faced our individual grief with the support of a community who understood the unique experience of outliving the person with whom we intended to spend the rest of our life.

Creating a community of other widowed people changed my perception of the word "widow." Instead of weakness I saw survival. Instead of victims I saw courageous warriors. Instead of only a well of sadness I was introduced to the crystal clarity of gratitude for each moment we are given to live. My widowed community changed my life, and I wanted to make sure other widowed people were provided access to the power of shared experience.

The founding of Soaring Spirits International, a nonprofit organization offering innovative peer-support programming internationally, is my gift to the widowed people who have come after me. Twelve years after the death of my Phil, Soaring Spirits has offered a community of support, a collection of relevant resources, and vital access to hope for three million widowed people. In this way Phil's love for me, and mine for him, has multiplied and continued changing the world.

I could not be more grateful.

I've learned so much about grief over the past twelve years. These two pieces are particularly meaningful to me, and I hope they offer others comfort in their own grief experience.

My Friend Grief

Over the past four years grief and I have reluctantly become friends. Grief is not the kind of friend I can call in the middle of the night when I am sad, but rather the kind of friend who sits quietly at the end of my bed while I cry myself to sleep. Grief may be away for weeks or even months at a time, but the knock of this friend is now as familiar to me as my own voice. There is no need to explain my sorrow to grief; she understands my process better than I do. Grief knows I will get up again no matter how hard I have been hit by her power, and patiently stands as a witness to my ability to regain my balance time and time again. When grief calls, I stop what I am doing because I have learned that she must be answered. When I quit trying to escape her, I find an unexpected comfort by her side. She calls me and repels me; guides me and confuses me; moves me forward and throws me back.

Some days I hate grief, and other days I miss her. I have discovered a safe place in her arms, though her twisting, turning path won't allow me to be still for long. Her presence has added a soft cadence to my day-to-day life that I have come to rely on as confirmation that I am, indeed, alive.

The irony of this does not escape me. I have realized that in my mind grief has replaced Phil, and that my fear of letting him go has created a relationship with grief I could never have anticipated. I am beginning to believe that this is why grief comes in waves.

If grief was linear and we could walk from one stage into the next, there would likely be large numbers of grieving people with severe stage fright. I would be terrified if someone were able to provide me with a grief graduation date. Instead, grief throws us from one phase to the next, with no predictable pattern or discernible course. Like boxers who learn to fight on their feet, our tortured, grieving selves wheel from one moment to the next, watching for the inevitable gut punch. And slowly, painfully we become stronger, faster, and more confident each time we are forced into the ring. That doesn't mean we won't hit the matt, or that we won't be tempted to stay down for the count. . . . but somehow our spirits find the will to fight one more time.

Grief holds the towel as we come out of the ring. Grief bandages our wounds and then sends us to face the opponent called death, again and again. Grief stands behind the stool in our corner and insists we go another round. There is a saying that speaks to the concept that some friends come into our lives for a purpose but do not stay long. I am beginning to think of grief as a friend who will come and go from my life. She will show me how to survive in the ring of sorrow, and then leave me with these hard-earned knocks, hoping they teach me something about living courageously. Grief will also point out that she is not Phil, and that he is not her. He exists in a separate, and timeless, place that she does not inhabit. Grief is wise. And eventually I must let her go, knowing that when she resurfaces, sometime down the road, I will greet her as a friend.

Grief Timeline?

The day Phil died I had no idea what kind of roller coaster ride I was about to board. In many ways I felt I was shuffled onto the first outgoing cart marked "grief," and told to put my lap belt on low and tight. Maybe I would have managed the twists and turns of the journey better if someone had handed me a grief timeline that mapped out the course that lay ahead. I would have appreciated having my grief start date clearly noted in red, the days when getting out of bed was going to be a challenge highlighted in yellow, all anniversaries/birthdays/holidays circled in green, and the most important thing of all . . . the grief end date . . . circled in bright orange highlighter so that I would know when my grief had officially come to an end.

Not only was there no mourning road map forthcoming, but grief kept me on a circular roller coaster ride. Riding through the dips and surprise upside-down flips might have been worth it if I felt I was going somewhere, but to end up right where I started and still suffer a case of nausea from the experience was infuriating. I remember very clearly after the one-year anniversary of Phil's death feeling that I should have arrived somewhere by then. Shouldn't I have moved to a new level of grief? I desperately wanted to graduate already!

Yesterday one of my widowed friends told me that her counselor said you can expect to grieve one year for every five years that you were married. She wondered what I thought of this idea. The first thing that came to mind was that since I was married to Phil for five years and two months, then I should have been done grieving his loss three and a half years ago. There have been so many times over the past nearly five years I have wished someone could tell me how long this whole healing process would take. I do understand the desire to calculate the effects of the death of a loved one on our lives, and even the desire to create some kind of measuring stick for healing. But if someone had provided me with a grief end date, I am sure I would have focused on nothing but getting to that day. If graduating from widowhood were possible, I would have taken whatever extra courses were needed to meet the early graduation deadline. And I think that I would have missed the whole point.

The brutal nature of grief forced me to live one day at a time. As a person who tends to jump ahead to the next thing, or tries to figure out how extra effort on my part can bring about a desired goal sooner than expected, the unpredictability of grief made living outside of the moment impossible. No other life experience has so firmly placed me in the present. When my babies were born I wasted precious time thinking about their next milestone, instead of reveling in the current one. When Phil and I were happily married I wouldn't take the time to sit on the couch and watch a TV show with him if the laundry wasn't finished. Accomplishments tended to be put aside as I reached for the next goal, because living in the moment was not enough. I was always focused on taking the next step.

In the aftermath of Phil's death, the inability to go back in time paired with the lack of desire to move forward into the future without him bought me some much-needed time. Time to allow the reality of his physical absence to sink into my shell-shocked brain; time to figure out who I was without him; and time to slowly discover that I was strong enough to weather this devastating storm. If I'd known that I was only expected to grieve Phil's death for one year I would have located the end date and run full speed ahead to get to the finish line. Flying past the lessons I needed to learn, the healing effects of camaraderie, the small blooming of the first flower in spring . . . all in order to say I was finished.

So, no, I don't think there is a measuring stick or a formula that can predict how long a person will mourn the death of a person they love. But I do think the small markers on our own personal measuring sticks are much more important than we might suspect. I think healing happens in centimeters, and each small dash is a triumph.

Wedding Rings

ELISA CLARKE WADHAM

On April 20th, which fell on a Sunday for that second anniversary of my husband's death, I moved my wedding rings from the ring finger of my left hand to that of my right. This had been my growing intention for several months. It was a symbolic act; there was nobody to witness it, and it was unlikely anyone else would notice.

Below the knuckle, the left-hand finger was eroded and pale. It looked naked, and vulnerable. The rings, two gold wedding bands sitting either side of a slim diamond eternity ring that served as my engagement ring, were enhanced by the addition of three diamonds in a simple setting, which I had inherited. Together, they had been doing their work on that finger for sixteen years. In the customs of our tribe, they signified at a glance that I was an apparently well-to-do married woman, following traditions that when considered seem almost as primitive as nose rings. They carried a value far greater than the precious stones and metal alone, for they were symbols of commitment, promises, and love. They were a statement that he and I had chosen, and accepted, each other in marriage.

I was in my late forties and he sixteen years older when the rings were placed lovingly on my finger by my second husband. These rings had rarely been removed, until now. A strange sense of reluctant self-exposure accompanied the changeover. When I held my left hand out in front of me, to look at it in its vacant state, I saw only emptiness and loss.

My husband slipped away on the merest wisp of a breath, after a long, cruel illness. He was suddenly gone, just like that. After a while, there was nothing left for me to do for him, except to organize farewells and memorials, to try to comfort his distant family and to begin the long process of dismantling and redistributing the tangible remains of his life. During his illness, it had been important to me that he knew, layer upon layer, how much I cared for him; somehow that did not change after his death.

A debonair Englishman, he had come to Australia years before with his then wife and two of their six children. The older ones remained in England and France at university or following new careers, and eventually the other two drifted away as well. His wife too returned to England with the much younger man she had run away with. We had all been friends during their marriage, and a couple of years after his divorce he asked me to design the interiors of the old house he was remodeling. That was when our romance began. Over the following years I became close to the children, the oldest of whom was not much younger than myself. None of them were in Sydney when he died, although several had visited earlier, and not even the oldest grandchildren were present at his Sydney funeral. He had hoped for that, perhaps the oldest grandsons, then in their early twenties, at least. In spite of the large group of friends and my family present, I felt very alone, both for myself and for him. A memorial service in London was also organized, at the little church in Chelsea that he and the family had attended. Afterward, we walked around the corner to a pub called The Surprise, where we had reserved the pleasant upstairs room for the occasion. The five daughters and his son reminisced about him for each other and their friends, and sang songs, their arms around each other, in their usual extravagant style. For them, this was a celebration of his life. For me, it was a painful reminder of all that I had lost.

In the early morning, very soon after my husband had died, a dear friend had, with a sixth sense, arrived at the hospice. He sat with me as I waited dumbly in the little room they keep for such occasions. My friend had lost his partner years before and knew just how to be with me. He spoke gently, his words carefully rounded in his mouth. "You have a new title now. You're a widow." I remember looking down at my hand with its rings, holding it in the palm of the other hand, running my right thumb back and forth over the ring finger. The hands would be lonely now, with no brow to stroke, no other hands to hold, but the metal of the rings and the tiny shining stones seemed to hold a shimmer of embedded memory of what that had been like. I couldn't imagine taking them off.

That first year of being alone was quickly complicated by the sudden death, in June, of my first husband. He was the father of my only child, and we had remained close after our divorce, three decades earlier. My daughter and her husband were living in Singapore with their three small children, the distance an added difficulty at this most difficult of times. The two deaths, so close together, sent seismic shock waves through our little family, and bore devastatingly into the core of my being. My daughter and I struggled to help each other with our different losses while also attempting to manage our individual grief, but our strong and loving relationship came under siege. It was for me a time of both psychic and physical pain, complicated by a desperate need to appear to be coping, and an endless river of private tears. There was little comfort to be found. I had to keep moving to stop myself falling into the black pit of despair, and later that first year made a road trip a thousand kilometers north and four weeks long, to Queensland and back, with my little dog Dido the only constant heartbeat against oblivion. I accepted with gratitude the company of others to push back the darkness, but in spite of the great kindness of friends I was completely hollowed out, and exhausted.

As the first anniversary loomed, my close friend Robyn, herself a widow who well understood the need to keep moving, invited me to join her on a private tour to look at outdoor sculpture. So it was that, alone on a gritty little beach in New Zealand, in a dreary overcast dawn, I greeted the turning over of that terrible year at the precise hour of his death. But, because I was there, in the midst of nature, sharing a time of wonderful things and big thinking, with interesting people, I felt that it might be possible to survive.

As the second year passed into a lonely, depressing winter, the presence of the rings began to weigh on me, like a chain securing me to the past. They signified a state that I no longer had a right to claim. I felt unmoored from relationship, love, partnership, sharing, and caring. I was both marooned on an island of loneliness and adrift in an ocean of little purpose. Having been productive and caring of others for all my adult life, I now felt useless. My work no longer came easily or gave me satisfaction. It became clear to me that in order to save myself, a transition must be initiated, a life raft to change invented. I needed to shift my course both emotionally and physically (the one enabling the other, perhaps). I needed to seek a way to heal and move forward into my future, whatever it held.

Some people treat the concept of "trusting The Universe" patronizingly and with intellectual derision, but I, having been taught by long experience to have faith in the process, embrace it wholeheartedly. Like invisible writing manifesting on a blank page, plans began to materialize. A Korean friend set a date for the trip that we had talked about for years, one that he would organize to Korea, with a small group of friends. Then, my tentative search for a small place to rent in the country, to serve as a temporary base, was almost miraculously rewarded.

The offer of a perfect cottage adjacent to a friend's house, high on a bushy ridge with extraordinary views to the sea, seemed heaven-sent. I spent six months living there, two hours' drive south of Sydney, enabling me to rent out my city apartment to finance these adventures.

The days were special, healing me gently in the peace and abundance of nature, even though I was often alone on the mountain, but once darkness fell, Dido the little dog and I retreated behind tightly closed shutters and huddled together in the snug bedroom, never opening the door until dawn.

And finally, like a reward for persevering, the long-discussed possibility of my son-in-law being offered a big job in New York became a reality, meaning that he and my daughter's little family would relocate there from Singapore. When the phone call came from my daughter to confirm this stunning news, I stood in my cottage, looking down over the Shoalhaven River winding its shimmering way though the valley to the sea, the sky a dome of shining blue above. With a sense of awe and gratitude, I, the tiniest speck among multitudes, saw that The Universe was indeed providing for me: having lived in New York as a teenager, having ever since wished to return, having longed to live in closer proximity to my daughter, her husband, and their children, it was a foregone conclusion that I too, would somehow move to New York.

Meanwhile, the rings were comforting on my left hand, although I wondered about the mixed messages they gave. Tentatively, I asked other women their thoughts about if and when a widow might take off her wedding bands. Robyn, my friend who is three years ahead of me in her journey of loss and reinvention, had chosen never to wear a wedding ring during the many years of her marriage, yet found herself putting a ring on that finger in the weeks after her husband's sudden cataclysmic death. Eventually, she bought in Paris a magnificent citrine ring the size of a matchbox, which, when she wears it, dazzles everyone out of thoughts of marital status or indeed any form of classification and simply demands admiration. An older friend who had been married for five decades before losing her life's partner, said that her rings were part of her, and she could not imagine ever taking them off. A lusty divorcee advised me, with a laugh, to get them off immediately and find a man, a suggestion that then seemed impossible, although I too summoned a laugh. Other friends, husbands dynamically alive, shrugged politely and shied away from an answer, uneasy as most are around the subject of grief and loss. I recalled that my mother and her fellow widows had worn their own rings until they too died. There was no etiquette it seemed, no rules, unless there is another marriage, when the original bands will perforce be demoted and probably tucked away in a box somewhere.

Part of my dilemma was, if I take the rings off that finger, where will I put them? I felt as if they must continue to be worn. The only alternative seemed to be on the ring finger of my right hand, but that was occupied by a large opal ring in a roughhewn silver setting which I had worn since my beloved godmother had died several years before. It had become something of a talisman to me, as if she was still with me. It was distressing when suddenly the opal split and fell from its setting, unable to be repaired. I replaced it with the egg-shaped ring that I had worn before my godmother died. It too had history: an old friend owned a gallery, for which she chose semi-precious handmade pieces with a certain earthy character. After I had tried the ring on one day, loving it but resisting temptation, she secretly put it aside, until my husband dropped by to say hello. . . . Somehow that ring felt special, chosen, and I was pleased to wear it again with its freighted significance, in spite of regretting the demise of the opal.

In Japan, I was wearing that egg-shaped ring as my ideal traveling companion Margaret Mary and I meandered along the Philosopher's Walk in Kyoto on an autumn Saturday. Perhaps attracted to the large, roughly faceted sea-blue stone bright under browning leaves, an unseen bee stung me on my finger, beside the ring. It was a shock, unsuspecting as I was, and I cried out at the sudden stab of pain. I brushed the bee aside with a slap; it fell small and dead to the ground. A Japanese woman selling hand-woven scarves nearby inspected it, then came to my rescue with a pair of tweezers from her handbag, deftly pulling out the stinger. Someone else dipped a tissue into water and pressed it to my finger, gesturing that I should hold my hand upright, like a policeman stopping traffic. After I ceased to be a public concern and the thanks and bowing were concluded, we continued on our way. Why I didn't think to take off the ring then is a puzzle to me; when we returned to the hotel that evening, the finger was swollen and the ring impossible to remove. The thought of negotiating—in a small hotel in Kyoto, in Japanese, on a Saturday night—a situation where blood flow to my finger had been stopped and the ring needed to be cut off, spurred me to action. Working with ice, soap, hand cream, and desperate determination, it took me twenty minutes to get the ring over my knuckle and off my throbbing finger. The swelling remained for many weeks, causing Margaret Mary to remark in her dry way that it had probably been caused by the brutal ring-removal exercise rather than by the bee sting. As a result, it was several months before I could even consider moving my wedding rings to my right hand, where a space had been unwittingly created.

An unaccountable tension rose in me as the second anniversary approached. It was a time demanding much action and hard work, as I was about to rent out my home, abandon my design practice, and leave my country for at least a year, but my thoughts returned again and again to my husband and the long odyssey we had taken together toward his death. Time had smoothed the jagged edges of grief a little, though as I sorted and stored the contents of our home (his clothes! his desk!) both gratitude and regret rose in me like a tide. In the last six months of his life, as he grew frailer and hope receded, we were drawn closer and closer to each other. In the absence of other family members with whom to share, who might have taken on some of the tasks of caring for him and cheering us both, we returned to the intimacy of two people joined as if bound by invisible silken cords. Our physical union became one of me tending to his suffering body, as a mother tends to a newborn. There was no more independence, separate activity, or individual planning: we were again as we had been at the time we fell in love with each other, only this time, our focus was singular, fixed on him, and revolving around making his daily life as comfortable and pain free as possible, with as much companionship and sensory pleasure as I could conjure up. The morning sun streamed deep into our apartment in those months, and when he was out of bed for a few hours and bathed, I would settle him in on a couch in its path, in a nest of pillows, and play his favorite music. His hands fluttering along with the beat, eyes closed, there was an air of serenity about him then. He became mellower, more gentle and more biddable, and therefore easier to care for. His youngest daughter, flying across the world to visit him a few weeks before he died, found him to be "the father I have always wanted." His sense of humor and chivalrous nature mostly stayed with him until consciousness departed, a memory that I burnish and treasure. Our world shrank to our apartment, at best a peaceful haven of sunlight and soft music, at worst a place of 3 A.M. torment and rage as his disorientation and confusion increased. The hours of his struggle and my nurture were broken by the visits of his doctor and professional carers who bathed him and produced items that I had no idea existed to ease the increasing physical challenges. Friends calling and visiting were the saving grace, distracting him and fortifying me, most particularly as his memory faded under the assault of the illness and drugs. But we were given the gift of time to be together, to live out our days as husband and wife. Unlike my friend Robyn, I was spared the terrible shock of sudden traumatic death, which for her folded into disbelieving grief, angry denial, and an evolving relationship with the memory of her husband that would go forever unrequited.

I know that my basic nature is optimistic, and that served me well now as I was able to stop dwelling on the memories of difficult times when both of us behaved less well than we should have. My gratitude is profound, for I was given a second chance to demonstrate my marriage vows to love and to cherish, in sickness and in health. I had made a commitment under which

I chafed when he was less than the man I had believed him to be (and I was certainly not my best self), but toward the end I was able to prove that commitment to the depths of my capacity until his life was over, and indeed beyond. Perhaps, when he first placed that engagement ring on my finger, that might have been his hope, though the ultimate end of our particular love story was blurry then for me, not something I cared to think about.

Reliving, for the second year, the weeks and days leading up to his death was bittersweet. I missed him, deeply, as well as the better parts of the rich life we had shared together. I regretted much and I continued to mourn the man who was, in essence, full of exuberance and fun, loyal and loving, and in many ways, generous-spirited; that man and I sadly passed each other by during challenging periods of our marriage, causing me to reflect unhappily on my own part in that. But I was able to balance these thoughts with my sense of us having come full circle, back to trust and acceptance, back to unconditional love: the best of what a marriage might mean. I hoped and believed that he died with this awareness. Now I knew that, like a wounded warrior, I would survive, weighed down but moving forward carefully with battle scars and painful lessons learned.

Into the third year after his death, my ringless ring finger and I were installed in a quirky loft apartment in Manhattan. Once in a while, on the subway, I would see someone idly assessing me, as I assess others. They may think they knew something about me because there was no wedding ring, but the lack of that symbol is a lie, an omission of fact. That feels both wrong, and as it should be. That bare finger does in fact symbolize an emptiness, and a time of change. I was on a blank page as far as a new relationship might go, although the possibility of one was a fragile, tentative hope.

My left hand does feel naked but not useless or unloved: holding my grandchildren safe on the sidewalks of New York, the two little ones with one of their hands in each of mine and the oldest with his hand tucked under my arm when crossing busy streets and avenues, is a consolation that brings with it a joyful sense of purpose. I have much to share with them as I build a new life, and much to embrace as their young lives evolve. Hands full, the present, rather than the past, has become my reality.

The Afterlife of an Archive

DEBORAH E. KAPLAN

My husband, Roy Rosenzweig, died in 2007 of an illness we had no reason to anticipate. In the United States, 10 to 15 percent of lung cancers occur in people who have never smoked; he was one of them. Giving us little time to prepare, the disease ended his life within a year and a half of his diagnosis. For several months afterward, I preferred to spend as much time as I could away from our house, returning only to sleep. But eventually I decided to move, a feat I could accomplish only by going through my—and his—things.

Roy had been a professionally active historian for more than thirty years, and most of his possessions were connected to that occupation. Among the rooms that I'd been avoiding, his study remained as he had left it on the day he went to the hospital for the last time. Even for a space dedicated to a single activity, it was unusually functional. By means of its accretions, it also suggested the span and style of his working life.

Lined with file cabinets and bookcases, the latter of which wound their way through much of the house, the room contained a door resting on two-drawer file cabinets, which he'd used as a desk since graduate school, and a newer, more expensive desk chair, acquired at a time when the only health problem he worried about was a sore lower back from sitting too long.

First published in *The Chronicle of Higher Education* (October 1, 2010): B13–B14).

For years a second desk chair had stood near his own, for hosting the friends and students with whom he had often worked.

The rest of the space was occupied by equipment revealing his embrace of technologies that aided and eventually became the focus of his academic research. He had kept the typewriter table, even after he'd given away the IBM Selectric in the early 1980s, and a photocopier sat on it instead. We bought a Kaypro computer in place of the typewriter, but it, too, had been replaced by a succession of better, more up-to-date machines. I suppose I will come to say in the not-too-distant future that Roy died in the era of the MacBook Pro, two of which rested on his desk.

To assess the physical and emotional task I was about to undertake, a friend suggested that I inventory the possessions of which I was least certain—what we had stored in our basement. Early in our marriage we had come to think of me as Oscar and him as Felix: I was messy, and he was neat. To be more precise, I was slow to put my things away and hated to part with any of my possessions, and he was well organized, though not fastidious, ready to let go of anything inessential in order to keep track of what he needed. In our post-9/11 age, it is commonplace to note how difficult identifying crucial information is when we are drowning in data—how ineffective a watch list becomes, for example, when there are half a million people on it. But Roy understood that problem at the outset of his academic career and routinely threw things away so as to focus and draw efficiently on the materials that enabled him to do his scholarly work.

Given our contrasting predispositions, I was astonished to discover that most of the boxes and file drawers in our basement contained stuff that belonged to him.

I'd always been so daunted by his clear desk, the never-overflowing In and Out boxes perched at one of its corners, the reams of used paper he often bagged and took out to the curb for recycling, that I had failed to notice what he'd been accumulating. Many cartons contained letters he'd received, bundled in manila envelopes that were labeled "academic correspondence" and dated. I found shoeboxes containing stacks of index cards, grouped by theme, research he'd done for the dissertation that became his first book, *Eight Hours for What We Will: Workers and Leisure in an Industrial City, 1870–1920*. There were boxes of audio tapes with interviews he'd conducted for that book; for a film he'd helped to produce around the same time, Richard Broadman's *Mission Hill and the Miracle of Boston*; and for oral history projects he undertook in the 1980s. File drawers were packed with folders whose contents were clearly marked and arranged. Some held data, maps, and slides for *The Park and the People: A History of Central Park*, which he wrote with Betsy Blackmar, as well as comments they sent to each other about their chapters. On a shelf near the file cabinets were several large plastic notebooks containing copies of nineteenth-century New York newspaper articles that he compiled while writing that book. In fact, I found folders pertaining to almost all the professional work he undertook, often with groups at the City University of New York's American Social History Project and at the Center for History and New Media, which he founded in 1994 at George Mason University, where he taught history. Still, the plastic cases of floppy disks, Zip disks, and CDs that I also discovered, along with a few outmoded computers he saved because they could read the earliest of these storage media, explain why Roy's paper files are more voluminous for work he did earlier in his career—and they reminded me to extend my inventory to the laptops in his study.

Why had my husband saved all this material? We had known scholars who kept all their papers because they expected their fame to live after them and assumed that others would want to read every scrap that they had written. But Roy was apt to laugh at fantasies of self-importance. Moreover, the stuff he kept seemed less about his development as a scholar—he almost never saved drafts he had written, for example—than about the projects in which he had been engaged.

I think he amassed this archive, in part, because he was conscientious. Collected, sorted, and labeled, it provided him with ready access to evidence he might need to check or to consult for other purposes. But more than that, I think he conserved his research because he was generous, ready to share anything he had acquired. I recall over the years other historians contacting him for information. After one such call, he disappeared, emerging triumphantly from the basement a little while later, holding the tape of an interview he'd done years before. He put it in the mail that same day. For an academic who had spent much of his adult life in a variety of libraries and archives, real and virtual, the benefits and pleasures of a rich and well-organized collection of documents could not be overestimated.

If he disliked the tedium of the hunt for evidence, he did relish the discoveries that sometimes occurred because of it, and he was pleased when the research, as well as the technologies that facilitated it, were recognized. In 1997 the New York Historical Society, drawing on *The Park and the People*, created an exhibit on Seneca Village. The displays included Roy's floppy disks as a way to call attention to his research, which brought to light the nineteenth-century African American community displaced by the building of the park. It is characteristic of Roy that one of the last projects he spearheaded at the Center for History and New Media was Zotero, an open-source tool that enables not only scholars but also the general public to gather, organize, analyze, and circulate online research. He sought to create digital software that could give searching, assembling, retrieving, and interpreting data greater swiftness and ease, but, above all, he wanted to develop software that would make these activities, as well as their results, both more collective and widely available.

In *The Comfort of Things* (Polity, 2008), anthropologist Daniel Miller refutes "the myth of materialism," the assumption that "our relationships to things" thrive "at the expense of our relationships to people." He argues, on the contrary, that our experiences with objects and people "are much more akin and entwined than is commonly accepted." Based on the ethnographic study that he conducted in a South London neighborhood, the book shows that domestic objects not only express their owners but also accrue meanings from the relationships that their possessors have with other people. Inevitably some of the objects in the households he visited had been intentional or unintentional legacies: they were left to their owners by family members or friends now dead, or, more simply, they were what was left of these loved ones. Photographs, clothes, jewelry, paintings, sports equipment, figurines, tools, and music CDs are typical of the objects through which survivors remembered, indeed, continued to relate to, those who were gone, and most of the objects were on display in their homes.

As with those things, Roy's papers became, as I looked through them, highly resonant, calling to mind not only what he worked on but when, why, and with whom. They brought back moments in our life together when we discussed the projects to which his research contributed, and I felt his fascination or frustration with the work he was doing. Moreover, some files contained handwritten notes in his large, barely readable script that still seemed to me charged with his energy.

Although a far less efficient means for storing research than computer files, those papers had, for me, much more affective power. When I moved, I wanted to take all the wrinkled and faded folders with me. Yet this dearly evocative material, suffused with so much personal meaning, had been of use to Roy in a profession he had made as collaborative as he could. I didn't think that I should attempt to maintain only its private, emotional effects by keeping all the filled-up cabinets, notebooks, and cardboard boxes. So I contacted George Mason—where I taught, and still do—to see if it was interested in his papers. I was lucky. George Mason's library has a Special Collections and Archives unit; not all college and university libraries do. In addition, some of the archivists had known Roy for years and were aware of his professional contributions and the impact he had had on the university. They were happy to house his papers, and I knew that they would make the material readily available on the main campus.

I do not know if that is what Roy would have wanted done with his papers. Even had I understood before he died what he had gathered in our basement, I would have been reluctant to talk with him about any plans for a world that he would not be in. But I hope that these arrangements are consistent with his practices as a researcher and that when I visit his papers in George Mason's library, they will continue to summon up memories of the life he lived and the home we shared.

A Healing Garden

P. C. MOOREHEAD

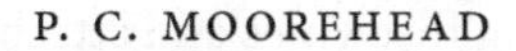

A month after I started a strenuous educational program in psychology, my husband died while working behind our garage. That was an area where he often stored building materials for his many projects on our home. He died instantaneously of a heart attack, with the caulk gun that he was using at the time still in his hand. Although Tom's death was unexpected in that he had not been in the hospital recently, it was not totally unexpected. He had a genetically based heart condition and had experienced three previous heart attacks and three open heart surgeries.

I thought I had prepared myself for Tom's death, but I discovered that grief has depths that I had not explored. It was for me, I realized, like a journey into a land where I did not know the language. My professors were generous in allowing me to use some class assignments to work through my grief. I wrote, I sculpted, and, after several months, I planted.

I cleaned out the area behind the garage where Tom had died, toting the building materials to various places around the property, and I pulled in a park bench from the backyard. I prepared the ground. Noting that Tom was a thrifty person, touched by a childhood of poverty, I took portions of plants already growing and moved them out behind the garage. I planted two trailing rose vines to grow up the back wall of the garage and a potato vine to grow on the downspout of the roof. Between the plantings, I placed white violets. The fence there was already covered with honeysuckle from years before.

For the time being, I felt finished with what I had accomplished. In the future, I hoped to add a little plaque of some kind to the fence or garage wall to note this sacred place and its special meaning. More plants could be added as the garden grew and developed.

I nursed the plants through their first dry summer. They did well, and almost everything survived into the winter. Sometimes I sat there on the bench and read the morning paper while drinking my coffee. Sometimes I meditated. Sometimes I just stared at the still-growing plants. It was easy out there for me to speak with Tom, asking him for advice, especially on financial matters.

With the next year's spring rains, everything flourished anew, including some huge weeds. I hoed and raked the area and added some new plantings. I put in the beginnings of a ground cover, added a batch of white violets to replace some that hadn't survived, and trimmed back some honeysuckle that had died from an oak virus spreading in the earth under the fence. I tied up the growing rose vines and attached the potato vine to the downspout for support.

On Easter Sunday, I took out a plaque called "Saint Francis of Joy," that I had purchased once on an outing with Tom. He was an ardent conservationist and animal lover, who gave generously to causes for each. His own spirituality had a definite Franciscan touch to it. He had, in fact, attended a Franciscan college after high school, before transferring to a technical institute. The plaque seemed just right for the area, and I mounted it on the fence, above one side of the bench. Putting up the plaque on Easter Sunday, the celebratory day of Resurrection, seemed appropriate. My belief is that Tom participates still in the energy of life.

As time passed, I found that I, too, could be more celebratory and more grateful for Tom's presence in my life, without mourning so much his physical absence. My mourning gradually turned into a morning. My healing garden helped me to a new day.

You See, I Told You So!

MIMI SCHWARTZ

I am not one for ritual; even New Year's makes me uncomfortable with its pressure to feel a certain way. So when Rabbi Julie asked if I would say a few words about loss at the university's Yizkor service of remembrance, I started to say no. "We need someone to speak personally," Rabbi Julie said, "and with my father dying, I just can't." My husband Stu had died the year before, in August—and I'd been writing a lot about grief; but these were private acts. To speak publicly about what my losing him felt like, and what my life meant now, was something I didn't know if I could do.

Then I thought of Stu, on the faculty for forty-five years, coming to this same Yizkor service every fall. He came for his departed parents and his grandparents, and for good friends, our age—Steve Goldfeld and Art Rich—who died in their early fifties, before we even considered the possibility. This Yizkor service, Stu would say, was a comfort, his way of dealing with grief and loss.

He'd stand to recite the Mourner's Kaddish, swaying with the congregation—and then continue in silent prayers for the dead, his lips moving to reach beyond what we know. Usually I was there, not out of conviction, but to be beside him, our shoulders touching. You see, my way of dealing with loss was not the ritualized Yizkor service of remembrance. Mine happened (and still does) anytime, anywhere. It is what Rabbi Julie calls *kavanah*, a spontaneous ritual coming to and from the heart without formality. Often it comes in dialogue, like the one that led me to say "Yes" to Rabbi Julie's request. *I can't* was my initial thought, but kept hearing Stu say, "Go ahead. You can do it!" just as he had during our fifty-six years together.

And afterwards. I'd hear him in the garage when the car acted up. And in his study, as I tried dealing with taxes, bank transfers, and bills. And every other time I needed to do what he once did easily, his voice soothing and guiding me to carry on. It was when I couldn't hear his counsel, when I had no idea what he would do or say, that losing Stu felt overwhelming, especially that first year. Fortunately, he was a man of strong opinions.

A month before the Yizkor service, at the Princeton cemetery, our family held a formal ritual of remembrance: the unveiling ceremony to uncover Stu's gravestone. It marks, one year after death, the official end of mourning, what Rabbi Julie called "the time to turn grief into memories." I went along with it, not expecting much—until my children and grandchildren began to speak. There was Stu's voice in their words, shaping their values to be upbeat, accept challenges, and, to use his favorite saying, "Play the hand that's dealt as well as you can." As thirty of us, family and close friends, stood in a circle, we offered more versions of Stu's positivism, together. And together we recited the Mourner's Kaddish, the prayer for the dead that never mentions death. Its rhythmic chant, mostly in Aramaic, not Hebrew, felt like a rocking cradle of sharp *v*'s and *k*'s softened by gentle *s* again and again. And with every repetition, I heard Stu reciting this chant, our shoulders touching.

Before leaving, we all placed stones—pink, black, yellow, white mottled, and mica-streaked stones—on Stu's gravestone. They'd been gathered by our grandkids from our garden and from the towpath where Stu loved to walk and some from New England where we spent summers. That morning on my front stoop, they had decided to wash them, put them in plastic bags, and pass them around so all could choose a particular stone of memory. As I placed my speckled white stone on top of the rough gray marble slab, I felt Stu's presence more powerfully than I ever had alone at home. This formal ritual, what Rabbi Julie called *keva*, was more important than I thought, giving communal strength to everyone there. I could hear Stu saying, "You see?" which made me smile.

Stu had another ritual for loss, his own, that took place every fall before the Jewish High Holidays. He and his brother Howard would choose a day to visit the graves of his grandparents and parents together. They'd drive to cemeteries in Brooklyn, Long Island, and Queens and end in Forest Hills at the graves of their parents, Rose and Charlie, and their grandmother, Bobbi Becky. Standing before the gravestones, they'd put a stone on the gravestone and tell their parents, especially Rosie who loved gossip, what was going on in the family: who had a bar mitzvah or a bad back or went on vacation or changed jobs. "It's the only time," Stu used to say, "that I feel connected to my parents without great sadness." The two brothers made this trip, even that last year when Howie had cancer and Stu's heart was failing. And afterward, as usual, they ended the day with their family ritual: eating pastrami sandwiches at Ben's Deli in Rego Park, their Dad's favorite place.

I never went with them. Nor did I go to my family's graves, even those buried less than an hour away. I'd connect to my mother whenever I'd pass her needlepoints that fill the house. I'd feel my father close every time a grandchild did or said something bold or witty. "Dad would like that!" I used to tell Stu, "I do not need to go to the cemetery or synagogue for solace. Those I have lost are around me."

And yet, after I spoke at the Yizkor service, saying much of what I have written here, I realized that private moments of remembrance are not quite enough: that I needed more than myself to get through losing Stu. I learned some of that every time my neighbors invited me for Sunday dinner during my first months alone, knowing to keep it short, an hour at most. And from the postman's kind words. And my children's embrace, and advice, and morning phone calls. And from all the friends who listened so well on walks and over coffee. But when I talked in public, partly in tears, to people who knew Stu and me together for so many years, it made permanent a memory of us that I knew would carry me forward into the future, whatever it may be.

So I was glad I said yes to Rabbi Julie. And glad I spoke to honor Stu's memory and all who grieve in individual ways, as they search for the best path to walk without those we have loved. And especially glad that on my way home after my Yizkor talk, I went to Princeton cemetery to tell Stu how the day went—and heard him say, yet again, "You see? I told you so."

Yes, I Miss My Husband, but I'm Also Discovering the Pleasures of Living Alone

ANNE BERNAYS

When my sweet husband, Joe, died after a years-long assault by Parkinson's disease, I found myself, at the age of eighty-three, living alone for the first time. After our wedding, I had gone straight from my family's townhouse on the Upper East Side to Joe's tiny Midtown apartment. We were married for almost sixty years.

After Joe died I felt, alternately, numb and raw, as if the top layer of my skin had been peeled away, leaving me with excruciating pain. I prefer the numbness. Thirteen months of this anguish, and I'm slowly beginning to unearth my old, cheerful, energized, opinionated self. I live in two distinct universes: The first is living without Joe (unspeakable) and the second is living by myself—which, I have to admit, has its liberating moments.

Imagine 22,000 breakfasts looking at the same face across the orange juice. Joe was always good company, funny, never tedious or solipsistic.

This was first published in the *Washington Post*, June 4, 2015. https://www.washingtonpost.com/news/soloish/wp/2015/06/04/yes-i-miss-my-husband-but-im-also-discovering-the-pleasures-of-living-alone/?utm_term=.1e92ee5e31bd.

Both of us spent hours a day writing: he most of the time, I when the children were at school. He didn't go to an office like other fathers. We took all our meals together; his idea of a break was to go with me to the supermarket. We also wrote two nonfiction books together, hardly a simple undertaking.

So his absence has made this the most terrifying period of my life. Sometimes, when self-pity takes over, I calculate that my emotional dislocation now is in direct proportion to how comfortable our marriage was. Over the months, the pain has eased a little. But I'm still confused: Who am I? Am I a widow, a doleful label that, as far as I'm concerned has nothing to recommend it? Or am I Anne, who grew up rich, hung out with many of the most notable writers of the 1950s, had a career in publishing, published ten novels, co-wrote three nonfiction books, and now teach Nieman fellows at Harvard how to exercise their imaginations? I've had fun!

Of course, I miss my husband terribly and cannot look at his shoes in the closet we shared without crying. Still, there are times when I can see a future that's not all woeful. I can, for example, do things that used to be Joe's jobs. No matter how many times I asked him, he was reluctant to let me share work that had to do with money. I kept saying, "What if you get hit by a bus?" But it didn't seem to make any difference. He paid the bills, dealt with our accountant, kept track of our modest investments, and, in general, was keeper of the purse.

He also did everything involving our wheels: getting our parking permit, paying the excise tax, renewing the registration, rejoining AAA, and so on. I do these things now, often with my pulse speeding up unpleasantly. But I do it, along with my oldest daughter, Susanna, who's helping me navigate the wilds of bills, record keeping, and tax paying. She claims to be holding the feds at bay.

Her two younger sisters, Hester, who lives an hour away, and Polly, who lives in Dutchess County, New York, are also super-daughters. They have my back. They keep an eye on me via phone and, more often, text messages, e-mail, and cell phone pictures. They take me out for lunch and to the movies. They give me advice, recipes, and gifts, but it's their concern and love that count the most. These three women make it easier for me to come to terms with the fact that I'll never see Joe again.

I live in a light, airy apartment with a stunning view of the Charles River and the Boston skyline. We moved there from the other side of Cambridge a year and a half before Joe died, sparing our children the task of emptying a too-large house where we lived since leaving New York in 1959. Still, being alone is the emptiness and sadness of clothes unworn in more than a year, of a refrigerator stocked according to the appetite and taste of only one, of the silent darkness of insomnia.

But here's the lighter side of living alone: I can do anything I want, when I want, how I want. I can go to bed without worrying about Joe, who was sicker than I recognized, mainly because he never complained.

The first line of a poem I have yet to complete goes, "Who would exchange worry for grief?"

Well, actually, I would.

But I no longer have to worry about whether or not he swallowed his daily ration of seventeen pills; about that funny rash on his head; about his next doctor's appointment; about why he had fallen in the kitchen again.

What's taken the place of worry? Food.

It's amazing how much food and its purchase figure in my life. When I'm feeling especially blue, I don't light the stove at all. Instead, I heat up half a bag of "oriental-style" vegetables in the microwave. When I'm okay, I'll fry tofu cut into cubes or a lamb shoulder chop or a Cornish game hen marinated in something called Soy Vay. I buy 4-ounce packages of smoked salmon and ration each one to last a week of breakfasts.

I eat things Joe didn't like: frozen yogurt, black bread, cheddar-flavored pretzels, ready-made chicken salad in a plastic container. And I avoid things he liked and I didn't: Jell-O, oatmeal, Vienna sausages (yuck!), canned corned-beef hash, any kind of tomato, canned soup loaded with sodium, lemons.

I eat breakfast while reading the *New York Times* on paper, and lunch while surfing my MacBook Pro. (When Joe was alive, my computer stayed shut until the meal was over.)

The best part of the day is cocktail hour. I sit on my 1950s Scandinavian-style couch with a vodka martini in a fancy glass, reading the *Times* (of London) Literary Supplement. This hour melds with barely a ripple into supper, which I eat still facing the tube; it may last an hour or so, sometimes starting with half an avocado eaten off the blade of a knife. Whenever I like to, I cook. Otherwise it's a bit of this, a bit of that—crackers and cheese, a small salad—whatever catches my fancy. When Joe sat across from me at the table, however, we always had a proper 1950s-style meal: meat, a vegetable, and something starchy. I gave up this antiquated habit without the least regret.

I have friends to walk with, e-mail, and text with—and an older sister who lives nearby. I guess I'm still in mourning because I'm reluctant to go out at night. Once a genuine party girl, I often prefer to stay home alone, protecting myself from anxiety, a state that has a nasty habit of appearing just when I crave serenity.

Do I have a message for other women who find themselves, at an advanced age, living alone, maybe for the first time? Not really. I could say that time heals all wounds—or time wounds all heels, as Joe would have it. I could talk about the restorative benefits of family and friends, and about the resilience of the human spirit. But that's not my style.

I would tell them instead: Don't let your woes swamp other people. Get plenty of exercise. And make sure you have enough ice on hand for that six o'clock cocktail.

Part III

Long-Time Widows

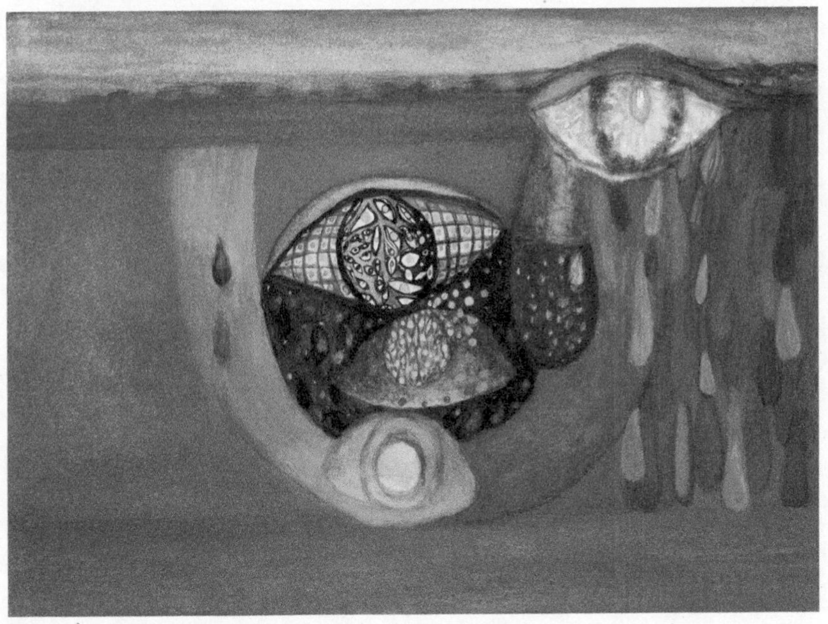

The Grief Convention

EDIE BUTLER

When Larry Parrish, my partner and the father of my two children died, the period right after his death turned out to be a confounding time. We had lived together for almost forty, unconventional, difficult years—more than half of my life—and we were not officially married. Now I was a widow, or was I? When you aren't officially married, are you? Neighbors and friends said the conventional, well-meaning things, and it took some time before I knew how to feel about his dying and how to respond.

Larry was diagnosed with stage-three lung cancer in March 2007, the day his father, Lawrence senior, died in Storrs, Connecticut. His father was ninety-three. Larry was sixty-one and would live another ten months. Larry died in hospice in Concord, New Hampshire, six months before his grandson, Asa, was born. The Parrish men would ebb and flow that year.

One of the personality traits that I found frustrating in my relationship with Larry was his trying to cheat on life. He smoked cigarettes, for instance, for twenty years, inhaled a tobacco pipe for about twenty-five, and smoked pot till the end. But he thought if he took a small mountain of mega-vitamins and supplements it would keep him safe. He ate a banana every day. He drank green teas. When his cancer did not metastasize, "See," he said, "it's the saw palmetto." When he was diagnosed, I was angry—at him. He and I were constantly back and forth about his smoking, but Larry was the first to admit his emotional paralysis. He needed a few crutches, he explained, to navigate life, and his biological family, in particular. We both used the drugs of the day: amphetamines, pot, LSD. I phased out my drug use as Lisa got older—it wasn't an example I wanted to set. I stayed peeved that Larry wouldn't even try to give up the drugs. He did switch from cigarettes to a pipe after awhile under pressure from our girls.

Larry died in New Hampshire, but we had met in Philadelphia in 1968. When I first met him, he was masquerading as working class—soiled old dungarees—scruffy, unshaven; he called himself a freak (he was called a hippie a few years later). We had two daughters, Lisa and Amelia. (I had Lisa when I was married at 18.) When I met his parents some months later, it was clear he was not working class. Born in rural Connecticut—white, male, upper middle class, into an intact family of gracious, educated, progressive Quaker parents, with a sister living in London and a brother in Colorado. After meeting his parents and seeing what and where he came from, we had a talk. It was never going to work, I told him; we were too different. He campaigned and eventually dismantled my misgivings about our staying together; we'll be fine, he liked to say, because he was so black and I was so white. He was, he said, the needy one.

He won the argument, but the fact remained that we couldn't have been more different. African American, I grew up far from rural Connecticut with my single mother, her two younger brothers, and my grandmother, in a little rented house in inner-city Philadelphia. My mother supported us all with a job as a clerk for the Veteran's Administration and then Social Security (She was a supervisor when she retired forty years later). By the time we moved to West Philly from an even more distressed neighborhood, black, working-class families were predominant in our new one.

The neighborhood was not dangerous, but my mother and grandmother were afraid at night, living without a grown man in the house, is how they put it. The police were the biggest threat, arresting local boys on suspicion of whatever they wanted and bringing them back beaten up. I absorbed the adults' fear but was taught not to show it. We were all conditioned not to call attention to ourselves. People usually misconstrued my quiet as strength. Larry misread my lack of affect as strength too. He said more than once that I didn't seem to need anything or anyone.

His parents were accepting of our interracial relationship. They were dismayed, though, that we decided not to get married, and they never gave up trying to convince us. Larry and I agreed on one thing—we didn't trust marriage. We thought it was a trap full of unrealistic expectations that ruined good relationships. I regretted not being married after he died, though; not being married made settling our joint business much more difficult.

Larry and I met in Philadelphia just after he had finished college at a small Quaker school outside of Philly. I had left New York University after the first year, moved back to Philly, got married. I left the marriage, had a baby, and moved on.

I moved with toddler Lisa into an apartment on my own. I was actually feeling good about my life. I had a couple part-time jobs that were enough in those days to support myself in our post-beatnik, pre-hippie neighborhood. I got involved with a woman, Rona, who lived in the same apartment house, and who turned out to be a classmate of Larry's at college. Eventually, Rona wandered off, and Larry and I became a couple. We moved in together after another year or so.

Larry knew that Rona and I were lovers. He told me then that he had slept with a man. We didn't say we would tell each other if we slept with other people, but I assumed we would—he didn't. I would have one other romantic, asexual relationship, which I told Larry about. He did not talk about his, but it was apparent that he occasionally saw other people. Trust was an issue for him, and I tried to understand, but his having a part of his life that I didn't share and he didn't share with me made us progressively less close. I found myself getting more uncomfortable and anxious as we got more distant.

We could talk to each other about everything but our feelings. We talked about movies, music, and politics. We analyzed *other* people, especially family, endlessly. We were idealistic and the Vietnam War was on, feeding our incendiary idealism. We spent hours together writing letters to senators, telephone companies, the Internal Revenue Service, announcing Larry's war-tax resistance, and demonstrating in the streets. Our lives centered around the University of Pennsylvania where he was in graduate school in what was then called Oriental Studies, and I was working on my bachelor's degree.

Then, in the 1970s, Philly became a war zone. The Black Panther Party had an office space a block from us. The Philadelphia police under Frank Rizzo, the city's shotgun-toting police commissioner, used the streets to take on the Black Panther Party as well as the Vietnam War protestors. The Move, a commune of black, urban homesteaders, had a shoot-out with Rizzo's police force and a cop was killed. I wanted to get away from the anger and violence. And I wanted a break from the anxiety and distance at home.

This was one of several times in our life together when Larry and I felt very far apart. We had periods of being very distant, yet we somehow found our way back to each other, but this was the first time we separated. I left Larry in Philadelphia, and with my daughter, Lisa, who was then eight, went to New Hampshire. I planned to stay for a year. I had friends there, a couple trying to start a pottery studio. After about six months in New Hampshire, I was lonely but found New Hampshire interesting, and Larry said he missed us, so he came up to New Hampshire instead of my going back to Philly.

Our potter friends had an offer to buy into a homesteading community. There was a piece of land with a cabin on it for sale that we could have. We bought in and lived in a community in the woods for the next four years. Our daughter Amelia was born in our house there. We liked the woods and living off the grid. We lived without electricity, running water, and central heat. We learned to garden together, and to work on our house. Then, in 1978, a house fire left us homeless. Rather than rebuild, we rented a handmade house in the next town and eventually bought a house there where we have lived since.

Ironically, Larry, the beer-drinking pipe smoker opened a natural foods store after we moved into town. He enjoyed the store. He believed in natural food with his whole heart, even if he couldn't manage his addictions. The natural food catalogs gave him information he needed on vitamins and other supplements to counteract the effects of smoking and drinking, but his habits caught up with him. A persistent cough and dizziness finally got him to go to a doctor. His lung cancer was advanced by the time we got there, but the oncologist offered chemotherapy anyway. We wanted to try everything—Larry even asked about a lung transplant, but the disease was too far along.

We tried to give Larry what he needed at home as long as possible because he wanted so much to be at home. When someone suggested he go to the hospital, we heard him say pitifully, "But I want to be home." Even after he later went to the hospital and then hospice, when it was not possible, he wanted to go home. I was glad he could stay home for as long as he could. Medical people came to the house to drain his lungs when he thought he was drowning, give him the meds he needed, and help keep him clean. But, on a snowy night in December, he had trouble breathing, and the town rescue squad plowed out our driveway and got Larry to the hospital in Concord.

Larry was in the hospital that Christmas. He called from his room in the morning to ask if we were coming to see him. Of course, I told him. We went with presents and company. Wally, one of Larry's close friends from Connecticut, had come up. My brother was visiting. And Lisa had come up from Philly where she was living. We all left for the hospital in separate cars; Amelia and I rode together and got there first. She parked the car while I went up to Larry's room. I went over to where he was resting on his bed—he looked beautiful, peaceful. I reached down and laced my fingers in his, spread out his arms and spread mine over them. Amelia started into the hospital room and froze. She and I made eye contact for a minute and smiled, and I leaned down again to Larry. Amelia came over slowly and stood by the bed with a hand on each of us. Then everyone finally got to

Larry's room. We gathered around his bed and opened presents, and managed a few hugs and laughs. Lisa has said it is one of her favorite memories.

Those moments in the hospital were sweet for me too. They were fleeting—especially those few minutes when Larry and Amelia and I were connected. To underscore how fleeting it was, a few days later Larry was moved to hospice and died after a couple days. People came by. Tom and Sue, friends who had helped Larry through the uncomfortable last weeks with Lakota therapy and sweats and singing, came in and sang to him as he neared the end.

We had two memorial services, one in the town where we lived and one later that summer at his family's cottage in Maine. The service in our town included people from all parts of his life and from our life together. It was a Quaker service with sharing and memories, singing and candles, food and pictures. It was beautiful. For two people who lived in a bubble of secrecy, it was beautifully public. The service was gratifying and lovely, but it was also the first hint that being the widow would take some thinking about, which I had not thought about before. Someone at the service said to me with a face contorted with sympathy, you must be devastated! Actually, I was dumbfounded by the remark. I could only nod and smile weakly—but not too much!—and realized at that moment that I wasn't "devastated." No, I wasn't devastated. I was sad that the girls had lost their father. I was sorry that Larry had to suffer. And I would miss him. I was full of regret for not trying harder to help Larry stop smoking. But I was not feeling a howling, devastating grief. How I was going to respond to expressions of sympathy without having to explain all of this confounded me at first. It seemed to me this was a time when I should be, wanted to be, as honest as I could be. I had to learn that I only needed to say thank you.

We wanted a memorial get-together in Maine because his family's house there was a favorite place for Larry. So later that summer at the cottage in Maine, Amelia and Lisa and I; Larry's sister Sue and her family, who flew in from England; his brother David, who had come from Colorado with his family; two of Larry's cousins; and Tom and Sue from home, helped us say good-bye in Maine with a Lakota ceremony and sharing. I sat Larry's ashes on the picnic table, and we had a last lobster with him. We spread his ashes into Casco Bay and swam with him one last time. I wanted to do my best to give Larry a ceremony that he would have liked to be part of, and I hoped I would feel better about not feeling more devastated.

I sift through the good memories and the regrets. Over the last ten years, I'm less confounded by what I worried was an inability to grieve properly. I haven't mentioned love, because I can't remember the two of us ever talking about it or saying the words to each other, except on greeting cards.

But I understand that the long, complex, productive, difficult life we lived together for half our lives was a life that we often loved—maybe it was that feeling that brought us back when we grew apart. Neither of us was emotionally articulate, sentimental, or romantic. I liked to remind him of the first time we went out. We were on our way home from a film at Penn; he parked the car, disappeared, and came back with a beautiful bunch of flowers that he threw on the car seat and said, "here." I got the message then, and I understand it a little better now. We didn't articulate to each other the meaning of living a deep, full, and difficult life together. But as this part of our life was ending, I think some pieces started to fall into place and we were able to see it. That moment in Larry's hospital room, for instance, was a moment when I hope we communicated to each other our appreciation for the fullness that we had lived together.

I see now that I don't need to play the widow like a part—I can't. I can think about Larry, remember him with the people that matter, and live the next part of my life.

10 Scary Things I Have Done since My Husband Died

DEBBY MAYER

Why scary? Why *scary* things, asked a friend. Be more positive, she said. These are *brave* things you've done, *courageous* things.

Because "10 Brave Things" would put half my readers to sleep and send the rest looking for the remote. *Courageous* is overwrought and overlong.

Still, why scary?

Here's why:

Spring . . . Dan had died the previous August, after our twenty-five years together; we were both fifty-six. Now I went downstairs to our small, dark, dirt-floor basement to do a load of laundry and discovered there a good-sized mouse dead on his side next to the dryer. The laundry and I went right back upstairs. I walked in circles around the deck, knowing that I must rid the basement of that mouse.

I needed to take a trowel—No! A shovel!—down to the basement to scoop up the mouse, hoping that its remains would not have seeped into the floor (eeuuww). Or a bag (ugh) or a cloth (Touch it? No way!), as the shovel would be very hard to maneuver out the wooden door, tight corner, narrow steps—what if the carcass slid off the shovel and I had to pick it up again, or, worse, what if the carcass slid off the shovel *toward me*?

I could not stand this.

The mouse could not remain on its side next to the dryer.

I got the shovel. It was big; we didn't have any small shovels. I made myself take the shovel down the steps.

I couldn't do it.

I went back up the stairs and stood on the deck in the tentative spring sun, discouraged because I was so squeamish.

Then I did what I had to do.

I went indoors to the kitchen phone and called for help. I called Chris, a young friend who seemed sturdy and brave. She answered her phone, and with apologies I described the situation, physical (mouse) and mental (me).

"Sure," she said, "I'll be right over."

"Right over" in our rural area meant a fifteen-minute drive, so I waited patiently on the deck.

Chris showed up on schedule. "Down here?" she said on the deck, outside of the basement.

"Here's a shovel, or a trowel, and a bag."

"That's OK." Chris waved them away and headed down the steps to the basement, where she had never been before. I figured she would assess the situation and tell me what she needed.

But moments later she returned, *holding the mouse by its tail in her bare hand.*

"Chris! Not in your bare hand!"

I made her wash her hands. I thanked her profusely.

"No problem," she said. "I'm trying to do one scary thing every day."

I'm trying to do one scary thing every day.

Never had I attempted to be so brave, so courageous.

In my admiration for that goal, for her tackling scary things, from the infinitesimal (my mouse) to the immense (whatever challenged her), this essay is titled in honor of Chris.

The 10 Scary Things

OK, I've done 110 scary things since Dan died, maybe 1,010, but I've culled here what for me are the top 10, in which 10 is the least and 1 is the most. Number 10 took place the day after Dan died, Number 1 three years later; everything else happened somewhere in between.

10. Got up in the morning

In this way, the widow not only acknowledges that life goes on but also that she accepts it, and the pain of grieving.

My father died in the evening, and my stepmother did not rise from the bed for a day. She had my half-sister and me downstairs, dealing with the concept and practicalities of the funeral.

Dan died at about 9 P.M., and after a few hours' sleep I got up the next morning; our two dogs had to be let out and fed—at seven o'clock, not nine or noon. At that point, you might as well make a cup of coffee and stare out at the backyard. Or go to the computer.

Since everything had gone so terribly wrong for the last four months, I was writing Dan's obituary myself, so that it would be correct, and would include what I wanted it to: the dogs and me as his immediate family; his canoeing the length of the Connecticut River, from the Atlantic Ocean to Canada, in weekend trips; his full academic scholarship to Columbia; his generosity to local causes.

I had to deal with the odd but kindly woman at the funeral home, which I had chosen only the night before, minutes after Dan's death (I grew to think of her, not unfondly, as Morticia). I had to call the gentle, marvelous people at the Buddhist cemetery across the Hudson River, the only place I could think of in which Dan might be happy to have his ashes buried.

In all these distractions I took some comfort. Because not only had I lost the love of my life, but also, in another part of my brain, I knew that each thing I touched—the kitchen sink with its mysterious gurgle; our three cars (his idea) with their total of almost 400,000 miles; our dogs, the ancient Cooper, the adolescent Lulu; my unremarkable paycheck—was now mine to deal with alone.

Not just the expense, but more important, the decisions, without Dan, the witty, practical man with cutting-edge taste in music who paid off his credit card every month. During the four months of his illness I had visited him daily in the hospital, worked full time, paid the bills, cared for the dogs, got the cars serviced, and neglected the house.

Now it was September, and I wasn't so much up a tree as out on a slender branch, among leaves that fluttered to the hardening ground.

9. Asked for help

I would rather that people offer help, instead of my putting myself out there and risking the discomfort, on both sides, of refusal, but when I needed help, I learned to take the chance.

Not only does the widow no longer have the mate to dispense with the dead mouse, but also there is the family to care for. I could bring Lulu to my dog-friendly office, but such duty was beyond Cooper. Instead, five friends came over, one per weekday, and let him out. In an added benefit, this extended our family. Cooper and I sent tulip plants to his helpers at Christmas and cards to them for Valentine's Day.

8. Paid for help

The frightening thing here is pushing past the specter of scarcity (what if I don't have enough?) natural for a widow or for a man who grew up poor. Dan would never have paid to get the gutters cleaned or the weather stripping replaced in the garage.

When he died, the only way to lock the two sliding glass doors was with sawed-off broom handles. Outside, the dog fence was rusty, and the second compost pile was locked behind the snow fence and contained our only pitchfork, beyond my reach. My chore list grew daily while I worked, cared for the dogs, and strapped on snowshoes to feed the birds that freezing, snowy winter.

As spring approached, I knew I had to Do Something. In desperation I consulted the classified ads in the local newspaper, and there I found: "Got a list of chores you never get to? Give it to me!"

I took a breath and picked up the phone.

7. Flew across the country by myself

I did feel like a child. I bought stuff—a new suitcase, a spiffy black duffel type with recessed wheels at one end, and a rain jacket that would double as a windbreaker.

Years had passed since I planned an itinerary alone, kept track of the tickets, got myself to the airport on time, but I retrieved my solo exploration skills. In three years, my suitcase and I visited friends in Washington and New Mexico and flew to two countries where I didn't know a soul.

6. Invited people over for dinner

If you don't cook, and for two-dozen years you've lived with a man who is a superb avocational cook, not only do your minimal kitchen skills atrophy but also solo entertaining becomes terrifying.

My heart was in the right place: I wanted to invite friends to my home, sit them down, give them some food, talk with them about interesting, intelligent matters. But I came up against a wall every time, of actually doing it by myself.

And then, a solution! Host a potluck dinner, and when I panicked at the last minute, get the ham from a caterer.

5. Put down his dog

I've known that phrase forever, since I was a kid in Schenectady. Or, we *put the dog to sleep*; one didn't use the politer *euthanized.*

You may say I killed the dog, but Dr. Tumulo, who had known Cooper since he was a puppy, said, "People wait until their animal is in pain. You don't have to," and that was my guiding principal.

We understood each other, Cooper and I, but he bonded with Dan. Cooper was sixteen when Dan died, and the winter afterward he was either asleep or bumping into things. Coming in from errands on a Saturday and finding Cooper comfortable on the couch, I would think *Dan must have stopped by and put him there.*

I had hoped Cooper might reach his seventeenth birthday in June and have some time on the deck, but in March, I realized June was too far off. I called Dr. Tumulo's office and made Cooper's last appointment there. Feeling like the witch in *Hansel and Gretel*, I fed Cooper his favorite dinner, chicken and rice, during his final weekend, and gave him half a Dentabone every evening. In bed at night, he curled next to my heart.

On Monday I went through with it. I had already driven Dan to Albany Medical Center, ten months before. I began to realize, over the winter, that in some bizarre way we had been fortunate, Dan and I; if he had to die, at least he went quickly, without months of misery in a nursing home.

Loss is sad, but sometimes death is not the worst thing.

Cooper went without protest, seconds after the shot, dying in my arms.

4. Became a Lay Eucharistic Reader at my church

All my life I had been aware of select men in my Episcopal church who took turns, one or two of them every Sunday, to move smoothly—no, glide, as if on wheels—around the altar. They actually read very little but rather assisted the priest, handing him the wafers and the wine just when he needed them, standing in precisely the right place at exactly the right moment, flawless in a silent liturgical dance.

I like to dance, and as a girl I was taught to help, so when women were finally, belatedly invited to become Lay Eucharistic Readers at my church, I volunteered. It was owed to me, but more important, I wanted to do it.

Ultimately, serving wasn't so much learning a dance as a new language, moving over the months from inarticulate, to hearing my mistakes as I made them, to communicating. People say they like to listen to me; maybe they're just being nice. But when our rector told me that he appreciated celebrating the Eucharist with me as lay reader, it was, simply, one of the greatest compliments I have ever received.

3. Learned to use the gas mower

With its fierce blade, its requirement for a poisonous, flammable chemical, of all the forbidding things that lurked in the basement and the shed, the gas mower was the most frightening. For two years I didn't touch it; instead I used our hand mower, a quiet, friendly helper that allowed me to meditate over the smell of new-mown grass. But in our third spring together, I had to admit that my friend and I couldn't handle half an acre of lawn—front-back-side. Everything was weedy and tufted and unkempt.

Dan did all of the mowing and most of the cooking. I figured out how to feed friends with a potluck dinner, and I learned to use that damned mower.

2. Dealt with the snake in the bathroom

Arriving home one evening at about nine o'clock, I opened the bathroom door, and in the second before I turned on the light, I thought, *I didn't leave a man's tie lying in the middle of the bathroom floor.* The snake—a big one, I swear—was struggling at that very moment to leave, to work its way back down the heat grate and into to the cellar.

I dealt with this problem by stamping my foot and yelling: "You, snake! Get out of this bathroom! Go back down that heat grate!"

Slowly, the fat snake complied.

It was September. Dan had been dead for just over two years. If it had been one year, I would have had to call Chris and her partner, Robin, the one couple I knew who stayed up late, and tell them that Lulu and I were on our way over.

I didn't do that. Instead, I pulled the bathroom rug over the heat grate. Then I found several large, heavy books, and I walked around the house, placing one of them on top of each of the other heat grates.

I could have peed in the yard with Lulu under cover of darkness, but daybreak would end that solution. I might as well become accustomed to my sole, snake-infested bathroom. We performed our ablutions that night, Lulu and I. We curled up in bed together. In the morning, light rose again.

1. Sold our house

Despite all its implications of dismissal and rejection (*don't need you anymore!*), despite all the smart financial reasons for staying (I paid off the mortgage and then put that amount into my retirement account every month), I moved on.

I didn't expect to. I loved our house. Dan and I had replaced everything, from top (roof) to bottom (septic tank). We had re-created the bathroom, enlarged windows, added the screened porch and deck. By myself, I had the kitchen remodeled. The house stood "finished," needing only the continual maintenance that every house requires.

I loved our pretty, quiet road that didn't go anywhere. I knew the neighbors, and if they were odd, or imperfect, so are we all, and their presence reassured me.

But the house, its gardens and field, its three acres of woods, were all in the wrong place. Once, I was pleased that Lulu and I could take a two-mile walk without seeing a soul, not even in a passing car. But with Dan gone, I grew tired of driving for every single thing I had to do, and I yearned for more human contact.

Was I making a mistake to want a world of sidewalks and streetlights? It was very scary. But that's the American way, isn't it: you light out for the territories, and years later, Mama wants a house in town—a sign, as the poet Frank O'Hara wrote, "that people do not totally *regret* life."*

That October, I dreamed about Dan. We were inside our house, preparing to leave. As we moved to the door, he said, "I'm glad I was here." I was glad to be there too. But now I was ready to shed grief-as-love. I wanted a place where my walks with Lulu offered new sights, not memories. If moving forward is a necessary betrayal,† well, my solo exploration skills were honed. Accustomed to the branch I had found myself perched upon, I was ready to move off it, onto a higher one.

* Frank O'Hara, "Meditations in an Emergency," in *Meditations in an Emergency* (New York: Grove Press, 1967), 38. Italics is O'Hara's.

† Caitlin Flanagan, "Warm Comfort," *New York Times Book Review*, May 14, 2017, 14. Review of *Option B: Facing Adversity, Building Resilience, and Finding Joy* by Sheryl Sandberg and Adam Grant.

Being Alone

SONIA JAFFE ROBBINS

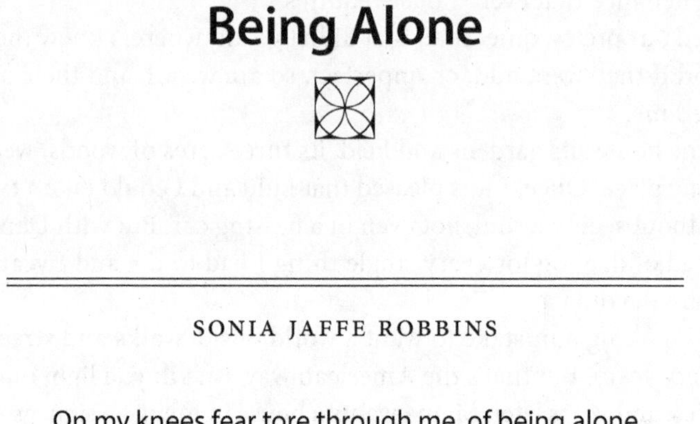

> On my knees fear tore through me, of being alone
> but mostly of not being alone, someday.
> —Laura Viviana*

I have never lived alone. I am seventy-five years old, and except for two weeks when I was twenty-one and occasional weeks here and there when my husband was traveling or I was traveling, I have never lived alone. Does that mean anything? Most people around the world live among a web of family all the time. In some Muslim cultures, a widow is never left alone for the first forty days after her husband has died. When I learned that, a few weeks after Jack died, I felt relief that hordes of relatives and friends hadn't moved in with me immediately. I needed solitude to absorb the fact that the man I had lived with for fifty-two years was permanently gone, never to return. He is ashes in a pale-blue cardboard box on a bookshelf in the guest room.

I'm a seventy-five-year-old feminist in 2017, and I don't know how to live alone. Jack and I were never joined at the hip—we did many things together (movies, baseball games, long walks), yet many things separately (he went to the gym every day; I traveled alone; we had our own friends). Being

* Thanks to Laura Viviana (lauraviviana.com) for permission to quote from her poem.

feminists meant, for us, that we each encouraged the other to be independent, while simultaneously being each other's main support.

Yet I feel not quite a grownup now that I'm fully alone. Sure, I know how to shop and take care of the money and rent a car and make appointments, all the things I did before, when I was sharing my life with Jack. But sharing a life means sharing the work, and now I have to do it all: shop, cook, clean up, do the laundry. Before I travel, I have to eat all the perishable food in the refrigerator; there is no one at home who will eat the rest of the potato salad or that last piece of chicken. If the printer doesn't work properly, there's no one to vent to about it before I tackle the problem myself. And when I kill a giant cockroach, there's no one to ask to dispose of it.

Some friends would be quick to remind me that these are first-world problems. I have sufficient money, I'm not in danger of losing my home, insurance has taken care of most of the medical expenses. But my life is unbalanced. I am disoriented. There's no one I can tell my day to, no one I can rant to about the current president and his cronies. I have to make a conscious effort to see other people, to have a social life, when I've been used to having a social life ready-made in the next room. Even when I felt constrained by Jack, I didn't realize how much I needed him to give my life structure. And I'm a second-wave feminist!

The first time I was totally on my own, I was nineteen. I went to a college that sent its students to jobs around the country for three months at a time twice a year. For my second job, I went to Los Angeles, where I knew no one and where there were only two other students from my school. I spent the first week at the YWCA, in a suite with two much older women. After I finished work, I looked for apartments, but apartments at all of the U-shaped garden complexes I looked at, with a swimming pool in the U, were too expensive. Finally, I settled on a room in a rooming house, with a half-refrigerator and a hot plate. I took my suitcases there on my way to work and shopped at a supermarket on my way home, buying way too much food. After I'd unpacked, put food away, and sat down on my fold-out bed, the silence pressed in on me. I had no radio. No music, no voices, no one but myself—I started to cry and couldn't stop.

The first months after Jack died were filled with practical minutiae: notifying all the financial institutions, hiring a lawyer to navigate the details of Jack's never having written a will, getting Jack's name removed from our co-op shares. I would cry, missing Jack's presence, his body in bed, his being there to talk to. But I felt on top of things, able to handle what I had to.

One day, about eight months after Jack died, I began feeling frightened. The fear wasn't attached to anything in my life at that moment. The fear was making it hard to sleep and difficult to get out of bed in the morning. After a few days of this amorphous fear, I remembered that day many years earlier, of being nineteen and alone in a strange city three thousand miles from home. Back then, I had scared myself into thinking I was having a nervous breakdown and the only alternative was to go home—not a place I wanted to be, but as the Robert Frost poem puts it, "Home is the place where, when you have to go there, / They have to take you in."

Now, I am home, but what does home mean? Home was Jack, and Jack is gone forever. Does that mean home is gone too? What is home when I am the only one in it? How do I come home to myself when I'm still learning to be a grownup? Home is now single, not double. No one will take care of me besides myself. It's hard to have only myself to depend on, but there's a power in that as well.* I'm not nineteen anymore, I have a whole life accumulated in me, a life I only dreamed of when I was nineteen. She still lives in me, but is no longer the only me.

Another day, I'm on a bus heading up Amsterdam Avenue. For weeks I have dreaded opening the door to a dark apartment, with no one to call out, "Hi, Sweetie." In the bus, I feel a psychic shift. I am going home, and the dread is missing. The nineteen-year-old can come home to me. I am coming home to myself.

* Many thanks to Louisa Ermelino for this thought.

Re-creating My Life

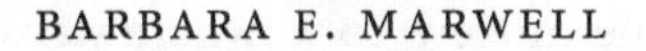

BARBARA E. MARWELL

Suddenly I'm alone. It was years in coming, thirteen years in fact, after the initial cancer diagnosis, but it feels sudden. My life during most of those years, with an uncertain end date, was focused on living the life we had always lived with travel, time with friends, dinners, theater, concerts, museums. Twelve years in, we knew we were in the last chapter, and we squeezed in every bit of normalcy we could—including a trip to Portugal and northern Spain. Then the last three months, in and out of hospice, twice back from the brink, helping to make his last months a good death. After all that it has ended abruptly, and I face a void.

There were no good-byes, no summing up of our life and love of almost sixty years together, no kisses or holding hands or a family gathered round in love, acceptance, and mutual comfort as the husband, father, grandfather takes his last breath. He had asked to come home from the hospital when it was clear that there were no further useful medical interventions. We were expecting him to die, but not quite this day, this week. His last words to me—"Can I have some juice?"—not what you think of as parting words. I slept in the room with him all night, in case he would awake and say something more. But there was no more. By the next morning he was in a coma. He died the following day—forty-two hours after he had come home. I shed no tears then. My tears, my grieving had come months earlier, when the decision to enter hospice was made.

My daughter, who lived nearby, had been with us earlier in the day, but went home for lunch with her family when the nurse from hospice assured us he would certainly not die before the next day. She came back; we hugged, she sat with her father. I called my son in San Francisco to tell him his father had died. We had told him not to fly in the day before. His dad was in a coma. There would be no more good-byes. He had come many, many times during the hospice months, and there had been many talks. No need for him to come now. He would be with us the next week at the open house and then again for the memorial service.

The after-dying arrangements had all been made in advance. Two friends were to be on call to contact the funeral home and sit with us when they came for the body. Ironically, both were out of town, so I made the call. I didn't watch as they carried the body out. I had done that with my mother six years earlier. I become stoic in those moments, or perhaps numb.

Jerry was cremated, as he had requested. We had an open house and two memorial services—one in New York, where we were living and one in Madison where we had spent forty years of our adult professional lives. Can I say they were joyful events? That seems absurd and yet they were, with so many warm and loving memories, stories of achievements, quirks and foibles, of deep friendships and crucial roles played in many lives, anecdotes funny and celebratory, a gathering of all the lines of our lives coming together in one crescendo.

Now, for the first time, I would live alone. I had gone from my parents' home to my marriage home. I was seventy-five years old. How do I make a new life? Daytimes are easy, evenings are hard. Days in the first weeks and months filled up with the busyness of tasks—planning the memorials, financial matters, cleaning out his office. The activity created a barrier to experiencing the new reality—a bit of denial, perhaps, but also a time to integrate a new life pattern. I buy too much at the grocery store. I am still buying for two. I cook dinners for myself and eat them accompanied by a book or the TV. I like having the TV playing; it's the sound of another voice.

The remnants of our life together: What to do with my wedding ring? I notice some women continue to wear it on the ring finger of the left hand. That doesn't seem right to me, so I move it to my other hand. It doesn't fit on the ring finger, so it becomes a pinky ring. What do I do with his clothes, the contents of his wallet? I remember Joan Didion keeping John's shoes, in case he comes back and needs them. It takes me two years to give away all the clothes, and then I cling to a few symbolic things—the Green Bay Packers Super Bowl hat; the Hawaiian shirt he wore, with a touch of respect and humor, to teach about Rick Warren and his purpose-driven evangelical church.

I have a frantic, almost obsessive need not to be alone. I aim for at least one social activity every day. Spontaneity has gone out of my social life. No more turning to Jerry and saying, "How about a movie tonight?" "Let's try the new restaurant in the neighborhood." Everything must be planned. Like the song from *Hello Dolly*, "I'm the woman who arranges things." Evenings alone are so long. How do you face dinner alone, when for almost fifty-five years dinner was the capsule to the day, the time we talked, shared, problem-solved, and planned? Who do I turn to now to recount the details of my day, talk about an interesting article, ponder the implications of a news story? I often think "What would Jerry say?" I miss his ideas—unique, contrarian, always interesting and provocative.

I learned mindfulness meditation during the most difficult year of Jerry's illness and took an intensive course during the first summer after he died. I practiced every day for a year or more and then slacked off. It brought a sense of calm to a life otherwise beset by doing. I return to it now when I am feeling tense. I probably should do it more often.

Six-weeks after Jerry dies, I return to Madison, our home for forty years and where we returned each summer after we moved to New York. Madison is the place with most of the memories of our long life together; where our children were born and grew up, where both of our professional lives were charted, where lifelong friendships were nourished. I walk the streets we walked together; I return to the restaurants and the movie theaters where we spent so many hours; I drive by the house we lived in for thirty years.

Alone in the condo we bought when we moved to New York, I see him sitting in his favorite chair; lying naked next to me in bed. I wear his bathrobe for the familiar smell. Sometimes on the street I see a mirage, someone who looks like him coming toward me. I blink and return to reality. I want to talk about him. In Madison I luxuriate in the people who knew him best, those who will share their memories. We reminisce, we mourn, we laugh, some cry. Here is where I can finally grieve, bring some measure of closure to the life that was and begin again, re-create a life not on the ashes of the old, but on its foundation.

When you're unmoored you turn to what you do well. I'd always been good at school, so I enrolled in University summer school classes—with twenty-year-olds. Hesitant at first, I soon realize that I can take risks and enter this world. I know more than most of the undergraduates; I'm not uncomfortable speaking in class; the professors are gracious and welcoming. The students, initially respectful, over time make overtures, if not of friendship, then at least of conversations that look beyond my seventy-five-year-old face.

Structure and routine anchor my days. I go to the gym, I go to class, I go swimming, I do my homework. I arrange to spend time with at least one friend each day, preferably for dinner or an evening movie, because evenings, which once were vibrant or cozy or comforting, are now long, on the edge of loneliness, and maybe too much TV. I begin to prepare to teach a class on contemporary sub-Saharan Africa in my lifelong learning program at The New School University in New York. I know nothing about the topic when I begin, but I am taking a class to get me started. The very enormity of the topic and the task is a shield against empty time, against the descent into morbid thoughts. As a psychologist, with a cognitive behavioral orientation, I believe that what you say to yourself drives your feelings. Instinctively, I think, I practice what I have tried to teach my clients. Dark thoughts, self-pitying thoughts—why me?—do come, but mostly I confront them and turn the other cheek.

Most of my closest friends in Madison are coupled. Conventional wisdom says that couples invite you once or twice when you are single. Then you fade from their social calendar. Luckily, that doesn't happen. These are deep friendships; the people I would call if I were in trouble; those who would call me. Year after year when I return to Madison, these friendships remain strong, even if there have only been a few phone calls or emails during my months in New York.

I begin to spend more of my Madison time with the women—the female halves of couples, professional colleagues who were once one level more than acquaintances but now become friends. Over time, the balance shifts slightly between time with couples and with women friends. I am more on the edge of the world of coupledom and feel the loss, not only of the interesting social time, but of a world that was mine for all of my adult life.

The frantic pace continued for about a year. I spent a lot of time on email making plans. Sometimes I hit a wall, when on short notice I look for a friend to join me at a movie or a museum exhibit. Two or three calls and nobody available. A wave of melancholy washes over me. I realize that I am alone. This is one of the hardest things about being a single person. Slowly, I learn to take a deep breath, maybe more than one, and go out by myself. Not as good as having a companion to talk with after the movie or while walking through the museum exhibit, but better than staying home and feeling deprived. How long did it take before I could go to a film or a concert alone? I don't remember, but it had to be learned and practiced. Even now, there is always a slight tinge of sadness and self-pity before I go marching on. I still don't go to restaurants alone.

Travel was probably the most daunting step to take as a single person. Jerry and I had traveled all over the world during our married years. He loved to plan our trips. He was a great navigator, willing to drive anywhere, a whiz at reading a map. We had always traveled during University winter break. Now I would do it alone. My first foreign trip was to Myanmar (before the persecution of the Rohingya) with a tour. I didn't try to find a friend to join me, partly as a test of going it alone, partly because I didn't know who to ask and didn't want to be rejected. I worried about making friends in the tour group or being left alone at "free meal times." It went more smoothly than I could have hoped. The group was small and friendly. I "circulated" easily and notched a central place in the group. There were no lonely dinners or staying alone in my room because no one invited me to join them for dinner. I enjoyed the trip and crossed that hurdle, but like going to a movie alone, traveling by myself, even in a group, was not as enjoyable as having someone with whom to talk and share at the end of the day. My next trips were all with friends.

For eight months of the year, interrupted by frequent travel, I live in New York City, our original hometown. We had moved back to New York when we retired, ten years before Jerry died. I re-created my life when we moved back to New York, shifting the center of my daytime life from profession to involvement with volunteer organizations. I made more friends of my own through these organizations, perhaps with the foreshadowing of the single life to come. I came to these new friends, as the mid-seventy-year-old person I am now, with an almost empty backstory of how I came to be. This tabula rasa is freeing in some ways, unmooring in others. My previous professional status is not part of how my new friends know me. My children are names to them, as are theirs to me, not kids we knew from birth or childhood and watched grow and bloom. Most of my new friends don't meet me as part of a couple where, despite my own accomplishments, I was in the shadow of a very dominant personality. The strong and independent person I was in my professional life now spreads to all of my life. Even my long-term friends see me differently.

I have a very small family: my son and daughter, their spouses, their children. My son lives in San Francisco. My daughter was in New York for the first two years after Jerry died and then moved to Chicago. I have been distant from my difficult younger sibling for many years, My living cousins are half a generation younger, and have never been a significant part of my life. One of our priorities for our children was the development of independence. The flip side of that is less enmeshment. After Jerry died, would I have liked to have kids who called me every day and monitored my social-emotional temperature? Maybe the phone calls. I'm sure they were watching to see how I managed, but their outward behavior changed little. There was no cosseting of their widowed mother.

It is now almost five years since Jerry died. I was the first of my friends to get married, and, ironically, the first whose husband died. Notice I rarely use the word widow. I prefer to think of myself as a single person, which seems to emphasize my individual agency, not my status as part of a couple. I have a busy, satisfying life, with a community of friends, a vibrant intellectual life, and a leadership role in an organization that plays a core role in my life. I get invitations from friends all over the country to visit. I'm a good guest and get invited back. Many friends have commented on how well I've adjusted to life after Jerry. "You are the 'poster child (or woman)' for re-creating your life." At a recent celebration of my eightieth birthday, my children and grandchildren talked with admiration about the role model I am for life after a searing loss, and life in the later decades of life. Reinforcing affirmations all, but would I trade this life for having Jerry at my side again? In a minute.

Strange to say at this stage of my life, but I have grown in the last five years, developed parts of myself that perhaps were dormant next to the powerful man I met at sixteen, married at nineteen, lived with and loved for fifty-five years. Now I am ready to have a man in my life, mostly on the weekends, which are often the loneliest days. I've been introduced to two men recently, one in Madison and one in New York. They are interesting to talk to, have dinner with, but no spark. Does that come with time? Am I looking for the "love at first sight" that I experienced at sixteen? Have I become too comfortable with living my own life, not having to adjust to someone else's habits, eating dinner at 8 if the spirit moves me? Do I want a man's trousers hanging in my closet? Open-ended questions all, with many more pages to write.

My nineteen-year-old grandson says that, with increasing technological progress for replacing body parts, he expects to live to 120. "You probably could live almost to 100, grandma," he says. Not sure how I respond to that prediction, but it can be put aside while I continue to take pleasure in my good re-created life.

Becoming Maggie

MAGGIE MADAGAME

Raised Catholic in a very small community in northern Michigan, I began my life as the seventh of ten children in a lower- to middle-class family. My mom's family was of German/French descent and my father's family was Irish/Swedish. Both families immigrated through Canada and settled in Michigan. My mother was raised Baptist and converted to Catholicism when she married my father. I attended a Catholic school through eighth grade. I attended church every Sunday with my family and followed some pretty strict guidelines on how to act as a sweet, Catholic girl. Our life was centered around the church calendar and around the constantly changing expectations of the church at the time. By the time I was thirteen I knew my way out of my small town was to get a college degree. I then put myself through college.

I feel I was raised to distrust people growing up, to fear anything bigger than a small town and anyone different. I feared God and mistrusted my own ability to make decisions. Too long I clung to the lies the small town maintained to keep people where they were, discouraging them from breaking free.

Before Harry and I married, he had raised three sons with his first wife (who died of cancer). When I started seeing Harry, I was divorced, with my two-year-old daughter, Elizabeth. He was nineteen years older than me. We shared twenty-two years of marriage before Harry died from an inoperable cancer around his heart on August 5, 2009. We raised our two children in a rural community. When they graduated from high school, they continued to university for higher education. In 2015, my youngest daughter, Heidi, came out as transgender (female to male) to become my son, Holden.

My journey the following eight years since Harry's death has taken me from a long-lasting grief to an acquired level of skills to cope with my fears and anxieties. The most difficult bridges I had to cross in order to find myself without Harry were to take back independence from family, community, and church. Many people said it would take a few years to get past my grief. At the time I thought three years was an enormous amount of time to grieve and get past losing a loved one! Now I know it's not about how to get past anything. It's just a matter of being able to put the loss in a place that's safe and doesn't destroy the present time and present decisions that need to be made. I had to get to the point of being able to redefine who I was, or who I wanted to be, without Harry.

I remember being reminded by many people (by small verbal messages and facial expressions) that it was time for me to move on. After just a year I sensed my colleagues and my community were avoiding me. I was tainted with death and sorrow, and no one wanted to come to grips with the possibility it could happen to them. The only people who didn't avoid my pain were my first-grade students. It was perfect. They forced me to live in the moment.

I prayed and sought guidance from Jesus. I thought he'd let me know what he wanted of me. "He will guide and strengthen me," I thought. In my case, I believe religion kept the wound open. It made me feel helpless. My fear increased for quite some time when I wasn't speaking to God anymore, but my survival instinct did also. I was told by my music director (at church) to start baking bread more and helping those who were in need. He said that would turn things around for me. A piece of advice I heard often: Help others when grieving. It didn't work for me; it was just another distraction that kept me from looking inside myself to see what I wanted to do with my life and how to proceed. I was afraid without my belief in God and belonging in a system of faith. I lost a church community, weekly routines of choir practice, and going to mass. It was a difficult transition to begin speaking to myself rather than to a deity. I felt alone and lost at times. I would look up to the sky out of habit, thinking heaven was there. But I was determined not to return to my unrealistic dependence on God to help me or make decisions for me.

I noticed I really enjoyed it when I got the chance to visit my son at college. I felt I could be myself in a more liberal, multicultured, university community. I remember feeling the power it gave me to feel autonomous. No one knew me. I didn't feel I was labeled with the persona of widow. I would cry, laugh, and be myself without being on guard for what role I felt I was expected to play. I liked the feel of not being judged by family or community.

I decided I wasn't Margaret any more. My father said often (when I was younger), "Don't ever let anyone call you Maggie! Maggie is a barmaid's name! Make them call you Margaret." I think that's one of the lies I've passively believed over the years. When I decided to move from my small town to the city, I was Maggie.

Family and Fear

When my son came out as transgender, I had a realization. The conservative, religious community I lived in would not be a welcoming place for my son. I wanted more for him and for Elizabeth. I wanted much more for myself too. When Holden took his freedom as the gender he is, instead of the gender he was assigned at birth, I felt a transfer of power to me. I'm still in awe of his determination to get through these struggles and become Holden. I have been empowered by both of my children to actualize myself and be free.

When I told my family about my plans to retire and go to Istanbul for a few months (my daughter, Elizabeth, was living there), I had a couple of brothers suggest I was nuts. A cousin said, "We'll have to do an intervention to keep you from going to Turkey!" I think silence and family members shaking their head back and forth were the worst reaction. I read it loud and clear, "You don't know what you're doing!" "You really want to do this?" "Is it safe there?" "Aren't you scared?" or "Are you kidding? You are *not* going to Turkey!" These were not supportive sentiments. Each time I heard negativity about my leaving, it strengthened my confidence to do what was best for me. I slowly realized many of the people around me didn't want me to interrupt their power of status quo. How dare I make a hole in their so-called normality and shift things? Wasn't I a bit crazy because of my depression and didn't I need them to help me get well again? Get well again would mean—don't change the rules in society, know your place.

I took a teaching job at a private, Turkish school. I was scared to death! My Turkish was minimal. The expectation for the teachers and the structure of classes were foreign to me. When I returned home from Turkey I was shocked by my own reaction. I was seeing a big cage around me which I was allowing to lock me in. I had new eyes. I didn't care about most of what I had. My possessions, my house, and property didn't mean the same to me. I knew how to be minimalistic and wanted to continue. I saw that all the things in my home were just things. I didn't miss them while I was gone. I didn't need them or want them. The process I started going through made me realize my house wasn't a home anymore. I had no loved ones in it; it wasn't a place I wanted to keep. It became a building with very little meaning. My mind was open to more possibilities. I wanted to live a lifestyle with challenges and opportunities. I wanted to live near excellent health care. I wanted to be near an international airport so I could travel without complication.

Even though I knew possibilities were open to me, I wrestled with a lot of anxiety and depression. I had internalized all the fears I was fighting with. My feelings of guilt were keeping me from growing. It seems like I was always taking three steps forward and then regressing two steps back. The only way I was able to latch onto my freedom was to learn where all the guilt I was feeling was coming from. I had to decide what I wanted my life to look like, rather than what others had in store for me and were willing to control. I took antidepressant drugs and sought counseling. Consequently, I suffered through fewer panic attacks and prolonged anxiety. I'm still learning to think through triggers from my old way of thinking, and I cope with more ease. The scope of this turnabout was huge for me. It began with how I deal with family and has overflowed to ways to manage my life with friends, community, and acquaintances. A change in my thinking began to transform how I could make decisions based on what I wanted for my life. Seeing a psychologist kept me on track.

Besides therapy, reading helped. *The Three Questions** calmed my racing mind so I could see things in front of me more clearly. *Riding the Dragon* encouraged me.[†] I still write down quotes and affirmations to remind myself not to fear the dragon but to climb on and ride. I'll always read to gain more insight for help. I've learned that when a book speaks to me, I'm ready for the information to sink in. Many times it was helpful to have my therapist discuss content when I was having trouble understanding new concepts from an author. He knew my desire to understand more about my grief and depression and suggested *Existential Psychotherapy*.[‡] This was pivotal in my transformation. It took months to read and discuss with my therapist, but I still refer to many of the charts and notes I took then to refresh myself.

Freedom

Holden and Elizabeth helped me see the limits of the small community they grew up in and encouraged me to do whatever I wanted to make a change or stay where I was. I remember one pivotal summer when the only used

* John J. Muth, *The Three Dragons* (New York: Scholastic Press, 2002).

† Robert J. Wicks, *Riding the Dragon* (Notre Dame, IN: Sorin Books, 2003).

‡ Irvin J. Yalom, *Existential Psychotherapy* (New York: Basic Books, 1980).

bookstore and the only local coffee cafe closed. I was angry. Enough to think about moving. I didn't want the house and property any longer. I was leaning toward getting an apartment or condo in the university town I loved. Finances were tight, so I had to choose to live within my means. I put a high priority on being debt-free and began to pay off whatever I could while waiting for my home to be sold. I began to see frugality was the only way I could pull off this change I wanted for myself. When my house finally sold I felt a huge relief. I was alone when I signed all the paperwork to pass my house over to new owners. I was elated. There was no turning back. I was determined to go forward.

Within a year I was living in the city. I found a small, affordable, one-bedroom apartment in southern Michigan. The sense of being on my own was invigorating. I was scared to death, but I loved it. Not to say it wasn't still very difficult, it was. But it was the best thing I did for myself. Selling my home gave me a boost of optimism. Whether I'd screwed up or not I knew I could begin to look ahead and adjust what fit for me.

I labeled my personal growth-work "Do The Work" (DTW) (It's also the acronym for Detroit Metropolitan Airport). DTW is freedom. This continuous work has helped me uncover which thoughts of mine were true and which were not true at all. I thought of it as my flight to freedom. I had to do the work. With help from my therapist I began to unlearn old thinking and unchain myself from my past. It was the only way I could be free to live my life genuinely. After seeing a loved one die it's easy to remember how limited our time is in this life.

When my small apartment was loaded with the things the movers piled in, I could hardly walk through it. Again, I had to downsize and sift through each item to decide what I wanted, needed, or could live without. It was much more difficult at this point. I wasn't just deciding for myself. I had to talk to my kids to see which things they could live without. I was at the point I couldn't fly solo on those decisions. There were possessions they had from childhood. I had a vast number of books. I took it step by step—literally. If I couldn't decide where an item had to go, I would force myself to walk it over to labels I had created: Throw Away, Give Away, Maybe Keep, and Keep. Another rule I demanded of myself was "If it makes you sad, get rid of it, if it makes you smile, keep it." I went through at least forty albums of pictures, removed the pictures, put them in photo boxes, and threw out the empty albums. No words can describe how liberating this felt.

Now I was free to explore cultural events, swim at the YMCA, become active in volunteer opportunities, and be Maggie—a new name for a new life. My new life hasn't come without mistakes. I knew my choices and decisions were open for screwing up. Not being afraid of failure is a benefit of letting go of the past. "Perfect" and "bored" aren't words I like to use. When

I found the book by Miriam Greenspan, *Healing through the Dark Emotions*, it finally hit me that the only way I was going to get through this was to not avoid the difficult, scary emotions that come with grief. Greenspan says, "The rupturing of our capacity to feel and honor dark emotions in ourselves and others is a symptom of our global illness."* In a January 16, 2010, journal entry I wrote: "It's so simple to say, I want this to *go away*! And then I proceed to push and shove and pound it into my heart that is numb and mushy. The grief edges its way into my heart like walking into muck; once your foot gets into it, you have to tug very hard to get it out, like a suction cup." I know I have to tug hard to get out, but I also want to be okay with the muckiness. The nature of grief seems to be just that, sometimes.

I have fought hard for my freedom. My experiences in the last eight years, since Harry's death, have helped me put things in perspective. They have helped me figure out who I am without my husband and how I can live my life as an independent woman.

* Miriam Greenspan, *Healing through the Dark Emotions* (Boston: Shambhala, 2003), 234.

Who I Am Revealed

RONI SHERMAN RAMOS

In the year 2000, at age fifty-five, I had an identity crisis. From 1972 to 2000 I was married to Paul Ramos, a Puerto Rican black man with strong ties to his culture. Together we had two beautiful daughters, and together we founded a health center on the Lower East Side. Betances Health Center provided us with health care and much, much, more.

I came of age in the 1960s, and my left-leaning ideology did not include pride in my own Jewish heritage. I was drawn to the Latin beat, the black resistance, the CAUSE. Attracted to the culture and to the man, Paul Ramos, I assimilated and became them. Our daughters identified with the Latina heritage, and that was OK with me. We were an interracial family who experienced all the worst parts of a racist society. When Paul and I got married, my Aunt Sophie said, "Fine, just as long as you don't have children." Living in Brooklyn shielded our daughters from a lot of that, but when we went on vacation the ugliness of people surfaced. We were shot at while rowing on a lake upstate, water pipes to our cabin were broken, and our tires were slashed. We found out later that an ordinance on the lake forbade rentals to nonwhites, and our landlord used us to test the waters.

So when Paul died unexpectedly at age fifty-nine, I was thrown into a crisis I never could have anticipated. Who was I?

I was fifty-five years old and a widow. The grief was unimaginable. No way to prepare for this occurrence when you expect to grow old together, buy a small house in Puerto Rico, reap the benefits of buying a Brooklyn brownstone before gentrification. All gone.

Just the sound of Latin music, the sound of the Spanish language, the sight of the Health Center we founded triggered panic. To the entire Lower East Side, Paul was a hero. He had come up in East Harlem where, a short Latin boy in an all African American school, he had to fight his way in the streets every day. When he was a teenager, his mother chose a man over Paul, which left him homeless. Abandoned and hungry Paul rode the subway all night, but he attended high school every day. A survivor, Paul rose up the ladder by perseverance, intelligence, and sheer tenacity. I was his wife. I graduated from nursing school in 1968 and immediately volunteered on the Lower East Side at a pilot program of the Judson Memorial Church. I was teamed with Paul, a community advocate, to go door to door testing children for lead poisoning. It was love at first sight . . . chemistry!

Once Paul died, at age fifty-nine, the staff and board members at the health center began to act strangely toward me. I wanted to keep my status at Betances and maintain my deep connection to the clinic and its community. Without Paul, I was no longer valued; I became an outsider. At first, they asked if I wanted to be the executive director, I was not interested. I think they did this to make me feel included, although they knew I did not want that job. Eventually, I began to realize they might have been afraid I would expose certain professional incompetence. The board of directors, some of whom were Paul's lifelong friends, refused to accept me, and refused to even talk to me, so I had to face the reality that I was no longer part of the Betances community. Hard as it was, the only thing I could do was detach from it and attempt to put it behind me.

For thirty years I had not understood or examined why I rejected my own culture and successfully adopted another. My children were grown at the time of Paul's death, but, uncomfortable as it was, I felt the need to look back on my marriage and face the tough understanding that raising our daughters with different views on parenting, different cultural expectations, and different ways of communicating had not been easy and in fact had made for a very rocky marriage at times. Since I had learned to lean on Paul as the strong, capable one, I had concluded that everything I was, everything I represented, added up to weakness, ignorance, and embarrassment. If abandoning my own roots meant adopting Paul's, I was willing. After all, I was an imposter, and the only thing about me that rang true was my husband, and that validated me.

So here I was, a widow, having been rejected in a concrete way by the man I loved and rejected by my adopted community.

I knew I did not want to spend the rest of my life alone, but who did I want to be with? Who was I? I struggled for months wanting my life back.

I went into therapy; I attended a bereavement group on the Upper West Side, which helped. My biggest comfort after losing Paul was a connection I made to a psychic. Her talent was undeniable, and her assessment of my relationship was profoundly helpful. No marriage is perfect, but in death one tends to idolize the lost partner. As I said, Paul was a folk hero in community health care, and bigger than life, but our marriage had challenges. Patricia pointed out those imperfections, and I came to realize we were not saints; our marriage was not without challenges. I now had to rely on my own resourcefulness to survive. I had to learn to accept who I was and celebrate it, for only then would I find happiness restored to my shattered life.

The first summer after Paul's death I rented a house in the East End of Long Island with three other women from the bereavement group. Their life experiences were so different from mine. Their husbands had left them financially secure, whereas Paul had left an unexecuted pension plan. A signature was all that was needed, but it was never signed, and so I did not receive his pension. It was discussed that when he retired, Paul and I would have health insurance for life and a modest pension. Of course, we had bought our brownstone in the early '70s, and now it was worth much more, and it was where I loved to live.

It had been over thirty years since I had dated, and so I approached this in an interesting way. This was an adventure, I told myself, and, in a way, it was. I found dates with men on Match and Concerned Singles. I met like-minded, interesting men who were genuinely looking for a life partner, and others who were financially insecure and wanted a woman who could take care of them.

I met David on Match, and on our first date I arrived late, having gone to the wrong address. The planned date was at a restaurant that was closed for a private Xmas party so we had to fumble to find another. It was not love at first sight. When the bill came, he asked, to be politically correct, if it was OK if he paid; I said sure. He lived only blocks from me in Brooklyn, but did not offer to walk me home. Our first several months together were fraught with turmoil. David was coming out of many years alone after two marriages; he was terrified of being betrayed and retreated whenever he felt endangered. I saw this as weakness and responded with anger. It took months for us to learn to trust each other, but it was a worthwhile investment. David is a therapist who helped me examine many of my own insecurities and helped me work through difficult times with my daughters. We helped each other to understand that we are very different people, and we do things differently. I know that sounds obvious, but I think I always thought if someone didn't do things the way I do them, they were wrong.

Today, I am married to David. We have a relationship built of love and trust. He and I spend long hours talking and reminiscing. He is not threatened by my crying while remembering Paul. He accepts my moodiness on the anniversaries of Paul's death or birthday. He does not mind having a photo of Paul among other family photos. It is with him that I have learned how to love myself for who I am. I have a full life with work I love, children I love, and friends I love; nonetheless, living with someone, whether a dear friend or partner, is important to me. It is not only the physical intimacy but, even more so, the emotional intimacy. Although I am convinced a woman does not need a man to feel complete, I am sure that intimate connections with others fulfill a need that cannot be denied.

Losing the Artist, Living with His Art

DORIS FRIEDENSOHN

Three of us were seated at the dining room table contemplating *The Mystic Marriage*. My husband's large oil canvas shows a pair of cherubic lovers in flight over a postcard-perfect Italian village. Above their heads, a pair of doves flutter. "Bliss. Uncomplicated love," Eli said. "Inspired by a honeymoon week at the Lago di Garda. Twenty years ago." Vivian, Eli's friend for half a century, had just announced her intention to buy the painting. What an odd moment, I remember thinking. A widow on the verge of a new life, Vivian wanted to transform her bedroom "into a chamber of love." Eli, after two decades of our happy marriage (his second), was ill with cancer. He died two months later, as anticipated, in August 1991. He was sixty-seven, twelve years my senior. Vivian lived another twenty-five years. After her death, as I had promised, I bought back the painting from her estate. Paul, my partner for the past four years, finds *The Mystic Marriage* as mesmerizing as I do. Lives change, but the dream of love—we both like to think—lives on.

Alone in bed in the late summer and early fall of 1991, I found myself checking the clock at 3:25 A.M.; and then again at 3:55 A.M. and 4:05 A.M. Sometimes, in a waking dream, I saw Eli standing on a subway platform—only to vanish as I approached. In other dreams, I was living alone in a grubby room in a dangerous neighborhood or back in my parents' apartment. Classic expressions of loss, I'm sure. Poor sleep and unsettling dreams didn't set me up for breakfast alone. My husband, like many college professors, enjoyed holding forth, especially around 7:30 A.M., as a way of clarifying his ideas. How to think about intimacy and the building of pyramids? About the power of religion and the sexual revolutions? About drugs and the death of figurative painting? All this while dividing his attention between a cheese omelet and the *New York Times*.

To escape the morning silence, I joined an Early Bird tennis group at our club. At 5:45 A.M., five days a week, I had my first coffee before getting on the court at 6:00 A.M. The hit of caffeine and the friendly chat eased me into the day. Male players, especially the best of them, were eager to warm up with me, and I appreciated the attention. An hour of hard hitting plus ten mindless minutes in the sauna rounded out the therapeutic session. At home, after a bran muffin and homemade coffee, I was ready for a trip down the turnpike and doings at my college. The routine lasted six years, until my left knee gave out.

Meanwhile, I was traveling often (while teaching) as a consultant on American studies programs—to Mozambique, Turkey, Poland, Argentina, Nepal, Japan, Guinea, and the Republic of Georgia. The task of enlightening—or at least entertaining—colleagues whose knowledge of the United States was likely to be uneven or out of date kept me buzzing and engaged. As my State Department hosts advised, I was careful about roaming the streets alone. But I took advantage of hotel pools, seductive buffets, speaking French or Spanish to waiters and strangers, and CNN in the room at night. Back at JFK after each adventure, my limo driver would be there, waiting patiently. If my flight was delayed, I often thought, at least Eli wouldn't be pacing back and forth, trying not to worry. Once in the limo, I couldn't wait to get home to my plants, my prose, and my calm, welcoming house.

Familiarity brings comfort. Living with Eli's art, I revisit our history and my own, along with his cultural, painterly, and personal preoccupations. His words—spoken and written—bang around in my brain, like some combination of a soccer match, ballet, and moon shot. His paintings also talk to me; they talk at me, and sometimes they talk back to me. I'm in the conversation but not running it. Except when I am.

The display of his work in my house is mostly as it was twenty-five years ago. Big, disturbing paintings of "apocalypse"—people maimed or drowning or flying out of windows—occupy the gallery-like front room. Barefoot Tunisian women carrying wood, and an urban Tunisian couple at loggerheads hang opposite one another in the living room, as if in conversation about their mysterious "otherness." Paintings from a romantic sojourn on Crete dominate the downstairs hall and my study. Naked lovers, their beautiful bodies showing signs of decay, distract me as I read in bed at night. Mixed among these canvases are playful pop sculptures from the early '60s, drawings of nudes, satiric lovers at war and play, and a variety of wood carvings.

The Artist and the Model

Fifty years ago, when our story began, we fell into archetypal roles: I posed nude, on a well-worn bedsheet, and the artist drew me, usually in pencil. "Bend your right arm and reach toward your left shoulder," he might say. I followed instructions. I was in his space, in his studio, and—at such moments—his single-minded focus. Studying my body excited him. He shifted my position, focused on my breasts, flat belly, or long limbs. Then he attacked his drawing pad.

I was flattered by the attention but ambivalent about modeling. It required a discipline I didn't wish to acquire. No matter. I was still a novice college teacher with a new PhD. In the faculty dining room at Queens College, I had snared a sexy artist with long sideburns, expressive dark eyes, and a great flow of language. His loft on Chambers Street, where he settled after leaving his marriage, had a lumpy mattress and dishes from Job Lots. He took me to cheap dim sum restaurants where regulars threw their napkins on the floor and to Pearl Paint on Canal Street for art supplies. He talked, eloquently, about Leonardo, Piero de la Francesca, and other beloved Italian Renaissance painters. He told me about living in Paris at the end of World War II and a transformative Fulbright year in Rome. While drawing me naked in a soft, floppy hat one afternoon, he mentioned Ben, his analyst from the '50s. "Ben," I said, abandoning my pose. "Not Ben W?" The same smart shrink I had been seeing for the past two years? The story played well at cocktail parties in a time when everyone had a therapist tale to tell. In fact, our connection to Ben made for sweet, sly jokes and more than a few useful revelations.

Recently, an old friend wrote to report that she had seen me "naked in Amherst." I looked quite fine, she said, reclining in a floppy hat. It seems that the gallery at UMass/Amherst had mounted a show of nudes from local collections. Among them was one by Elias Friedensohn, titled *Doris*. She emailed the image to me. Not the best of his nudes, but a striking likeness. There I was, happily compliant, captured by an artist who was only beginning to know me.

Utopian Moments and Recurrent Nightmares

In 1973 on the mythical island of Crete, we walked the beaches, gazed out at the marine-blue sea, and celebrated one another. The air smelled of rosemary and occasionally of pot. Eli's autobiographical paintings of that voyage show us as fit, energized, and comfortably naked. Idealized, in a word. One double portrait from the Crete series hangs next to the front door of my house. No visitor passes it by without a second, possibly envious glance. I'm envious too: of that uncomplicated couple—without obligations or intimations of mortality.

Still, the painting has an edge that's hard to identify. Is this a dream? A wish rather than a more nuanced view of who and how we were? The two of us are confidently in motion, but not touching and not looking at one another. Maybe touching is unnecessary in Utopia where the point is to escape conventional behavior. Surely this freedom is what most vacationers hope for. It's dreamtime before reality kicks in once again; before the kids flounder and the furnace fails; before projects stall and our bodies deteriorate—as they will, all too soon.

The underside of love is anxiety about one's lover. And about one's own readiness to commit and to give. Will the lover be there, tuned in, eager for communication and sexual commerce? Eli's needy, tortured lovers from other periods always grab my attention. I feel the demons of desire exploding within them and their wacked-out ids: the stuff we repress to sleep at night. They unsettle me. How do we humans deal with our lusts and attachments, our fragile egos and power struggles? For "explanations," Eli drew on the Bible, Greek myths, Holocaust history, and Freud.

I envied his courage. And his learning too. Much as I might have fancied a plunge into the darkness, I was wedded to conventions of "reason"—even after three intense years of psychoanalysis. This emotional balancing act is not uncommon in relationships. The dark partner needs the relief offered by a lighter companion. The so-called reasonable one needs a regular, reality reset. On my own after a quarter of a century with Eli, I made adjustments. My voice became more ironic, my narratives almost at home with the gloom.

But it took some doing. I joined a writers' group—of smart, politically serious people. They don't like "lite." For a quarter of a century now, I've benefited from their tough-minded responses to my work. Once a month, we gather around my dining room table for a salad and dessert before circulating hard copies of the latest works-in-progress. Soon enough, with these friends, I was commenting on all sorts of national and global shenanigans, often of a threatening kind. I was also sending drafts, revisions, and miscellaneous jottings to a faithful correspondent in California.

When the World Trade Center was attacked in 2001, I was preparing a keynote address for a conference in Poland on "America and Globalization." Glued to the tube, I watched the towers implode, chaos in the air, and body parts mixed with industrial refuse on the ground. Alone in the house, I ran back and forth from the tube to the phone. Talking with my stepdaughter Shola, I was reminded that Eli had worked this turf. In the late '80s, following the '86 stock market crash, he produced a series of satiric watercolors. *Defenestrations*, he called them. The paintings show two-dimensional men in suits diving out of tall buildings as people on the street stare, scream, and gesture wildly. Shock and confusion are palpable. The scenes have a hypermanic quality that somehow allows viewers to stay cool. Human folly (e.g., trusting the Market, lusting for More) is the subject here, not good guys and bad guys. With the smell of disaster still wafting across the Hudson, I let Eli's imaginings merge with my politics. We powerful, vain Americans may have been victims, I would tell the Polish scholars, but we were not innocent. Greed and sanctimoniousness have shaped our fate. Our demons, like the proverbial chickens, have cost us dearly.

"Nail Head" and Other Maimed Creatures

In the early '70's, Eli bought a collection of old wooden pieces—used for steaming men's hats. With these hat-blocks, he created a portrait gallery of the depraved and their victims: men (generally) lacking ears, eyes, or a nose; or with an eye or ear where the nose belongs. One piece has shiny, removable false teeth; others have nails pounded into their faces or thick brown-red paint, like blood, smeared over their heads. Maimed creatures all, even the smiling, red-lipped woman with nails decorating her face who flirts giddily with a similarly maimed but coy male companion.

For a long time, I kept the most gruesome heads hidden in the basement. Then, about three years ago, the *Times* critic Holland Cotter praised a show at the Met of African sculptures with a family resemblance (nails on the bodies and heads) to Eli's. Cotter's article sent me directly to the living room bookshelf. Reaching above eye level, I removed a dark wood, male head, well-shaped but featureless, and covered with nails. Settling him on the coffee table, I ran my fingers over the flat nail heads and half-smiled. "My nail-head," I said out loud. From the basement, I retrieved four other wounded pieces and placed them among the ceramic pots and the African objects scattered around the first floor. These stand-ins for the human family are sense deprived, seriously flawed. Weird and demanding to be noticed. Comic in the right light. Or when I'm in the right mood.

This is how art works, I thought. It seduces us and accustoms us to evil we can live with, albeit not easily. I wrote to a former dealer of Eli's, citing

Cotter's piece and urging her to come to Leonia for a look at the hat-blocks. "Why not?" Luise said, as we sat in the studio two months later. "No one is buying, but these pieces should be shown." And they were, to the delight (and confusion) of many friends and fans of Eli's work.

These days, "Nail-Head" (a piece Eli titled *Eye Fetish*) occupies the front line of my understanding. Depravity is a human constant (along with decency and humor). From starvation in South Sudan and destruction in Aleppo to poisoned water in Flint, Michigan, I know what humans can do. What *they* do, of course. And what *we* do. What *my* taxes support. Still, each morning I take comfort from granola with extra-rich yogurt—while paging through the *New York Times* for the latest, chilling reports.

Blissed Out—With "The Bella Telephone"

Bombs fall, temperatures soar, and floods of biblical proportions wreak havoc. After a glance at Nail-Head and his cohort of destroyers, I wander into the dining room and behold "The Bella Telephone." Eli's madcap autobiographical subject is a large, smiling head and an arm in a bright red-orange sweater. I see this '60s pop figure, made from epoxy, snuggled up to an enormous, old-fashioned phone. The man and the phone sit on a solid, black base—about 12 inches by 30 inches. He is alone but in contact. His lady love's ear can be seen in the phone's receiving unit. The caller grins effusively. I grin too. She's only an ear, some women friends say, passive and listening to him. Right. But wrong. Whatever the gender clues might suggest, sweet connection is the salient point.

Day and night, married and alone, I've relished Eli's humor and his insistence that we humans can make it through. Especially if we're lucky in love. "The Bella Telephone" presides over a low breakfront in my sunny dining room. Succulents, crowns of thorns, and a wandering Jew thrive there, lined up along three large windows facing the garden. For over twenty years of solo living, I've relished the company of the fellow on the phone. He seems so present and alert to my presence; and he offers no back talk. Perhaps someday, I thought, I'd be joined by a new man using a smaller phone. Indeed. Now as I set the table for a meal with Paul, I'm still grinning. Paul assures me that he's grinning too.

Advertising Is Us: Consider *The Grass Goddess*

The Grass Goddess, a large oil in bright pastel colors, hangs in the dining room where *The Mystic Marriage* once presided. Fleshy, sly, and provocative in the fashion of the late nineteenth-century ads, she holds aloft a marijuana plant. Ah, the seductions of packaged happiness, good health and well-being! In the 1960s and '70s, when we occasionally relished this alternative to booze, *The Grass Goddess* seemed like Our Far-Out Woman. But no longer. Today, consumers of cannabis are happily shopping around, and the marijuana business is big. Some California entrepreneurs might want her for their packaging—or at the door of their Grass Bank. For this advertising coup, they might pay a fancy price. I wonder, is she more or less magical now that grass is medicinal—and legal? And with "regular" businesses grossing more than $6 billion in 2016? Should I make copies of *The Grass Goddess* for my grandchildren while I still own the original?

Terrorist at Heathrow and Other Airports

These days, I travel only for pleasure. I say this even as the pleasure has gone out of flying. The airlines, ever more devious, seem to offer bargains while laying on endless new charges. The food, if they serve any, is vile and the service brusque. Still, our sanity requires the fiction of calm in the lounge and tolerable delays; of a decent drink at a chain restaurant and liquor bargains at the Duty Free. The airports in Eli's final series of paintings, completed in 1990, lull me into that fiction while alerting me to dis-ease beneath the surface. Travelers gather at huge windows to watch a plane being refueled or the cleaners at work. Rows of orange-red plastic chairs seem welcoming.

Yet hiding behind one row of chairs is a devilish, small child fondling his cap gun. *Terrorist at Heathrow*, Eli titled the piece, years before we had reason to fear—or to notice the ethnic backgrounds of our traveling companions. In the painting, I'm sitting, with my back to the viewer, not far from the five-year-old with the gun. Eli is standing near me, a midlife man with a Lincolnesque head and a soft hat covering his balding head. What are viewers witnessing, I ask myself? Our passivity? Man (and woman) at the mercy of the (flying) machine? Arrivals and departures out of our control? Time slipping away as we wait? No, that's the old news. Today, anxious travelers jam airports everywhere, hoping for safe haven in a world run increasingly by maniacs. They curl up in sleeping bags and change their underwear in the rest room. I wonder, did the little kid with the cap pistol join a war-making militia or a peacekeeping army? Or is he, too, on the run?

Active and Passive: What Shall I Do about Eli's Art?

It's a half century since I first lay back on a mattress in his SoHo loft and posed for Eli. Before I appeared on the scene, he had enjoyed considerable success as a New York painter: more than two dozen one-person shows, purchases by museums and individual collectors, and reviews in the *New York*

Times, *Art News*, and elsewhere. Then, during twenty-four happy years together, marked by giddy adventures and extraordinary creativity, his career seemed to stagnate. The art scene expanded and turned away from figuration. Eli, indifferent to trends and "commerce," defiantly experimented with new subjects and new modes of narrative painting. What a bad joke, we both thought: an abundance of domestic pleasure and so few professional rewards.

Right after Eli died, there were several gallery and university-based shows featuring the *Airports* (his last project) and a glorious retrospective at a New Jersey regional museum that no longer exists. I was consulted by the curators. I wrote supportive copy and kept a circle of Friedensohn followers informed. What else could I do? What should I do with all the drawings, oils, watercolors, and pieces of sculpture stored in my house?

In fact, while feeling somewhat guilty, I remained busy with my own work: traveling often to western Europe along with Latin American, South Asia, East Africa, and eastern Europe for American Studies; publishing a food memoir (2005) and then a small book about a food service training program in New Jersey for very poor people (2011). Between projects, I attended nonfiction writers' workshops in Mexico, Italy, and at Goucher College; and I worked on my Spanish during repeated visits to a language school in Antigua, Guatemala. One afternoon in Antigua, a day laborer standing ahead of me in line at the bank asked in Spanish, "Who are you?" "I'm a writer," I said. I didn't add that since I no longer had to worry about students and their generally incompetent prose, I was free (and thrilled) to focus on my own.

On Eli's behalf, I did what was comfortable, what I knew how to do. With my stepdaughter Shola, an artist and graphic designer, I organized a number of exhibits in Eli's light-filled studio, just five steps down from the living room.

When offers for shows came our way, I wrote what was needed in support of the art on the walls. An unpublished book by Eli on aspects of his work as a figurative painter was my principal source. In the mid '90s, Shola and I turned that overwritten manuscript into a full-color, twenty-four-page brochure, "Secrets of Elias Friedensohn: A Painter's Reflections on Making Art." More recently, our family launched a website, eliasfriedensohn.com. With my son Adam managing the technical side, we've already publishing fifteen newsletters, designed by Shola, for which I do much of the planning and writing.

In an era in which narrative painting is seriously undervalued, I want to be sure that Eli's nuanced themes are well understood. Unwrapped, perhaps. To do so, I take liberties with his dense, occasionally idiosyncratic prose: shortening and simplifying his sentences, eliminating obscure references, and modulating some of his more obsessive preoccupations. Yes, I often clean Eli up. I worry that I sometimes get him too clean—in a way he would hate.

Unfortunately, I know more about clear prose than promoting art. And I share Eli's discomfort with art as commerce. Somebody else, not in the immediate family, should be resurrecting Eli. But who? And at what steep price? Who knows the work as well as I do? As well as Shola, Adam, and I collectively do? I remember another artist named Elias, a close friend of my father's, who died young and left three kids, a wife, and hundreds of beautifully crafted etchings. I grew up with a dozen of his scenes of classic New York, Paris, and Rome. To pay the rent and support her kids, Elias's widow pulled out her address book and began ringing doorbells. I was relieved not to be at home when she visited.

The equivalent of ringing doorbells for Eli's estate is writing letters to unknown dealers, editors, art critics, and curators. Most of these people are interested in Young Unknowns, Signatures, and Tested Commodities. Eli's humanism and subtle narratives don't resonate in today's market—just as they didn't thirty or forty years ago. But they resonate for me, more than ever.

To my astonishment, the more I write about Eli's art, the sweeter the challenge—and the greater the thrill. I didn't count on this particular benefit: on making his work mine—my writing challenge, my subject, my creative excitement. Yes, I still occasionally knock off a piece on food; and I still pay attention to changing manifestations of American diversity (topics on which I once lectured around the world). But nowadays, Eli's painting and sculpture are at the center of my writing, as the members of my writers' group can testify. I write for a small audience of readers, mostly friends, who respond—critically and generously—to comments on works they might have seen or wish they could see.

Writing about Eli's work, I see it better. And sometimes differently. I see the antic vision, the dark insights, and the struggle to make sense of so much that is elusive and conflicted in human experience. I'm fortunate to start each day with *The Bella Telephone* and have cocktails most evenings surrounded by original treatments of terror and transcendence. Who needs TV news when I have my very own, high-speed connection to hell and back? Yes, I'm willing to let go of some of the art on my walls and other pieces tucked away in the house. They belong, like many early works of Eli's, in collections and museums. Still, the task is daunting, and I'm not in a rush to let go.

After the Aftermath

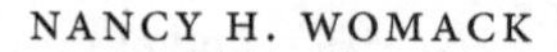

NANCY H. WOMACK

Soon after you died I gave all your clothes and shoes to charities, flushed the medications hospice hadn't already destroyed, and began to consider what to do with your personal effects: tie tacks, rings, books, paintings, wood carvings, coin collections, antique bottles, duck decoys, arrowheads, model cars, baseball cards, cat's eye marbles, rocks and minerals; a bicycle, a metal detector, an abacus; a telescope, a vial of volcanic ash from Mount St. Helens, a piece of the moon.

A few years later, I took over your office—little by little got rid of your hundreds of videos—hauled boxes and bags to every thrift store I could find, gave them to other men coming in and out of the house—electricians, plumbers, exterminators; removed all the shelves but two, one for your mementos; another for mine; repainted the walls, hung new pictures, bought a new sofa, a table, a lamp, but kept your corner bookcase and the desk you salvaged and refinished years ago.

Cleaning out the desk drawers took months—so much to deal with: files of family history, report cards from your childhood through college, a handwritten log of money you once borrowed from your sister, detailing when and how you paid it back; payment records on the first house we ever bought; a desiccated fountain pen someone gave you as a graduation gift; tools from your brief foray into engineering—drawing pencils, protractors, gum erasers, a slide rule; and birthday cards from other women, mostly generic greetings from colleagues and friends.

It's been over a decade now. Little remains visible of your ever having lived in this house—a few keepsakes from your hobbies and careers, pictures of us at our daughters' weddings, snapshots in small frames among books and memorabilia.

The top drawer of your dresser, the last of your secret places left untouched, still contains your wallet, several pairs of your dark-rimmed glasses, papers, and mystery. I open it occasionally. It smells of old leather and pipe tobacco. It smells of you. Just as quickly, I close it again.

Three Poems

JOAN MICHELSON

Dawn

In this hour, they say, the dead lie still,
weary from their all-night graveyard walk.

But came a knock. She opens to the Law.
Two police ask her to sit down.

They stand between the couch and the piano,
a polite young couple looking uncomfortable.

She can't take in their words. She goes upstairs,
turns the tap that won't stop dripping.

What next? She's made the bed. Step by step
she descends. They say, "You need to come."

They drive her in their small official car,
point her to a room that's flush with dawn.

It's empty save for one bulk on a trolley,
an image that will not stay buried.

He's dressed for work. Clothes smudged with dirt.
On him she fell. And falls. And feels the cold.

Dancing to Our Tune

It's Christmas 2012. You're fifteen years dead.
Dancing to "Green River," our Christmas gift
from early years, I watch my knees
in the bedroom mirror bend to follow yours
the whole long steady track on the cassette
we used to play. Later, I leave the carol concert
in front of Budgens and climb Crouch Hill.
The night is balmy, the houses dark and lit,
the wide road still with cars that seem asleep.
As in a dream, I hear our song begin.
It comes from further up the hill. A woman
in a car is listening to "Green River."
From the shadows, I watch her swaying.
She has a look so inward, I'm drawn in
to the familiar dialogue with absence.

High Noon

Dead almost twenty years
he was striding along the ridge
strong as young, and tall as ever.
Clouds dispersed. I felt the sun
and saw that light was in his eyes
and he, like me, enthralled.
Around us high desert plains:
sagebrush, grasses, mullein, stalks
of flowering gold rush golden rod.
No one here but the hidden,
and black tail deer (mule deer)
who bounce beneath sky so huge
it brings him down to climb.
I rose, lifted by his joy.

Part IV

Unique Takes or Digging Deeper

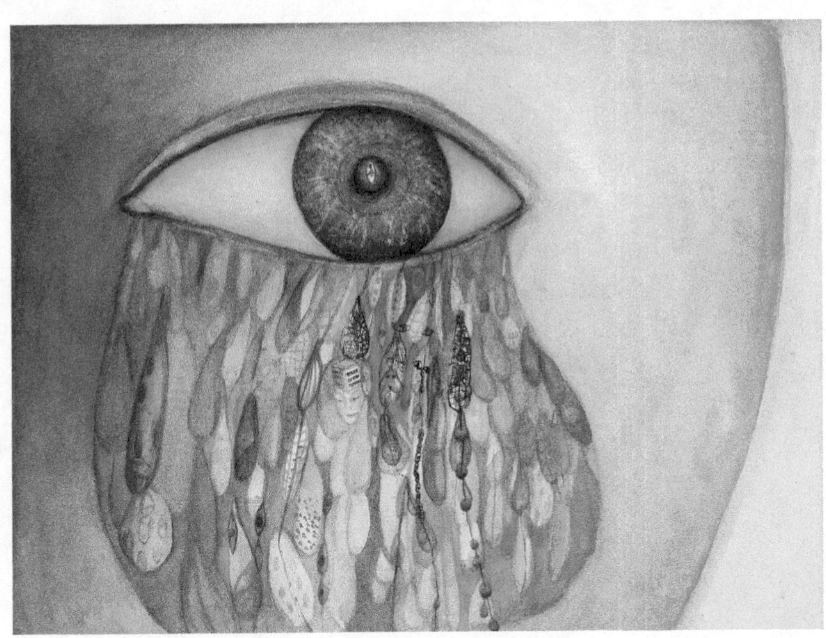

Widow-to-Widow

TRACY MILCENDEAU WITH MERLE FROSCHL,
ANDREA HIRSHMAN, MOLLY MCENENY,
AND HEATHER SLAWECKI

When I was thrust into widowhood at the age of thirty-one, after my husband's horrific months-long battle with brain cancer, I found myself in the early days playing out in my head the different ways I wish it had happened, or the different things I wish we'd done prior to his getting sick. At the time, I thought to myself, *it would be so much easier if it had been sudden.* (I wouldn't have to replay the experiences of taking care of the most basic of needs for my suddenly incapacitated husband.) *I wish we had had children.* (I'd have a piece of him to hold on to.) I thought that if the circumstances around which I had become widowed were different, it would somehow make it easier—to process, to move forward . . . what, exactly, I'm not sure. I was just so convinced that there was a way to change the experience by changing the circumstances under which it had happened.

As time went on, it became less of a game that I played with myself and more a matter of fact that I was curious about. Does the circumstance under which you lose your spouse somehow make one loss easier to move past than another? Are you better off having lost your person suddenly, or are you lucky to have the opportunity to say good-bye? It led me to the overall question of how our life circumstances shape our experiences as widows. These are the lenses with which I began speaking to the group of women whose thoughts have contributed to this analysis. Through discussions, email exchanges, and individual written reflections of their experiences, these women have shown me one thing: there is no "better" way to lose your spouse. There is no circumstance that makes it easier or somehow less painful. However, there are some aspects of a woman's life that can make the experience different, or perhaps facilitate the process of creating a new life post-loss. This analysis will cover the experiences of five women widowed, in each one's mind too soon, and how those experiences shaped life after loss.

Part 1: Surviving the First Year

Much is made of the first year in widowhood, and for good reason. Whether that loss was sudden or long foreseen, widows are facing the first of everything alone: the big days such as Christmas, Thanksgiving, and the other obvious holidays; days of celebration like birthdays and anniversaries; and then the less-thought-of-but-still-difficult ones that must be faced. The first time something good happens, like a work promotion, and you can't wait to tell your spouse. When you find out one of your best friends is expecting her first child. Your own child is graduating from high school. The list of firsts that are encountered without being able to tell your husband are countless, and often unexpected, but we are forced to face them, nonetheless, and deal with the emotional fallout that is sure to follow. That first year is often a blur of emotions, and all five of us shared in many of the same feelings, but all had a unique perspective to offer on how we managed to survive—a little worse for the wear, but all having made it through that year.

All of us were working women. Returning to work was a topic that brought up differing viewpoints among the group. One point of discussion was around the distraction that it did—or did not—offer to our pain, and the other focused on the comfort—or discomfort—that our colleagues offered. At a fundamental level, one would think (ourselves likely included) that returning to work would offer structure to the day, a way to take our minds away from the pain by focusing on a meaningful purpose. After a week spent with family mourning her husband Joe, Merle thought the best thing to do was to return to work and found that "being distracted was a salvation." For Andrea, work was a way to take her mind off her troubles, and Molly was thankful to have a reason to get up, dressed, and out of the house. There was certainly a consensus that we might not have been on our "A" game immediately upon return, but for the most part, our employers and clients, at least initially, were willing to bear with us as we adapted to our new normal. Andrea, a collaborative divorce attorney and mediator, was fortunate to have a colleague who assisted with client correspondence and questions until she felt prepared to begin receiving calls and emails. I was given space and freedom to work from home upon my initial return to an employer I had started working for mere weeks prior to my husband falling ill and who had been incredibly understanding during my absence while I was caring for him.

This initial grace period, however, didn't prevent us from common pitfalls that widows might experience in the workplace. Molly speaks of a loss of focus, interest, and concentration in the months following Kevin's death. "Coworkers, accustomed to coming to me for strategic advice or quick decisions, got instead fumbling and incoherent responses. I'd realize halfway through a conversation that I hadn't been paying attention and had no idea how to respond to the issue before me. That made me think that I had lost cognitive competence, and it scared me. I didn't recognize it for what it was—the early and most painful stages of grief." I experienced similar lapses in concentration, or perhaps interest. I had hardly figured out my new job before I unexpectedly disappeared from the office, and trying to get back into the swing of things felt like trying to walk through quicksand. I would sit staring blankly at my computer, unable to generate the interest or energy to ask the questions I would need to have answered, not even to excel but to adequately complete the tasks associated with my job. Had I known my colleagues or my manager better, perhaps I could have approached this with more honesty, but unfortunately that wasn't the case.

The key differentiator in those who ultimately had a positive experience returning to work and those who didn't was the strength of each widow's relationship with her colleagues prior to her loss. Merle found a safe haven at work, as though she were surrounded by her family, being in the company of long-term colleagues who offered invitations to social events and kept her busy. Molly relayed a story of breaking down unexpectedly in front of a colleague not known to be a sympathetic guy, who sat with her for over an hour, reassuring her that she was doing a great job. While there were a few compassionate colleagues who offered words of support for me, not having formed personal relationships prior to Chris's death, people didn't know where to start in offering condolences, and for the most part skirted around me awkwardly. Perhaps I felt awkward too.

For two of us, Heather and I, that uncomfortable environment, coupled with other factors, eventually led us to leave our jobs. Heather stated, "I didn't want anyone to feel sorry for me. I changed jobs after months of tilted heads and pitying looks from my colleagues. They all meant so well but it wasn't helping my cause to move on." My breaking point came after a superior advised me that I wasn't to mention Chris's name at work, after I stated I'd rather avoid a particular restaurant for a business dinner as it had been our "special place." It is interesting that Heather and I, as the two youngest at the time of loss, were the ones to leave our jobs. It could be that we felt especially dissociated from colleagues who didn't know how to handle someone who'd suffered loss so young, which can make others realize both their own mortality and that of their significant other. Perhaps, as neither of us had children, we felt less financial burden in taking that risk. I personally felt that I needed to take some time to give in to the loss and grieve before feeling ready to focus my attention back on work. I realize that this was a luxury that widows with children and greater financial responsibility would not have had the option to take, and for that I am thankful.

Merle continues to work part-time with many of the same colleagues and reports feeling that after Joe's death, her work became an even more important part of her life. Andrea, most recently widowed, continues running her own practice as a divorce attorney and mediator and is now fully reengaged in her work. After three years, Molly finally reported feeling reengaged, but has reevaluated the position work once played in her life. Heather has established a thriving career as a copywriter, and I, six months after leaving my job, found a new home at a company that partners with pharmaceutical industry clients in managing their marketing programs. While the five of us had mixed experiences with our employers following our husbands' deaths, one thing several of us have in common is a changed perspective on the role that our jobs play in our lives. For some, experiencing loss on that level causes a shift in what is held most important in life, and work becomes a means to that life, rather than the purpose.

The Beatles so beautifully captured it in their 1967 classic "With a Little Help from My Friends," and it has been oft-covered ever since for a reason—friends and family are an essential part of getting through the tough parts of life that are inevitable to us all, and especially when coping with such a life-altering loss. The first thing the five of us mentioned when discussing how we got through that first year was the help of family and friends. Most vocal about this was Andrea, who lost her husband unexpectedly on an October day in 2016. If not for the people she surrounded herself with immediately after Mike's death, she fears she wouldn't have gotten through those dark days. She speaks of her ongoing desire to be around those who knew and loved Mike best. "I don't want to lose the life I made with him, so I'm holding tight to . . . our closest circle of family and friends. For now, I simply don't have the motivation or energy to be with anyone other than those who loved Mike as much as I did." Andrea's friend circle has remained her constant as she navigates these early months and years of grief.

This is in interesting contrast to the experience Heather and I, the two youngest at the time of loss, shared. We both struggled with returning to the friendships and social gatherings that had once been the center of our twenty-something lives. We were now the third/fifth/seventh wheel among couples who were planning their own weddings, starting to talk about having babies, and caught up in the general living that they were entitled to. It only reinforced to us what we had lost and left us feeling confused. For me, I'd take steps forward in dealing with my grief, only to be set back after spending any significant amount of time with the friends who meant so well but only reminded me of the person missing from the party. Heather abandoned many of her "couple" friends and made new, younger single friends. These friends didn't know Eric, and didn't remind her of how off-track her life had been thrown. I isolated myself, spending a lot of time alone, and making new connections with other widows who I felt I could relate to, or perhaps could simply handle my sadness.

This contrast, feeling a need to be around those friends we shared with our spouses, and finding that being around those friends was too difficult to bear, boils down to a primary difference: the women who were widowed after having been married to their husbands for longer viewed their friends as family, having had children together, raising children at the same time, and experiencing so much of life in parallel. On the other hand, when widowed younger, we don't have the opportunity to have those formative life experiences with our friends. Heather and I had only known many of our friends for a few years, and there was so much of life still to experience together. Those relationships were missing some of that foundation that comes as you experience your thirties and forties together. As time passed, I was able to reengage in some of those friendships, but I've realized that many of them will never be the same. I've also completely lost contact with some people who Chris and I were very close to. I'm still coming to terms with that.

Another key differentiator in getting through that first year came for Molly, who still had one son at home and a daughter in college at the time of Kevin's death. Brendan, a high school senior, received support from friends who made sure he went on college visits, and teachers and school staff who helped him finish out his senior year and celebrate his accomplishments. Meanwhile, Molly's daughter, Cat, fought a deepening struggle against depression, requiring Molly to focus her care on getting her through that difficult period. Molly said, "The kids were both an excuse, and also they kept me from having to face something I wasn't ready to face." As a result, Molly was well through the first year of widowhood before she found herself an empty nester and in a position to start her grieving process. "Then I was truly alone and had to face my loss in silence and solitude. It was then, finally, that I crawled into bed with the covers over my head."

Interestingly, for a few months after my husband died, that was something I wished for. That Chris and I had had a child together, and that was for a few reasons. First, I felt it would serve the purpose that it did for Molly: a reason to function, something to keep me from falling apart. A reason to "be strong" when I felt I had no strength within me. Second, I wished for a piece of him. It would be a way for Chris to live on in my world. Experiencing the loss that I did played heavily into the decision I later made to not have children at all. Just another way in which loss continues to impact my life.

Part 2: Life Beyond the First Year

As the five of us talked through how our lives changed after our husbands died, the word "identity" came up time and time again, and it had many far-reaching and rippling effects on various aspects of our lives. Molly, Heather, and I were caregivers for our husbands through cancer. Being a full-time, or nearly full-time, caregiver is a huge sacrifice, but it's also a huge honor. To walk with a man through the most painful days of his life, to endure surgeries, manage medications, and hold that person's hand as he transitions out of this world—there aren't necessarily words that can describe the beauty and the pain of it. But when it's all said and done, and one day you're no longer that caregiver, it can feel like the bottom has dropped out from under you. And not only are you not a caregiver but now you're no longer a wife either. It turns your world upside down.

It hit Molly perhaps most acutely, as she was dealing with several major life changes at once, with her children moving out around the same time. She felt the roles that gave her life meaning had all disappeared around the time she lost Kevin—nobody needed her any more. "Being widowed, an empty nester, and contemplating retirement all happened at the same time. I felt, and still feel, profoundly, the loss of role. I'm no longer a wife, part of a couple, a mother (at least not in the same day-to-day practical way), caregiver, striving professional, or dog owner. Some have told me that's wonderful as I can create the world I want for myself, but to me it's too much freedom. I listen to friends talk about where they might live in retirement, and can't imagine picking up and going someplace on my own. I have to resist the urge to be overly involved in my children's lives."

Merle spoke of finding her way after Joe's death, and described feeling that in attempting to find her new identity, she was constantly trying on new roles to see what would fit. "I felt like I was always rehearsing. I was rehearsing new roles. It's like my old roles were gone, and now I'm going to rehearse being on my own . . . being someone who dates . . . being independent . . . being in charge of the finances. So I always felt like I was rehearsing. Until that role became . . . mine." She recalls feeling like she had to become somebody different, because she was no longer the same person.

We all related to that, and the three of us who are more recently widowed agreed that we're all still evolving into our new identities in widowhood. Seventeen years later, Merle no longer feels that being a widow is her main identity. In fact, many of the new people in her life are not even aware that she is a widow.

Andrea added an interesting perspective to the subject of identity. She struggles with how to act around single men, explaining that she has a naturally playful and flirtatious personality, which can sometimes be misinterpreted as something more than friendliness. When married, she felt that if she was in conversation with a man who mistook her communication style as something of a come-hither interest, she could simply laugh it off, saying, "I'm married!" as a fallback, even though she didn't wear a wedding band for the last fifteen years of her marriage (for no other reason than the ring needed repair). After Mike's death, she feared the way her animated communication style might be (mis)interpreted by the opposite sex, and she was even more surprised to find how significant her wedding ring became to her. "With a ring on my finger, I am assumed to be married and unavailable. That keeps me from feeling vulnerable and empowers me to be my exuberant self with a lot less concern about being misunderstood, which makes it a whole lot easier for me to be in the wide world. Understanding that, I bought myself a plain gold wedding band and, though I didn't wear one for half of my marriage, ironically, I now wear it all the time. The ring has come to represent my past, especially how I was once married, loved and cherished for decades by Mike. I wear it with pride, it's my 24/7 testament to the life I once had. And, with that ring around my finger, Mike is always with me, and I feel closer to him."

It was interesting to hear Andrea speak about how she felt differently now about her marriage than she did when Mike was alive, not only in her newfound desire to wear a ring, but in her perspective on their relationship now that she has the "benefit" of hindsight. It led into a discussion around the lost (and unbeknownst to us, last) hopes that we each had for the future of our marriages. We all experienced a sense of lost dreams for what was yet to come in our relationships, but for unique reasons. Molly and Kevin were at the tail end of their child-raising years, years which inevitably take their toll on every relationship as the focus must turn from romance and each other to raising children to become healthy and happy adults. She spoke of how they were looking forward to saying good-bye to the years of shuttling kids to and fro, missed date nights, and interrupted plans, and finding new and exciting parts of their marriage again. Late dinners, quiet nights at home, time rediscovering what brought them together so many years prior. To lose her husband on the cusp of that chapter felt an especially unfair blow after the years of selflessly putting family first. Similarly,

Andrea's husband had recently retired, and Andrea planned to do the same within a few years. They were beginning to dream of how they'd like to spend those long-awaited years. They had worked so hard, both professionally and personally, to reach this point in their life together and in the blink of an eye those hopes and dreams were gone. For both Molly and Andrea, the unfairness of losing their husbands at such a pivotal and exciting time in their lives will likely never fade.

Heather and I feel a different kind of frustration in the futures we lost with our spouses. For us, both just two years into our marriages, the "what ifs" were our crosses to bear. I feel that I was robbed of a future filled with the hopes and dreams Chris and I never got to see come to fruition. I'll never know what our children would have looked like, where we would have lived, where careers would have taken us, or even whether we would have had a happy marriage. I like to think so, but how does one ever know? Similarly, Heather, though now more than twenty years removed from her loss, still from time to time ponders what her life would have been like had Eric not died. How could she not? We go into marriage with a vision of the future, and to have it taken away so quickly creates a blank space where those dreams were. Building a new and different life, no matter how happy, can't quiet those lingering questions in our brains.

Building that new and different life when you've been dealt such an immense blow isn't easy, but it is an inevitable part of being a widow. As far as this was concerned, there was a clear divide in this rebuilding process between Heather and me, widowed at twenty-nine and thirty-one, respectively, and Molly, Andrea, and Merle, widowed at fifty-eight, fifty-nine, and sixty-one. In the year following Eric's death, Heather moved cities, changed jobs, integrated with a new group of friends, and started dating. She met a man named Adam a year after Eric died, eventually married, and had a daughter. She struggled with feeling judged in the aftermath of Eric's death and, as a result, has taken it upon herself to reach out to dozens of women who find themselves newly widowed, myself included. She feels her message is important. "Date if you want to date. Don't date if you don't want to date. Move. Don't move. Change jobs. Change your hair. Redecorate the house. There is no rulebook."

I, as previously mentioned, left my job and, largely prompted by loneliness and a desire to meet people who knew nothing of my story, started dating roughly seven months after Chris's death. I feel fortunate to have fairly quickly met Ed, an incredibly empathetic man who I recently married and with whom I'm building a life and future where I previously couldn't have imagined one. Interestingly, to the point of identity, I haven't felt ready to give up Chris's last name. It's something that is mine of his, and a way that I feel I can keep him alive. In loss, I've also discovered characteristics within myself that I wasn't aware of before. I have an incredible appreciation for the smallest joys and have discovered how little I really need, from a material standpoint, to make me happy. And when I'm happy, I make a point to revel in it and say it out loud. Both Heather and I feel that our age and childlessness upon our first husbands' deaths was a strong contributor to the speed at which we made changes in our lives. We both felt unfairly cheated out of our great marriages to Eric and Chris, believed we had a lot of love to give, and wanted to have a second chance at creating that bright and happy marriage.

Molly, having finally had the time to grieve after focusing on caring for others in the initial period, is starting to reclaim a life for herself. She redecorated her apartment, has taken a trip to Italy, and started to make friends who didn't know her in her former role as a wife. She's starting to contemplate that there might be another chapter for her, but has yet to envision what that might look like. As she put it, "I think about my husband every day, but I accept that this is my new life. I no longer feel so acutely that something is missing, but neither do I feel like my life is complete."

Merle has built a life of contentment for herself as well over the years, and is thriving. She has found new passions like singing; she has been in and out of a relationship, become a grandmother, and has made many new friends over the years. Still, she says, "I often wonder what I would be doing now if Joe had not died—how my life would have been different. Each year, my daughter (and now granddaughter) and I visit a beach in Montauk that was Joe's favorite fishing spot, and where we spread his ashes. We collect heart-shaped rocks, and now have a large collection. At those moments I do miss him terribly, and I am so sad that he never got to know his grandchildren and, even more importantly, that they never got to know him. He would have made a wonderful grandfather."

Andrea, the freshest into this experience, recently passed her one-year mark. She is still coming to terms with the reality of Mike's absence and is focusing on remembering the happy times shared together while beginning to look to the future, but can't currently imagine what that future will be. She says, "I dread the upcoming year anniversary. . . . I fear that I will be hit even harder as the permanence of his death sinks in and time marches on. Mike is gone, and there is no more Mike and Andrea. And, if I haven't made clear yet, I'm in the process of coming to grips with 'good-bye my love, my knight in shining armor.' "

Closing

So, you see, the absence is never really gone when someone you love dies. We all lost our husbands in different ways—suddenly, unexpectedly, and after devastating illness. Some of us were at the very beginning of our marriages, and some had weathered the years of raising children, experiencing the ups and downs that come with that, and were entering those welcome golden years of marriage. Those circumstances impacted the way our journey into widowhood evolved, both in that first painful year, and then as time unfolded. They led us to perhaps make different choices—leaving jobs, friendships, and cities—and caused us to find our new identities at different speeds and in different ways. Yet we all have one thing in common: we lost a love that can never be replaced and will honor that love through our remaining days, however they may be spent.

Parenting as a Widow

KATHLEEN FORDYCE

One of the blessings and the curse of having a toddler while grieving is that they won't sit still. And they won't let you, either. No matter how desperately you try to stay in bed with the blinds closed, they bound into your room at 6 A.M. full of energy. They plead with you for breakfast, babble a mile-a-minute and pull you to the door, showing you that the sun is shining and begging to go to the park.

While the temper tantrums and endless energy may make you cry, at one point during the day they will run into your arms and put their little pudgy hands on either side of your cheeks and plant a kiss. They will make your lips rise into a smile, even if just a small one. They don't allow you to wallow or hide from the world. Despite your best efforts to force the world to stand still, they prove that it goes on.

My husband died of testicular cancer at the age of twenty-nine, two months shy of our son, Logan's, second birthday. After beating cancer when he was just eighteen, he was diagnosed again a decade later, three months after our son's birth. We spent eighteen grueling months traveling from our home in Miami to oncologists and hospitals in New York and Houston for rigorous, and often experimental, treatments. We rode the highs and lows of the roller coaster ride as a new treatment would work for a short time, buoying our hopes and spirits, only to have them dashed, leaving us with one less option.

The cancer was aggressive; there was already a large tumor in his abdomen when doctors spotted it. But aside from the masses seen on CT and PT scans, my husband did not appear sick. He was tired, yes, but we were new parents to a then newborn. His back hurt too, but we attributed it to an old mattress. Quickly, the masses spread to his lymph nodes, lungs, and brain. Three months into his first treatment, when the cancer bounced back from the chemo, doctors said he would die. They would continue to try treatments, but chances of a cure—or even remission—were unlikely.

We lay in bed that night in shock. I laid my head on his chest, listening to his heart, trying to comprehend how this young, healthy-looking man could be so sick that the doctors could not fix him. We said little, pulling each other close as we both cried. The next day I went back to researching experimental treatments, other oncologists, and making healthy meals and juices. I was too busy to think about the fact that one day, sooner rather than later, I would be raising our young son alone.

In the weeks after my husband died, Logan would run into the house and straight to our brown leather couch, calling out, "Daddy!" The right couch cushion still held the indent of his body. But his dad was gone and he was too young to understand he would never see him again.

While he remained blissfully ignorant to how our life had changed, I struggled to hold myself together. I had not planned to fall in love young, marry, and be a young mom, but found I thrived in these roles. I felt brave heading out into the world knowing I had them to come home to. Now, who was I? Our life, love, and dreams felt so intertwined after nearly ten years together that I couldn't remember who I was without him.

I moved through my first year without Nolan in a daze. I rose every morning, went to work, and cared for our energetic two-year-old son. I followed my therapist's advice and tried to find some small moment of joy every day—even if it was just the taste of a hot cup of coffee or the two seconds I got to sit on a bench at the park while Logan played peacefully nearby. At first, I relived Nolan's death every day at a quarter after 5 P.M., trying so hard to understand how everything in the world could be the same, yet terribly different.

Slowly, yet at a heartbreaking pace, one day turned into a week. A week turned into a month. And a month turned into a year. While well-meaning family members and loved ones feared the big occasions and time markers would be difficult, I found the routine, daily events more traumatic. Sitting down to eat dinner—just the two of us. Afternoons at the park, when Logan would run up to any man, wanting to play with them. And our almost nightly walks around the lake near our house. It was the lake where my husband and I routinely walked hand-in-hand after we bought our first house. We walked it nightly when we brought home our first dog. Then, in the weeks after our son was born. Now, I was walking it alone, leash in hand while pushing a stroller.

I watched Logan hit each new milestone with a sense of loss, pride, and awe. Each time he did something new, went through a growth spurt, or learned another word, I was reminded of everything Nolan was missing. I felt guilty that I was here to see it, and he was not.

After a few months of crashing on the couch each night because I could not face our bed alone, I craved change. As a person who likes a plan, I felt adrift with no goal. Nolan and I were supposed to stay in Miami for a few more years, while he worked his way up in the company and applied for jobs at his company's corporate office in Tennessee. When he was finally tapped, we would move—with our one, two, or three kids, depending on the year. We would buy a house in the suburbs with a cozy front porch and a sprawling green lawn. I would quit my job to stay home with the kids and freelance—eventually writing a novel—with the help of a babysitter.

But now, I had no reason to move to Tennessee—especially as a single mom who knew no one—and I couldn't see myself staying in my corporate communications job indefinitely. By the end of the year, I decided instead to sell our home in Florida and moved closer to family in New York. I secretly hoped the new start (new job, new house, new hairdo) would give me a clean slate.

Instead, pain and unease followed.

In the days following Nolan's death, I spoke to a child psychologist and asked for help in explaining our situation to Logan. Aside from the basics (like not comparing death to sleep) he explained that Logan's grief would be different from mine, and he warned me not to project my loss onto him. Logan was not grieving the life, plans, and dreams I was. He didn't even know or understand that they existed. But he would be dealing with his own sense of loss, and it would unfold over time as he grew and grasped his father's death.

As he got older, Logan asked more in-depth questions and cried in my arms as the answers sank in. They started out to be rather simple, like "Where is Dad?" "I know he's dead, but where is he?" They got more complicated as each year passed. "Why couldn't the doctors save him?" "Why did he have to go?" "What happens to his body underground?" "Why can't we bring him home?" "Are you going to die too?"

Periods of guilt and sorrow washed over us, interspersed with everyday life. When I became overwhelmed, I followed the advice of a friend who said, when you can't bear to think about the week ahead, focus just on today. When the day seems like too much, just think about the next hour. When the hour seems too long and painful, focus on just the next minute. I also kept what that psychologist said front and center. I had a choice: I could dwell on what could have been, or focus on what I had left.

The old adage "fake it until you make it" helped me through. When Logan mentioned the full family trees of his kindergarten classmates, I brushed it off and said we had more room just for the two of us (three with our dog, Charlie). When he said his friends were lucky to have playmates in their siblings, I shared how much young siblings fight. Instead of wishing we were a family of three or four or five, I tried to embrace our duo. We cuddled in my bed, enjoyed candlelight dinners, had less laundry, and traveled. When friends marveled at some of our adventures, I reminded them it was more affordable when there were only two tickets to buy and easier to shepherd one increasingly independent kid than a herd.

As my friends shared their marriage woes, I secretly let out a sigh of relief. While the pressure of being the sole supporter and caretaker was taxing, it could also be liberating. I set our priorities, budget, and schedule—and no one fought me on it.

We grieved Nolan, but not our little family. We acted as if life as a duo was normal, and it became just that. A year of difficult firsts turned into our family traditions. Soon, it was all we knew.

The part about grief that only its inhabitants know is how surprising and unrelenting it can be, and how tricky. As the days, months, and years wore on, I found the good stretches would last longer. But sometimes, grief would blindside me out of nowhere and knock me down.

Like at the first back-to-school nights, when I was the only parent sitting alone on a tiny chair in front of Logan's desk. Or the day a boy teased Logan on the playground because he had no father. Or the time another mother made a comment about the single mom in the class probably being the one who didn't contribute to the class party, not realizing the single mom was me. (And I was not only contributing to the party but helping coordinate it.)

After a difficult day, I would put Logan to bed and curl on the couch with a glass of wine, wondering when it would get easier. When it would stop hurting.

One sunny day over lunch, I was excitedly telling Logan—who was five years old at the time—about our upcoming trip to the Grand Canyon. He quietly listened, nodding along, and then retreated to his room to curl up in bed under his covers. After a few minutes of coaxing, he shared that he felt guilty going on another trip and seeing another wonder of the world that his dad would never see. Through tears, I told him how happy his father would be that he is seeing and experiencing the world. I said that wherever he went, a part of his dad was with him. That talk was years ago now, and a turning point for us. Every place we visited after that heart-to-heart, we didn't focus on being sad that Nolan wasn't there, but instead happy that we brought a small piece of him along.

I was a single mom for almost seven years. The first years were rough and brutal, but the last few were happy, fulfilling, even liberating. The trick about searching for a bright spot throughout your day is that the more you look for them, the more you find. I somehow survived, found my way to a new career, made new friends, and got into a new rhythm of life, balancing it all on my own.

I don't know if I believe that everything happens for a reason or that some higher being gives you only what you can handle. But I do know that everyone has good times and bad. Some are worse than others. But some little bright spot can be found in the darkness. For me, that bright spot was Logan.

Postscript

After almost seven years as a single mom, when I had fully settled into our new normal and loved every minute of it, I met someone new. He literally danced into my life on a rainy, summer night while I was out with friends. I had dated on and off occasionally, but found myself less than interested in a new relationship. But everything with Shane was different.

While I was ambivalent about falling in love again, I quickly found that I was no longer the same woman who married Nolan. Loving him and losing him changed me in small and profound ways. I am now remarried and we have a daughter, Mackenzie. Logan is a spectacular big brother, he clicked with Shane in a way I never could have imagined, and we celebrate the fact that he now has two dads.

For me, it's not happily ever after, just a transition to a new phase of life. Life unfolds in seasons, and as widows, we know how fleeting they can be. I am trying my best to fully embrace every moment of this next chapter.

Memories of a Widow's Daughter

PATRICIA LIFE

"Aw, the poor dears." This was the sentiment generally directed toward my mother, my older sister, and me when my father died of cancer at the age of thirty-four. I was not yet two years old and my sister not yet six. My mother, Muriel, left alone at thirty-three to raise two daughters, must have seemed a truly tragic figure with her tiny frame, shy demeanor, and delicately beautiful features. The tragedy was my father's, but Muriel's role was to endure throughout his illness and all of what came next, and I wonder sometimes whose was the greater misfortune.

My memories now of Muriel's early widowhood, of my sister's and my upbringing, and of the years of my adulthood up until my mother's death are made up of my own early memories overlaid by later memories and filtered over time. These memories of mine are also all mixed up with the stories remembered and retold by my mother and by other family members over the years. Facts and feelings have a way of sorting and resorting themselves over time. I cannot vouch for the precise veracity of all that I will report to you, my reader, but I will try to relay how things felt at the time, how they seemed later on, and how I view them now.

By all accounts of family and friends, my mother was devastated when my father died. She was also exhausted from juggling the needs of her children and those of her ill and then dying husband. My older sister,

Sandra, and I were less emotionally shattered than my mother because we had her strength to support us (and because I and, to some extent, my sister were relatively oblivious due to our immaturity), but the immediate trajectory of our family and all of our futures were radically realigned.

Since he died two months before my second birthday, I have no memory of him or of the loss of him, although I must have felt the distress and unhappiness in my home at the time. Sandra remembers our father's death and remembers happy family times with him before his illness, and so has always felt more deprived of our father than I do. I have seen a home movie of me learning to stand by clinging to my father's pant leg, but I find it hard to identify myself with the image because he does not seem familiar to me. My family tells me that during his illness I was sent to live for a few months with my mother's sister Roberta and her husband Ernie in order for my mother to better care for my father. I don't remember this either, but I had an extremely close relationship with them for the duration of their lives. After the funeral, my mother took me home again. I must have been glad to be returned to her because she later told me that she awoke early the next morning to find me crawling into bed with her. According to her, the best possible way to wake up to a world that no longer contains your beloved husband is to wake up being cuddled by your baby daughter.

Looking back at photos of the three of us when my sister and I were teenagers, I can see that Muriel was a strikingly attractive young woman, although as a child I disregarded her appearance. In retrospect, I would judge that she upstaged my sister and me. The word "pretty" is too mild to describe the eye-catching beauty and ladylike air that were hers. She had black curling hair, a milk-white complexion, a slender graceful figure, and unusual gray-blue eyes with gold rims around the pupils. She dressed with propriety but also with an eye attuned to fashion and the highlighting of her appearance. Having grown up in the depression of the 1930s and its financial constraints, she became skilled at sewing her own outfits as a young person. She was a city girl and disliked sports and outdoor activities in general. Even gardening involved too much dirt for her taste. My grandmother always said that Muriel looked like she had "just stepped off a bandbox," which I guess means she looked like she was always on stage.

Muriel was deaf in one ear since childhood, a fact that she always hid and that as a young woman had made her shy with young men prone to whispering into that ear when dancing close. And. as the family put it, she had had "trouble with her nerves" at the age of sixteen, which had required her to remain off work for a year. In later years, she was diagnosed with depression. Despite her looks, and maybe because of her shyness and shaky mental health, she never married until the age of twenty-five—surprisingly late for the 1940s. She must have loved my father very much to be brave enough to leave her family and home to follow him to a series of remote outposts where he was employed as an air traffic controller for the Canadian government.

My father died in 1956 at the age of thirty-four, the first indication of his disease being a small purplish mass on the side of his face. At the time my parents discovered it, they were outposted for his work to a small community north of Quebec (in Goose Bay, Labrador) with not much available in medical care and far from their extended families back home in southern Ontario. The cancer progressed quickly. Suddenly my mother, who had been a dependent 1950s-style wife, was challenged to become chief caregiver to a newly helpless patient. They were forced to move home to Toronto and accept the help of both sets of parents. With his death, this fragile woman was left alone to raise two young daughters in what was then very much a man's world. She chose never to remarry, not for lack of opportunity, but out of choice. I still wonder whether she made this choice in order to dedicate her life to the upbringing of her daughters or to protect herself from further harm. Perhaps the answer is a bit of both.

I'm certain that all new widows feel alone, but Muriel was more alone than most. Statistics indicate that most women will eventually become widows; late-life singlehood is known primarily as a women's issue. But my mother became a widow at the age of thirty-three and in the year 1956. The many young women widowed due to Canada's involvement in World War II were already at least ten years into their adjustment. In 1956, thirty-three-year-old women made single as the result of divorce were also still rare. My mother had no peer group. There were married ladies and there were a few never-married ladies, but there weren't many other newly single thirty-three-year olds with whom she could find common ground. Her parents and siblings and my dad's parents and siblings crowded around to help, but once he had died, she was left surrounded by an extended family composed of five happily married couples. Although she needed their help, her loneliness must have been excruciating. As I recall, all her lady friends were also married.

As far as I was concerned, the early years of my childhood were blissful, and I remained largely ignorant of my mother's considerable challenges. My father's life insurance paid off our mortgage, so we could remain in our little two-bedroom bungalow in the suburbs of Toronto. Both sets of grandparents and all my aunts, uncles, and cousins lived within a couple of miles of us. I might have lacked a father, but I never really had cause to notice. There was love in abundance and no shortage of playmates. My mother received a governmental supplement and made some money babysitting neighbors' children, which meant that my mother was available to me almost without interruption. My mom, sister, and I spent all summer every year with my maternal cousins, their parents, and my grandparents at the family cottage. That place was every child's perfect playground.

After my father's death, Muriel sold his car because she did not know how to drive (and never learned), but her brother and wife drove us to church on Sundays, and her sister and husband took us shopping. When we were all back in Toronto during the school year, we spent many weekends at various cousins' homes. The neighbor next door, whose daughter my mother babysat, partly reciprocated by cutting our lawn. He and his wife had lost one of their two baby daughters, and the two families were good supports for each other. I recall sitting on my front lawn with him while he built a bicycle for me out of a box full of parts that my mom had no idea what to do with. Why would I miss having a father when there were more than a half dozen wonderful men actively involved in my life?

My mother insisted, though, on keeping her own home and on making us a small family of three within the larger extended family. My sister and I knew that she was our parent and the center of our world, and we loved her best. I recall having a habit for many years as a little child of lying quietly in my mother's lap for a while each night after supper while she read the paper and before she did the dishes and made lunches for the next day. It may be that I was troubled by the upheavals in my young life and needed comfort or it may be that I was an exceptionably affectionate child. Maybe I just sensed that she needed me close or maybe I needed her and she needed me a little bit more than in most mother/child relationships. Our bond was strong throughout her lifetime.

The involvement of our extended family was both a blessing and a challenge for my mother. It must have been very tempting just to relinquish control and become a childlike dependent along with her children. When we were staying on our own in our little bungalow, my maternal grandmother phoned my mom every night without fail. My mom stretched the long black telephone cord completely out of shape by holding the phone tucked under her chin as she talked while washing the dishes across the kitchen at the sink. As time passed, she increased her independence from the family. She appreciated the privacy of her own home and the opportunity to make her own decisions. When I turned ten, she decided that I was old enough to come home on my own for the lunch break from school and that she needed enough money for my sister to have something better than hand-me-downs to wear as she entered high school. That summer she went back to school for a brief course in the operation of a pre-computer business machine called a comptometer. My sister and I presented her with a handmade diploma when she finished, and she reentered the job market after seventeen years as a homemaker. With her first paycheck, she triumphantly bought each of us a new outfit. Fashion mattered to Muriel, and this was her chosen celebration. I remember that she glowed with pleasure as we enjoyed the spoils of her success.

In 1967, when I was thirteen, Canada was celebrating its one-hundredth birthday as a nation by holding a great fair, Expo '67, in Montreal, Quebec. All of my sister's and my school friends were going with their families during the upcoming summer holidays. My mother must have felt dismayed by our obvious yearning because she saved enough money for tickets and took the three of us on a seven-hour bus ride to Montreal where we stayed in a hotel for two nights. While my cousins and aunts and uncles routinely went on vacation trips, this was the first and only time that we three ever afforded such an extravagance. My mother packed one small suitcase with our clothes and another with apples, peanut butter, and bread. I recall that we purchased lovely ice-cream cones during our enjoyment of the fair and one souvenir each for my sister and me. We came home ready to compare notes about the fair with our other classmates. At the time I thought that we were just doing what families did, but later I realized that this was another moment of great daring and accomplishment for my mother.

Before my father's death, my mother had been introverted by nature. Afterward, she had no choice but to become bold in some ways as she assumed the mantle of responsibility for my sister and me, but she remained extremely cautious and wary. Dating was one possibility she would never consider. She said that she had heard too many worrying stories about stepdads and daughters. She was certainly not interested in a fling or casual affair. Her generation was pre-birth-control pill, and she followed the views of her Christian religion, which viewed casual sex as sinful. Over time she developed an idealized image of my father. When I began to reach double decades in my own marriage, I realized that she had never had an opportunity to experience a mature relationship with a man. They had only been married seven years in total.

Being as young and beautiful as she was when widowed, Muriel definitely received interest from men. Once I was an adult, she told me that she used to get frequent phone calls from a male voice that she suspected belonged to the neighbor whose home backed onto ours. The message usually consisted of heavy breathing, but on one memorable occasion he informed her that he had "eight inches for her" if she were interested. She seemed appalled but somewhat amused by this when she told me about it later, but at the time she said it had made her nervous. When I think about this now, I remember the multiple locks on our front and side doors, and I imagine how anxious she must have often felt as she, the guardian of her children, slept alone in an unguarded house.

When she returned to office work, she received unwanted attention from her married boss, who persisted in mentioning his various affairs to her and pointing out that he was available to her as well. She used to say that the world of men assumed that, since she was single, she must be available. Years later she told me that there had been one man in that same office in whom she could have been interested, but that the qualities that attracted her were the same ones that made the relationship impossible: he was a faithful husband and a practicing Christian. If the perfect man for her had appeared, she might have been interested, but she was more afraid than acquisitive, and so she did not take time for any pleasures beyond those of her family and religion. As a result, she developed a slight air of martyrdom, but it was self-awareness, I think, that led her to make this choice to protect her mental health and meet her responsibilities. She found sustenance in the love of her daughters, her family, and the children she babysat, while her Christian faith provided the ground on which she stood. For Muriel, church was more than a Sunday activity. She drew great strength from reading the Bible and from daily prayer. Yet she never took part in activities outside of Sunday service, instead keeping her focus on the Christian upbringing of her daughters. She saw the support of the larger church community as important mostly for its role in helping her with us.

By the time I was a young teen, I had realized that the three of us were a duty to be shared among the family. Though still convinced that my family loved us fiercely, the recognition of their sense of duty was a gradual and shocking revelation. My sister and I began to see that the favors went mostly one way and that we were the "poor dears" of the family, always being looked after by the more capable, better, stronger, but always kind relatives. Sandra and I began to feel a sense of shame—shame for being lesser and needy and shame for having been duped and unaware for all those years.

My sister and I came to realize too that our mother had always felt this shame. We began to notice that she always approached our relatives with careful humility, considering which relative to call for a favor, pondering which one she had called on least recently. Her sister's husband Ernie was aware of his wife's slight resentment of Muriel's beauty and neediness, and so always treated his sister-in-law with very slight disdain, to do his part in supporting his wife, at least in his own mind. He and my mother were the same age, and I gather that my grandparents initially assumed that he would wish to date her rather than her older sister. He was never mean, but as teens my sister and I felt the way he subtly demeaned my mother to make sure his wife felt his favor. I doubt that there was anything more in the past than some disgruntlement, but my mother once advised me never to hug my brother-in-law for fear that he or my sister might get the wrong idea. There were undercurrents within the extended family of which my sister and I only gradually became aware.

When our maternal grandparents parted with their share of the cottage compound, one cottage went to Muriel's sister and husband and one to her brother and wife while our little family of three received some cash. We hadn't really understood that the cottage didn't belong to us in the same way that it belonged to the others. Nothing was said by anyone. Not about our dependency and not about all of the ways we owed our relatives for our upbringing.

Once when I was in my twenties and had taken on the task of driving my mom to get her weekly groceries, her sister thanked me for taking on the duty, and when I thanked her for having done it for so many years, she acknowledged that it was a relief to pass the responsibility on to me. After my grandmother had died, my aunt acknowledged to me that she had sometimes resented being considered as the necessary "rock" of the family while Muriel had been the coddled beautiful one. My aunt could not have performed her duty with more dedication or love, but I guess she was only being human if she sometimes wished to be free of her sister's neediness.

While Muriel's dedicated attention to my sister and me was welcome when we were children, her single-minded focus became suffocating when we reached our teens. She was overly wary and fearful of losing her children as she had lost her husband. I recall that she talked our family doctor into removing a perfectly normal mole from the top of my head because it reminded her too much of her husband's skin lesion. She imposed some ridiculous rules to keep us safe too, such as only allowing us to ride our two-wheeled bikes in our suburban driveway. If you have ever tried learning to ride a bike, you will understand the impossibility of the situation.

My sister Sandra married at twenty-one and moved to another city, which left me alone with my mother when I was seventeen. All her considerable maternal devotion clamped down around me, the remaining child. I moved out with a girlfriend and did not phone home for over a month. Now, having been a parent myself, the memory of this cruelty toward my mother makes me cringe. Once I had accomplished my independence, I reestablished contact, and by the end of that year we began to resuscitate the deep bond we had previously enjoyed. She grudgingly began to let me make my own decisions, and so my sense of desperation subsided. We needed a bit of time for healing but then continued forward with just as much love but more distance and mutual respect. I always knew that I could count on her more than anyone else to have my back through the challenges of life. As I matured into adulthood, her mothering role gradually diminished and our friendship grew.

Once the extraordinary challenge of raising her children had been accomplished, Muriel slumped with exhaustion as if she had run a marathon. Over the next few years, she suffered numerous health issues, first physical problems associated with menopause, Morton's neuromata, diverticulitis, Meniere's disease, and surgery for a benign thyroid mass, but then also intermittent mental health problems. As a consequence, she retired from office work in her fifties and resumed part-time babysitting. She would have made more money had she not retired young, but her health could not withstand the three-hour public-transit commute necessary for her to put in her eight hours of office work. Since it meant that she could live a quieter life and return to the type of work with children that she preferred, she chose frugality and improved health over full-time work.

When she was in her early sixties, my husband and I moved two hours away from Toronto to accommodate new employment for him, and my mother remained in Toronto in her little bungalow. However, two years later she suffered a serious mental health setback and moved in temporarily with us. After Muriel recovered sufficiently to live independently, she bought a condo near my home where I could be available to her when need arose. However, four years later, dementia symptoms compounded her mental health issues, and she moved from her condo to a care home that she and my sister and I had selected when she knew that she was going to need more help with daily living. Eventually the dementia progressed, and she was transferred to a dementia lockdown unit in a long-term-care facility. She died in 2007 at the age of eighty-six.

My mother's widowhood had a profound effect on her life and on my and my sister's lives too. Our lives spilled forward like domino chains in reaction to the initial event of my father's death. Had my father lived, we would have grown up in a different province, gone to different schools, and probably eventually chosen different friends, husbands, and careers. In her later years, my mother's situation continued to influence my life. Since my sister lived in a different city, I assumed most of the responsibility for Muriel's care. During these years, I was also raising my son, and so I switched to part-time work. I subsequently joined the family councils of the institutions in which she lived in order to remain aware of the issues in her life. Ultimately, my experiences with my mother motivated me to return to university to write a PhD dissertation on the topic of age and long-term-care facilities. The chain of tumbling dominoes had a very long run indeed.

Most people who hear of my mother's life see it as a sad story of loss and struggle. But no one can judge whether a life with my father would have been better or worse for her than the life that she lived as a widow. Had my father lived, she would probably have benefited from having a loving partner with whom to share life, and she would probably have had more material wealth and consequent opportunities for toys and trips. But perhaps their marriage would have failed in some way over time, leading her to an even greater unhappiness than that which she endured as a widow. I wonder though whether she would have had better health if my father had lived. If she had had a partner and some relaxing hobbies and if she had been less tired out, would she have become so ill? This is of course impossible to say. Some might judge that, pursuant to her widowhood, she had the satisfaction of maturing from the middle-class subservient fifties wife she had been to a fully responsible adult in charge of her own life and ours and with the opportunity to enjoy a career. Those, however, were not the types of achievements that gave my mother personal fulfillment.

I would assert that, in Muriel's own judgment, her life was one of contentment and satisfaction. She had chosen to live her life in accordance with a clearly held set of personal values, and she felt confident before her final illnesses that she had lived according to the most important priorities in life. Muriel did not find sustenance in worldly ambitions or possessions but in her loving relationships with her family, with the many children she helped raise, and with her god. After my father died, Muriel embroidered a poem from one of the bereavement cards she received onto a sampler. She framed it and gave it a prominent place on the wall of my sister's and my pink bedroom. It read: "There is a home, not made by hands. Beyond its golden doors, awaits the one who's now away, not lost, just gone before." She lived her life confidently believing that she would some day be reunited with her husband in heaven, and she had a deep belief that she would be rewarded in the next life for willingly fulfilling her duties in this life.

Widowhood is never a state one would choose. But it is the widow's choice afterward to decide the extent to which she will welcome the reconfigured present and future. My father's death and my mother's responses to it affected the development of our lives both positively and negatively. She could not control the tragedy of her partner's illness and death, but she coped with her loss and the repercussions of her loss during the ensuing years with perseverance and selflessness. She chose to prioritize duty and love.

Lost Acts . . .

NANCY SHAMBAN

This is about loss and loss and loss and loss—ten years of little and big losses. I was forty-five years old before I found the love of my life. She was fifty years old. Her name was Marilyn; she had four grown children, had had a twenty-one-year marriage to a man, and a seven-year relationship with a woman before me. I had had a brief marriage to a man, lots of encounters with men, and a couple relationships with women.

One night, after twelve loving and caring years together, when I returned from my office where I practiced psychotherapy, Marilyn met me at the door and announced that she could not join me the next morning to go on our vacation to Costa Rica because the test she had had that day showed she had cancer in her ovaries. Trip, a little loss; cancer, a big one. She had not been feeling well for a few months and finally had forced our doctor into ordering a sonogram. Really, she had not been OK since 9/11. She was very traumatized by that event and never really recovered from it. We then had a year of surgery, chemotherapy treatments, no work. Marilyn returned to work after a year but she wasn't OK. Something was different about her. She wasn't all there somehow.

We started going to doctors to figure out what was wrong. It took a year, during which I got annoyed and angry; I thought she was acting out against me. We fought a lot. I got crazy and ran off to get my own apartment in Jersey City. I even put money down on an apartment, which I canceled the next day. One day I got a phone call informing me that Marilyn was found somewhere wandering around. I knew she was going to the dentist downtown that day. She was at a dental clinic, having been brought there by a lovely young man who found Marilyn looking very confused outside the subway entrance. She knew where she was going but not where she was. He walked her to a dental place (but not the one she was supposed to go to). They were kind enough to keep Marilyn there and call me. I went as soon as I could get a break between therapy patients. When she saw me, she started to cry and came into my arms with such great sadness; it broke my heart.

Another time I woke up early in the morning and found Marilyn gone. I got up and waited until she returned. According to her, she had woken up several times during the night thinking she needed to go to work at her school on the Lower East Side. She said she left our house three times during the night and took the bus to the school. Each time she was told it was too early and she came home. She told me this with great amusement. How much was true, I never knew, but it was a bizarre event. Another time when her daughters came to visit her while I was at my office working she was very bizarre with them. She wouldn't just sit and visit until I got home. She insisted they go out for coffee, then wouldn't let them drink it. She insisted they come to my office even though I was not available. During this time she was asked to leave her job. She could not organize or do her job as a drug prevention counselor in a high school in Manhattan.

Her personality changed dramatically. She went from being a very private person who would only use a public restroom if I stood in front of the door to someone who started peeling off her clothes in front of her kids when she needed to use the toilet. She went from a news junky who was the mayor of our block, knowing everyone, getting people politically involved, volunteer at God's Love We Deliver to someone who never turned on the TV and hung out on the couch. A friend of mine who was visiting from out of town one day described Marilyn, who kept coming back and forth, seemingly to not let us be alone, as tedious. I was so annoyed with my friend yet knew her observation was true.

With all these events going on, I felt Marilyn's kids should know and be involved. I was going out of my mind as she seemed crazier. I needed help and support, so I elicited it from them. The children reacted in different ways, but within two weeks, three out of the four got it, understood, and were present from then on. Her younger son became enraged, wrote me a horrible letter telling me that if I wanted to be treated like a married partner of his mother, I should handle these things myself. If his wife was ill, he would not be asking anyone to help him. He believed I just wanted to dump his mother and therefore should just get out and leave. The situation deteriorated. It was horrible watching Marilyn as she got sicker and sicker, meanwhile, she was aware that something was wrong between her son and me. It was horrible not being able to fix something that caused her pain. When she died and I organized the funeral service, he seemed to have a brief period of knowing he had misunderstood my intent. Still, our relationship has never returned to what it once was, and that pains me.

All along there had been an absence of certain friends of Marilyn's who didn't help or come through for her at all, even when I asked them to. They basically disappeared from her life and mine when she got sick. This was a major loss for her, hurting her terribly. She was always there for people in her life. It was a loss for me because I needed help, people to stay with her when I had to be at work or just needed a break. I really never got over my anger at these people.

It took a year to get the diagnosis. On the day we received it Marilyn's daughters were with me. Marilyn didn't seem to understand. The diagnosis was frontotemporal dementia (FTD), a group of related conditions resulting from the progressive degeneration of the temporal and frontal lobes of the brain. These areas of the brain play a significant role in decision making, behavioral control, emotion, and language. "Dementia" is an umbrella term to describe a series of illnesses, including FTD and Alzheimer's, along with others. There is no recovery, and little could be done to delay it. It is a death sentence—a major loss. The doctor told us Marilyn's IQ was 88. In the film *Still Alice*, when Alice (played by Julianne Moore) and her husband are eating ice cream, her husband, who wants her to move so he can get a better teaching job, again asks if she will leave with him. She looks up and so innocently says, "Oh, I can't finish my ice cream?" That's when I cried. She so convincingly captures a mind that has become concrete, no longer able to understand concepts. My darling, imaginative, humorous, funny, wise Marilyn no longer "got it." That's when I cried and thought I would never stop. That's when I got that she would soon be "gone."

With the help of caregivers, I kept Marilyn at home with me as long as possible. But at some point, after a series of declines in functioning, it was no longer possible to keep Marilyn home. We had to move her at least four times because each place was a step down in terms of whom they would take care of and how much she qualified. They also were not all to our liking and kept trying to infantilize her before it was necessary, like putting her in a wheelchair because they worried about her falling not because she was really at risk. Marilyn was first moved to a place near her daughter in Pennsylvania, then to another place farther away in Pennsylvania, then to another place in New Jersey, and finally to a nursing home in Massachusetts, near her elder son. Wherever she was I went to see her at least every week or two.

She went through many changes over these years. She got violent for a while, she took things, she stopped recognizing people, although she knew me the longest. One horrible day, I arrived at the place she was in, and she was out in the courtyard frantically walking around in circles with a look of sheer terror on her face. I think that probably was one of the worst days for her because she was so confused, couldn't figure out what was happening to her. She knew something was wrong, and she couldn't fix it. It was her worst loss and terrifying for me. I could do nothing.

One day I got a call that Marilyn was "acting out" at the place, and they had sent her to a hospital to "calm" her. At the hospital they put her on an antipsychotic drug. I had told them that she was very sensitive to medications and to give her half doses, but that didn't matter. They gave her a full dose, and literally overnight I essentially lost the rest of my precious partner. She had a severe reaction to the medication, lost the ability to control her bowel and bladder functioning, and never knew me again. Major loss!

When Marilyn got cancer, our dog, Ms. Elbe (El for Libby, my mother, and Be for Bessie, Marilyn's mother), clung to Marilyn, she wouldn't leave her side. As Marilyn got sicker with dementia, the dog and Marilyn started to reject each other, as if each had become a stranger to the other. Our dog knew Marilyn had left. It was painful to witness.

So the years, ten altogether, went on. Years of watching her mentally and physically decline until she was balled up in a chair and had to be fed, bathed, toileted, moved by others. It is funny, each of these additions were losses of the essence of her to me, yet each time I went to see her I believed she knew me for a split second and would smile. It kept me going, helped me feel less loss. This is all ambivalent loss, loss that is and isn't happening. I just adjusted to who she was in any given moment.

Then, when I was away on vacation, I got a call that Marilyn seemed to be out of sorts; they would keep me apprised of how she was. Before I could get to her, she had died. Her elder son was with her and called to tell me. I flew home and planned her funeral. I can't say I was relieved. I felt utter sadness at her death. I felt tremendous anger for all that couldn't be done and for her suffering. I was furious with her friends who had abandoned her when she needed them and did not inform them of her death. Now, I am sorry I did that because Marilyn had such a pure heart, she would not have wanted that. It took a long time to get through my missing our visits, missing her, wanting to hold her. It took a long time to get over feeling the pain when I realized that some members of my family did not see my loss as equal to that of any heterosexual who has lost a loved one, did not treat me with the same respect and kindness I should have been afforded. It has taken until recently just to remember our life together before I lost her. I am now dreaming about her quite often, happy dreams of our life before her illness.

In all the loss Marilyn went through and the loss for me, first because of her dementia and then because of her death, it was not only and all about loss. In all our hospital situations, I was never kept from Marilyn, even though we were a same-sex, unmarried couple (marriage did not exist at that time as a possibility). I was always treated as a partner, with respect, and I was always allowed in and consulted. In all this loss, there has been a major, major gain. Three of Marilyn's four children are actively in my life, and seven out of eight grandchildren love me and call me grandma. (The eighth lives elsewhere, and I have not seen him for many years.) I adore them. I am fortunate beyond words.

Dealing with Double Loss

Husband and Hearing

SUSANNE BRAHAM

Imagine this. I'm walking home through Central Park on a beautiful June evening as the New York Philharmonic Orchestra is about to perform their first public outdoor concert of the year. But I cannot linger. I must pass through quickly because the memories are too painful, the music too disturbing.

My late husband Robert, who died suddenly at age fifty-six, had always enjoyed the ambiance of music under the stars in Central Park. Joining thousands of other music-loving New Yorkers, some indulging in rather extravagant catered dinners, we'd picnic on a blanket on the Great Lawn. Since Robert passed away nearly fifteen years ago, I've learned to enjoy many activities with other people, something that was not possible when I first became a widow. Music, however, is no longer one of those pleasures. What I hear now is not music. It's simply noise. Cacophony.

Robert and I had enjoyed an unusually close relationship. When he first called to ask me out on a date, I didn't remember having met him at an International House party just a few weeks earlier, and at the time, I wasn't inclined to accept blind dates. But I had been a violist for many years. So when he said he had concert tickets to hear violinist Isaac Stern at Hunter College, I happily accepted his invitation. Had it been love at first sight, most likely I would have recalled our having previously met, yet during our first actual date, my earlier, vague impressions of Robert came back to me and were confirmed. He was an incredible match. His ideas, philosophies, interests, and opinions comfortably aligned with mine. Our thought processes seemed magically similar. We talked freely, uninhibited. Hours passed when we were together without my needing outside distraction. And in time, we had few secrets.

Seeking out someone with whom I felt so totally comfortable was no accident. My own parents had been terrible role models and eventually went their separate ways (after fifty-two years!), leaving me with few positive expectations about marriage. But, in many ways, the closeness between Robert and me became a dangerous liability. With the exception of our separate jobs, we did almost everything together. Our individual friends became mutual friends, and, partly owing to Robert's intellectual curiosity, we took several summer classes together at Cornell's Adult University (his alma mater), sometimes studying subjects that appealed to both of us, but often alternating between my interests and his, always coming away enthused about having shared the experience. There were enough challenges in life without our relationship being one of them. What could have been more beautiful and satisfying?

And then one cold November night I awoke a bit past midnight. A light was shining and Robert was standing at the foot of our bed. He told me to call 911 saying, "Tell them I'm a physician, that I have WPW syndrome, and that I think my heart stopped beating." He then collapsed on our bed. I asked him what I could do to help. Unable to speak, he motioned with a loosely clenched fist that I should pound on his chest. Remembering his tales about stat calls (emergency alerts in the hospital) from his days of internship and residency, I did as he had indicated while trying to follow instructions on the phone—breathing into his mouth, sealing it off with my lips, pounding on his chest. But I panicked. His face was turning purple well before an EMS crew arrived. When they finally came, they shocked his heart into beating again and took him off to New York Hospital. But the beat could not be sustained.

I had known early on that Robert had WPW syndrome, an electrical conduction problem. He had failed his army physical; it had kept him out of Vietnam. Lying close to him, I sometimes sensed the strange way his heart fluttered—so differently from mine. We also knew he was prone to developing a berry aneurysm, the hereditary problem that had taken his mother's life when she was only thirty-six, following the birth of his younger sister. So Robert always carried a medical alert bracelet in his wallet, and he told me what to do if he ever developed a sudden violent headache. Unquestionably, these risks intensified our passion. But we lived for the moment, doing as much as we could while we could, never dwelling on morbid possibilities.

Nevertheless, following sudden loss, I developed posttraumatic stress disorder, reliving those final moments of struggle as I tried to administer

CPR. My nightly dreams were haunted by images of bringing Robert back to life—until I finally stopped dreaming, altogether. For almost three years I rarely entered REM sleep, but unaware of what was happening, I never sought help. Rather, I focused on soldiering on, settling Robert's estate, and going to my job as an editor at Columbia University, albeit I was not a very good parent for my children, sixteen and twenty-two at the time of their father's death.

Throughout that early period of grieving, the intensity of my emotions was unlike anything I had ever experienced. A frenetic need to preserve the memories of our time together made me intent on writing a memoir, keeping Robert alive through reliving the good times and our exciting political and social adventures. Because one perk of Columbia employment included tuition-free classes, I was able to take several creative writing courses. I figured they would be helpful.

But the memoir got sidetracked when, a few years after Robert's death, I became involved in a bizarre relationship with a man twenty-two years my junior. He became my addictive escape from the pain of loss. As he was much younger, I didn't fear losing him to old age or infirmity. The fact that he was a confirmed bachelor and an unremitting playboy made me think he would always be available—although he constantly reminded me we could never become a serious couple. This didn't stop me. I knew I wasn't ready for a lasting relationship, but I craved his beautiful body (our physical intimacy lasted for a few years). He reawakened within me something that had died along with Robert, and a reason to get out of bed in the morning. But with things suddenly veering in an embarrassing direction, I no longer felt compelled to reveal my life story. Instead, I began writing poetry about widowhood, while this much younger man, himself a novelist and poet, encouraged me in that direction. He even helped me find publishers for five of my poems in two different anthologies about widowhood.

This was all very cathartic and brought me into contact with a group of women poets who were similarly working through their grief by writing. Many of us traveled to different parts of the country to read our poems together, and a group of us formed a panel to discuss healing through writing at Seattle University's School of Theology and Ministry.*

Ironically, my memoir was tentatively titled "If the Beat Stops, Can the Music Go On?" referring to both my husband's heartbeat and Isaac Stern's role in bringing us together. Soon after Robert's death, I spent hours listening to music, one of very few indulgences that soothed me. On certain

* My three poems are "Ties," "Widow's Daughter," and "Widowed, Turning Sixty," in *The Widows' Handbook: Poetic Reflections on Grief and Survival*, ed. Jacqueline Lapidus and Lise Menn (Kent, OH: The Kent State University Press, 2014), 197–201.

Tuesday afternoons I'd leave my Columbia University office for St. Paul's Chapel on campus, where a resounding organ filled the air with noontime concerts. Also at lunch hours during 2007–2008, the Pacifica Quartet performed the complete Beethoven string quartets, all eighteen of them. I was enthralled. It was free, magnificent, and absorbing. But little by little my days of listening to music were coming to an end. At first it simply seemed like a question of volume, which I was able to boost with the help of hearing aids. But something else was going on, a phenomenon I might have recognized years back had I been paying attention when Robert and I had a subscription to the Metropolitan Opera.

Robert had loved soprano voices. He collected recordings of soprano arias and was especially fond of the crystal-clear sounds of Joan Sutherland. I, too, enjoyed her singing, but twenty or so years ago I began to find soprano voices less and less appealing, distinctly preferring men's voices or contraltos. I should have noticed that the violins were beginning to sound equally strange.

And then one day, some six years after Robert's death, I picked up a telephone receiver and realized that the sound of the dial tone in my right ear was quite different from what I was hearing on the left. The pitches were off by about a quarter to a half tone. My left ear was hearing a fairly pure tone, but the volume was incredibly low compared with what I could hear on the right. The louder sound in my right ear was both off pitch wise and muddled, like a radio station pulling in several stations simultaneously. So it was no wonder that Sutherland had begun to sound like a screech owl in her upper ranges, even while Robert was alive.

At higher frequencies I was beginning to hear the equivalent of A in one ear, A-sharp in the other, plus a lot of interference. As time went on, with both ears operating on different planes, I heard double or more of everything, including my own voice—and the more instruments or singers, the greater the dissonance. In addition to playing the viola and having near-perfect pitch, I used to perform in synagogue and church choirs. I had sung Handel's *Messiah* at both Carnegie and Avery Fisher Halls. So this was terribly frustrating, in fact, terrifying. Sitting through a religious service with music eventually became unbearable. Most music became unrecognizable, so I avoided it.

Nowadays, drums are my instrument of choice, percussion being the least bothersome. And I can still enjoy parts of Phillip Glass's percussive works, as they don't wreck havoc with my harmonic expectations. But learning to live in a world void of most music has been tough. I wrote to various ear specialists, even to the late Oliver Sacks, when he was still at Columbia, asking what, if anything, could be done. They all had a name for my problem (binaural diplacusis) but no idea how to fix it.

I had had my first episode of hearing loss (sudden deafness syndrome) almost thirty years ago, when I was in my early forties. The ENT doctor who cared for me attributed it to a viral illness and put me on a very high dose of steroids, which reduced the inflammation causing the hearing problem, but for a time it had been both scary and upsetting. My daughter, around two years old, was just learning to talk. I desperately wanted to encourage her verbal development through our communication, as I had done, very successfully, with her older brother six years earlier.

Luckily, that first incident of hearing loss left me with only minor damage, but over time, things began to deteriorate. In my early fifties, during an employee wellness-day hearing exam at Columbia, I was told to see an outside expert, as there was something obviously wrong with my hearing profile or audiogram. My father had been profoundly hard of hearing by the time he was in his sixties, but his doctor assured me that his loss was entirely different from mine. He eventually had a cochlear implant but unfortunately died a few months later of lung cancer, unrelated to cochlear surgery.

Following Robert's death, many of my social activities revolved around attending concerts with friends. But as time wore on, that was no longer an option, increasing the isolation of being widowed. I gave up my opera subscription. Going to theater, eating in restaurants with background noise, even talking on the telephone, became more and more difficult. I struggled at my book group, one that Robert had belonged to at the College of Physicians and Surgeons (renamed the Robert Braham Seminar in his memory). Unlike the usual age-related hearing loss, where the higher frequencies are gone, I had lost the ability to hear within the human voice range without significant amplification. And the degree of concentration required for making sense of what I could hear began to sap my energy.

For a while, with the exception of a few friends and relatives who came to my apartment for brunch (where I could at least hear them if they talked one at a time), I had very few social interactions. Going to restaurants for family get-togethers was dreadful. Trying not to look bored, I'd eventually feel infuriated because I couldn't participate in conversations. Moreover, for some reason, people with hearing loss at certain frequencies often perceive other frequencies that they are able to hear as much louder than normal, and on top of that, hearing aids amplify the distracting sounds no one wants to hear (cups clattering on saucers; silverware striking glass tabletops). As the noise level ratchets up during the course of a meal, notably at weddings, I've been driven to remove my hearing aids and flee to the ladies room, remaining there until ready to confront the chattering crowds I can barely understand. My only escape has been in dancing! If my hearing aids are plugged into my ears but the is volume turned off, I hear the percussive beat while the rest of the racket is silenced. The beat alone is needed for dancing—a great outlet for stress, allowing me to participate in celebrations.

For a few years, in my late fifties and early sixties, I thought I might possibly meet an eligible widower. However, being disabled presented problems. (Falling in love in my youth had been so much less complicated.) I had trouble accepting myself as impaired or damaged merchandise, yet I realized I might not appeal to a nonimpaired partner. Nor could I imagine dating someone seriously compromised. Finding a normal-hearing mate would have been wonderful, but there were so many activities I could never share with a partner who loved music or theater. As I've aged, many in my cohort have become "defective" in one way or another, so I no longer feel that same degree of self-pity. In fact, I appreciate what still works and continue to be fairly athletic. And at this point, quite a few friends my age have lost a spouse or divorced. I now have greater empathy for them and no longer see myself as the big exception.

Luckily, recent improvements in hearing-aid technology have kept me from total social isolation. With my new top-of-the-line hearing aids (not inexpensive), I can communicate fairly well, at least under favorable conditions. While my social life is not exactly blossoming, in noisy environments for strictly one-on-one communication, by wearing an antenna around my neck while a companion wears a microphone on their lapel, I can now hear more reliably through a Bluetooth connection that carries the sound directly into my hearing aids. This also works for gallery talks at museums. While at home, I use a captioned landline phone, and a shaker under my bed functions as my alarm clock, because once I remove my hearing aids at night, I hear very little.

By joining HLAA (Hearing Loss Association of America), a wonderful support group that helps with coping skills, I've made new friends who are also hard of hearing. Through HLAA, I've become an active advocate for people with hearing disabilities, going to hearings and participating in marches and other awareness activities—another beneficial way of helping myself as well as others.

And I've found some fortunate replacements for the music in my life. Before Robert died, he and I would visit my elderly mother at her beachfront Florida apartment. We'd take long walks together along the ocean. After his death, going back there by myself was unbearably lonely. My mother, struggling with heart failure and no longer strong enough to join me, had also loved the seashore. One day I decided to bring a hand-me-down camera to the beach, where I began taking photos of the ocean, the sea birds, and other creatures, capturing the varying moods and colors of the sunset and changing weather conditions. After downloading the photos to my laptop, I shared my walk along the coastline with my mom, a most appreciative audience. Something was brewing. In time, my skills grew and I began sharing pictures with family and friends on Facebook. My camera became a constant companion, opening up a new means of communication, while the loneliness of widowhood began to dissolve. Focusing on photography, my eyes had replaced my ears as channels for pleasure, while museums and art galleries also took on greater importance.

In terms of that memoir I'd once envisioned after the beat had stopped: well, the music failed to go on, but the pleasures of photography, other visual arts, and my continuing to write have replaced it, making my life symphonic in other interesting ways. But as far as replacing Robert, it has taken and will take a village to supplant all that he had meant to me, so my time ahead must be spent constantly reaching out to others as well as I can.

Synchronicity and the Secular Mind

ALICE RADOSH

Almost a hundred cards jammed the narrow box in my rural post office the first few months after Bart's death. Another hundred greetings were posted on his memorial website. Messages came from close friends, from Bart's former students, from members of the rescue squad where Bart had volunteered for many years, from community people like the couple who run the garage where Bart took our car and pickup truck for eighteen years.

The topics ran the gamut. How kind and patient he was: "Bart was a kind, gentle man who always cared about others through action and deed"; how principled: "He set the bar for what it means to be political and principled and thoughtful and just plain nice"; what an extraordinary relationship we had: "You two were quite a formidable pair—and clearly so right together." And some spoke my feelings at a time when I could barely speak at all: "I feel all the constellations have shifted, changed shape since Bart has died."

But very few included a reference to spirituality or anything supernatural. A few cards tossed in a phrase along the lines of "you are in my thoughts and prayers," but even those were few.

It does not surprise me that people did not reach for religious references and images. That there are even two or three in the mix is a bit of a

Originally published in *Jewish Currents*, August 24, 2015.

surprise. Bart was dismissive of anything that came close to religious belief. Sugarcoating it or softening it by conflating God with a deep love of nature, or calling it spirituality or determinism or any other Woodstock term, did not change anything. It was simply not who he was, and, on this topic, he was not going to bend in order to consider a different point of view. Not an inch.

Notwithstanding the OMGs that occasionally creep into my emails, or my occasional fervent and heartfelt "Please God, don't let this or that happen," I am as clear as Bart was that there is no spirit that looks down on us. Nothing happens in this world because of a presence that is gently—or sometimes not so gently—guiding events. There are amazing coincidences, and amazing things happen that we cannot explain, but neither Bart nor I would jump to a God conclusion.

Not long after Bart's death, my friend Joan admitted to having "religion envy." Joan's husband, Bill, was Bart's closest friend for decades, and in many ways the four of us had been a unit. Although it might have been numerically impossible, the four of us felt like a single couple. Bart's death shattered that. I understood what Joan meant by religion envy. It would be nice to think that Bart was smiling down on the three of us. Death would reunite us. He will be an angel guiding us as we finish out our lives down here. How could you not be envious of such beliefs? But such beliefs are unavailable to us. Nothing—not foxholes and not Bart's death—brought us any closer to these comforting thoughts. We were stubbornly and, yes, proudly, stuck with our atheism.

How to explain, then, the condolences that arrived from Bart's mother three weeks after his death and thirteen years after hers?

I loved Ida. She had embraced me and my children from the first time Bart "brought me home." Initially we had external reasons for loving each other. At first she loved me because she loved Bart, and she could see how happy he finally was after a ten-year failed marriage. At first, I loved her because I still needed a mother's love—something I had not gotten enough of as a child. Over the next thirty years a genuine and deep love developed between us. We could tease each other; we could listen to and confide in each other. And we could comfort each other.

The first weeks after a death are consumed with administrative details. Although not intended to be, it is a useful way of holding off a total emotional breakdown. There are insurance papers to find, health care bills to decipher. The car had to be transferred into my name only, where is the marriage certificate that I need, and do I have an original of Bart's birth certificate? I was constantly running to the filing cabinet. And then, in one of the drawers, I saw a folder labeled, in Bart's careful script, "Parents' Memorabilia."

Toward the back of the folder was a paper I had never seen before. Typed on the front was, "Rhetoric 12B, Theme No. 26, May 3, 1929, Ida Bush." Below that, was a grade, A–. In 1929 Ida would have been a seventeen-year-old high school student. The topic for the rhetoric paper was, "The Most Effective Short Sentence I Ever Heard." Ida wrote about a talk she attended in the high school assembly, and about her inability to listen to the speaker because, "Certain circumstances had conspired during the past few weeks to place me in a state of utter dejection. A cherished dream had been shattered."

Dejected and shattered, I read on. "Suddenly there penetrated into my consciousness, never to be erased, the words of the speaker, 'You will not always feel this way.'" Ida had underlined that sentence. You will not always feel this way. She continued, as I stood holding the paper, stunned. "The sentence took on animate power and offered me consolation and hope. Truth whispered in my ear, 'Do not deceive yourself by your mental anguish of today. Tomorrow you will have forgotten a little.' Many times since I have drawn on the power of those words to help me face the realities and disillusionments of life."

I knew from the date of the essay what cherished dream Ida was referring to. But now it felt as if she were talking directly to me about the reality that I was being forced to face. She was adding her voice to those of family and friends who tried to reassure me that time would make the pain manageable. But hearing that message from a woman who loved Bart and me so much was deeply affecting. "Tomorrow you will have forgotten a little."

But it was also a bit creepy. Her words had been written almost ninety years earlier. Bart had not yet been born, and here she was consoling me on his death. I called my friend Naomi and read her the essay. Similarly amazed by the paper turning up, she laughed and asked if my hard line on spirituality was shaken. No more than hers, I assured her, but I could not stop marveling at the coincidence of hearing from Ida when I most needed her comfort. I taped a copy of Ida's rhetoric essay to the refrigerator, where it stayed for the next few months, encouraging me to believe that I would not always feel this way.

Other consoling notes have appeared unexpectedly—from Bart, not his mother. We both left notes for each other—always a note under the pillow if we were going to be away for any length of time, but also a note might be left on the kitchen counter if one of us was going out before the other came home. Some of the notes were saved, and since Bart's death they have popped up in socks and underwear drawers, desk drawers, and various baskets and files where they had been tucked away over the last forty years.

By nine months after Bart's death, I had assumed that I had found all the notes. But one appeared very recently, just when I was spiraling down into the dangerous territory of, "this is unbearable; life without Bart is worthless; I am worthless," and so on downward.

This note had the "strange coincidence" quality of Ida's note. I had just come home from seeing a moving documentary about Henry Paulson, Bush's secretary of treasury. I emailed a friend about the film, stating that Paulson's wife, Wendy, was the real heroine of the movie and that everyone in power should be married to Wendy Paulson. "Heroine" is not a word I use often. "Heroine" was not a word Bart used often.

Very likely the downward spiral was set off by watching the Paulsons work together to navigate difficult times. The permanent loss of such a partner felt unbearable and now too familiar. I went up to my bedroom, in tears.

Before leaving for the movie I had upended a basket onto my bed while looking for a scarf. A small square of white paper now lay on the bed. I turned it over and read, "Honey, dinner is on top of the fridge. I cleaned up the little bit I had time for. I think you are a heroine."

A heroine? The note was written twelve years ago. I have no idea what prompted the note at the time Bart wrote it. But I do know that, while he might not use the word "heroine," Bart was always there to encourage me when I had to face a daunting task. It might be anything from a major speaking engagement to just facing my weekly piano lesson when I felt unprepared. Bart would march me to the front door, saying in a deep, stentorian voice, "You're Radosh and You're Proud" and push me out. It became a useful and not infrequent phrase throughout our marriage.

But, how strange to be reading "I think you are a heroine" at the very moment that I was emotionally imploding and despairing of ever again being or having a helpmate like the wife in the documentary, whom I had just labeled a heroine. "Nothing happens by accident" we are told by people who believe such shibboleths—the very people my friend Joan sometimes envies. But what are the odds of accidentally finding this note, with this word that Bart and I rarely used, at the very moment that I needed so badly to read it?

Actually the odds of such fortuitous accidents are the focus of numerous scientific and psychological studies. Carl Jung coined the word "synchronicity" in the 1950s to label the simultaneous occurrence of events that appear related but have no discernible causal connection. Things do happen by accident. Far more amazing things than finding the right note at the right time.

So, while I was startled, I cannot say that chills went up and down my spine. I did not feel Bart's presence as a breeze in the room. But my spine did straighten up. Brakes were put on my collapse into despair. Bart's right, I can stand up to the grief dragon—maybe not slay it yet, but not be crushed by it either. The heroine note has been added to the front of my refrigerator.

Here is the last story that tempts one to be a believer. Here is my mother-in-law's cherished dream that was shattered.

Ida, a very bright woman, was brought up in Washington, D.C., in a large and very poor family. Each year, every public high school in Washington, or as Bart would remind me, every white public high school, awarded a full four-year scholarship to George Washington University to one girl and one boy. Ida won the scholarship for the girl from Business High School.

That same spring, Business High's baton twirling team won the city championship. The scholarship was taken away from Ida and given to the captain of the baton twirlers. Ida never went to college. Twenty-five years later her son, Bart, was awarded the same four-year scholarship from his high school. He graduated from George Washington University and went on to receive his PhD.

I think maybe on January 27th I will light a yahrzeit candle.

Mourning American-Style

PARVIN HAJIZADEH

Let me take you back to the day before Labor Day, September 2013. It was a hot day. Both my husband and I worked in the garden; then he went for a jog and I prepared dinner. Starting at about 11 P.M. there was a very bad storm, and since my husband knew how much I get scared from lightning and the noise of the thunder, he came upstairs to our bedroom so I would not be alone. He held me 'til I went to sleep. My husband always stayed up late to make the list of the stocks that he was planning to buy the next day. He was a teacher and day stock trader. He loved both of his jobs, but I could tell he loved the excitement of trading more.

That next morning, I came downstairs to find him lying on the kitchen floor. I was devastated and did not know what to do. The last thing in mind was that he was dead; I called his name over and over, and then I called 911. They did not let me go with him in the ambulance, so one of my neighbors gave me a ride.

He was dead, and I could not scream. I could not scream, for I knew I was in America, and did not know what this culture does in the face of death, but I sensed that screaming was not part of the American way of mourning.

People came quickly to be with me while we waited for the boys to get to town to view their dad, who was still lying on the hospital bed. I, their helpless mother, could not even look at them. I started talking to everyone as if nothing had happened. I was so numb and confused. We left the hospital and got home late that night; I do not remember much about that night.

The next day, family members and friends came to the house. I could not explain to them what had happened. For the first time in my life I learned the meaning of the word "unexpected." He was sixty-four and only two days into his retirement. How had his life been cut short so unfairly and taken away by surprise? Questions still haunt me: What could have been done? What if I had come downstairs earlier? Did he want to be saved?

Going through the phases of mourning can be almost the same for everyone, but what made it more difficult for me was that since I am Iranian and all the mourning that I had seen in my life took place in Iran, I knew only one way to mourn, and that was not the American way. I was twenty-four upon my father's death back home. There we did not do anything related to arrangements; whereas, here, my boys and I had to go to pick where we wanted him to be buried; it felt like shopping for a grave. My niece helped me through a lot of the other details, but she also did not know the American conventions. He was her favorite uncle. We had to make decisions about a Muslim burial and bring an Imam from Boston. Thank God that I did not have financial issues to deal with.

A week after his death, we buried him. The day of the service I stood next to my sister and my husband's brother, who was standing next to the boys with some of their cousins who were able to be there (my family lives in Iran). I had to stand in a receiving line and face the shock in everyone's eyes and the quiet crying. When we bury our dead, we don't put the body in a casket, so I could see his body wrapped in white cloth. After the religious ceremony our older son (twenty-five at that time) went up front and talked about his dad. I do not know how he did it. When they put the body in the grave, our younger son (twenty-two) held one side of the platform and helped them to lower his dad. Later on, they told me that was the plan that the boys had agreed upon: one speaks and one puts him in. Throughout the whole ceremony, I was sitting on a chair quietly, silently watching, but I wanted to get up and scream, to cry loudly, and get my feelings out the same way we did back home, the way I learned watching at families' deaths, but I knew that I shouldn't. For I am in America, and what will people think if I do that? I am sure that was in my boys' heads too: "What if Mom just loses it and mourns the Iranian way?"

After almost four years, I still wake up in the morning and realize that he is not sleeping next to me. I then make my tea and go to the cemetery and have my tea with him. I love my morning tea time with him. I decided to stay in the same house as I have lots and lots of good memories and am not ready to leave them behind. I am driving his car; I mow the lawn and plow the snow as he used to do, and proudly tell him any developments in our life without him.

But that scream is still sitting in my throat.

The Rocks That Bind

JEAN Y. LEUNG

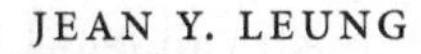

The night after my husband's sudden death at sixty, I lay in bed, not only grief stricken but anxiety ridden. How was I going to bury him?

Peter had never been one to follow rules, particularly those of a religious kind. Yet he'd given his parents religious burials. He was proud of being a Jew. We'd raised our son Jacob as a Jew. But I hadn't been born a Jew. Although his family claimed to be secular, they had sent him five days a week for a religious education to an Orthodox synagogue. My version consisted of one six-week summer Bible camp at a Lutheran church. His European family had settled in Africa; my Chinese one had settled in America.

Jewish death rituals were not unknown to me, since I had been around when my husband buried his father. As part of the Jewish community, I had gone to shivas and burials yet had never paid any attention to the details.

I had arranged both of my parents' funerals. But this was so different. Chinese burials didn't involve much choice. You went to the funeral parlor in Chinatown that was associated with your last name. These parlors have reserved plots within cemeteries. There is generally a wake the day before the funeral with an open casket and a wake the morning of the funeral. A eulogy is held, then the casket is closed and everyone goes to the cemetery, where there is a brief ceremony. Afterward, you treat everyone to a sumptuous banquet in a restaurant to thank them for coming.

From the moment someone dies to a few months later, the person's home is considered off limits. No one visits. If someone has to interact with the deceased's family, it takes place outside. I have memories of my sister-in-law waiting outside my sister's apartment to pick up her children after her father's funeral. The deceased's family is to stay at home, wear dark clothes, and be in quiet contemplation. Socialization is deeply discouraged. After my father died, I moved back in with my mother. It was a very lonely time.

It was a shock to me, as word spread about Peter's death, that people didn't stay away. The door would open and arms would envelope me, and we would cry together. I thought about how my mother and I would sit at the kitchen table and silently eat, listening to the clock tick away for months after my father had passed away.

At first, I was torn by this. By culture and tradition, this behavior was heretical. I had to keep reminding myself that this was Peter's passing, and that I needed to honor his traditions. Peter had been proud that he was a particular kind of Jew, a South African Jew. I knew, as with the Chinese, that there were slight variations in custom and tradition as people migrated around the world. Friends and family informed me that the variations were in what happens after the funeral and had more to do with the shiva. "Shiva" is the Hebrew word for seven, which is the prescribed amount of time for people to come to the deceased's home to morn with the family. Seven days? I shivered, thinking of the months my mother and I couldn't have visitors. Rutha, Peter's South African friend of over forty years, told me this was entirely up to my discretion. Jacob and I decided to hold shiva the weekend following the funeral. This was religiously wrong. One of those days would be a Saturday, the Sabbath, but we wanted to accommodate everyone, especially those who worked.

When we started looking for burial plots, I was certain of only one thing—that I wanted two plots next to each other, so that I could be buried next to my husband. As we widened our search, I began to think of what Peter would have wanted. He always liked places with a view, especially one of water. It began to dawn on me to consider my own needs as well. Chinese prefer to be buried on top of hills and mountains. Closer to heaven, they say. Jews have no such distinctions. Like Peter, Chinese prefer water views, said to enhance the financial futures of their descendants. I preferred a secular cemetery because we were a multicultural family but soon began to realize that secular cemeteries felt Christian. I worried that Jewish cemeteries wouldn't allow Jacob to perform Chinese cultural rites, such as burning candles and colored paper at the graves. I knew, however, that if this was a problem, he could perform these same rituals at home or elsewhere. Chinese tradition bends toward the practical.

Eventually we found a plot within a beautifully landscaped cemetery owned by a reform congregation. It sat on a hill and faced Manhattan. Two trees at the foot of the plot gave it shade. Because it was a family plot, there was room not just for Peter and myself but also for my son and any future spouse. Knowing how my life had turned out, I was leery of restrictions. "Should my son not choose a Jewish spouse . . ." I gently asked the cemetery caretaker. "All you would need is a letter from a rabbi that stated that she participated in the Jewish community." "What about, would I be . . . ?" I asked him. "No, you would not be the only Chinese buried here. We have, maybe a half dozen buried here." I breathed a sigh of relief. Still I told him we needed to think about it.

On a day when the sun was playing peekaboo, Jacob and I got some sandwiches and headed to this cemetery. We sat down where Peter would lie, ate, and looked at the view. A breeze ruffled through the trees. For the first time since Peter's passing, I felt a tiny tinge of peace. "Let's do it," I told my son.

We decided not to have a wake for Peter. Instead, Jacob and I had our own private viewing in the chapel. Peter looked peaceful, even angelic, in a shroud, the pain of three years of dialysis wiped away. So different from all the embalmed bodies in Chinese funerals. They looked artificial, like mannequins, with layers of pan makeup. Per Peter's request, in accordance with Jewish tradition, we'd chosen the plainest of pine coffins, with wooden dowels. As Jacob would say later, the Chinese way is to fight nature, to try to preserve things the way they were. The Jewish way is to acknowledge nature, to let her do her work, to let the body decompose. I much prefer the Jewish way. It helps me reconcile myself to what is happening.

Chinese funerals emphasize flowers. Arrangements are delivered to the funeral parlor and are placed along the walls of the chapel. They are a signal to the community of your stature and your relationship to the deceased. The richer you are or the closer you are to the deceased the bigger and fancier they get. The flowers always have ribbons with the names of the donors on them. I have always considered them to be tacky. Mourners get little corsages of a single flower, sometimes just a crocheted one, which they throw over the coffin in the cemetery before they leave. There were no flowers at Peter's funeral.

Unlike at Chinese funerals, mourners were encouraged to participate in the graveside service, to say whatever they wanted to. After the last one spoke, the rabbi grabbed a shovel, took some of the dirt, and poured it over Peter's coffin. He handed the shovel to Jacob. We began as a group to fill in the space above Peter's coffin before leaving. At Chinese funerals, this task is left to the grave diggers.

Before we had left that morning, I had to suppress an urge to run to the grocery store or call in an order to a restaurant. Everyone from the funeral was invited back to our house for refreshments, but I was not to supply the food, only the drinks. My Chinese upbringing lashed inwardly at me. I had been taught to always have food around to feed whoever showed up at your home. To not do so was a stain of honor on your family. There are folktales of people who went without just to feed their guests. When we got home from the funeral, people were already waiting for us with food. Tons of it! My Chinese relatives were aghast, however. Many had come long distances (one from California) for the funeral at short notice. This was it? Finally, my cousin from Albany took matters into her own hands. She took everyone who was still there in the evening to a proper sit-down meal with formally prepared food in a local Chinatown restaurant.

The funeral parlor had given us two large candles. We were to light the candles when we got home. They would burn for seven days and mark the beginning and end of our mourning period. I loved that there was a clear, definitive time keeper. Of course, my pain would follow its own path, and no candle could end it for me. But the candle's progression reminded me that I have one too.

On the morning of the shiva, I set out the leftovers from the gathering after the funeral. Once again, as instructed, I bought nothing. The doorbell rang. Food deliveries. People began to arrive, all, it seemed, with armloads of food. For the rest of the day and the next, neighbors, friends, family, children, and pets would fill our house. Not all the food was for the shiva. They also bought food for me, prewrapped for the freezer—nourishment for the months ahead. Visitors also filled the house with flowers. I couldn't help but think of all the garish flower arrangements at Chinese funerals.

We have one more step in the Jewish mourning process and then an ongoing one. Within a year of Peter's passing, we will unveil his tombstone. After that a candle is lit once a year on the anniversary of his death. There is no prescribed time to visit the cemetery. It is presumed that the cemetery will maintain the plot. Not so in the East. Families take care of the plots. They clean up the ground around the tombstone and plant flowers twice a year, once during the spring and once during the fall. A picnic is held. It is a festive occasion, with family uniting with each other and the dead. My mother would always update my father on what was happening to members of the family: births, graduations, marriages, and the like. Children play hide and seek between the grave stones. Before you leave, each member of the family leaves a rock over some paper on the tombstone. Every time my husband and I visited his parents' graves, I couldn't help but feel the contrast. We'd stand in quiet contemplation, put a rock on the tombstone, then walk away. Before leaving, we'd wash our hands.

For Chinese, it is the time around a death that is solitary. For Jews, it seems that the solitary period comes after the first year. Since my husband and I are a blend, I want to take the solitary out of our hereafter. When I visit my parents, I will visit him also and include him in a meal family and I will share. I take solace in giving my son the freedom to be able to grieve with family and friends at home and not have to wait months to be with people. But I also want him to picnic at our gravesite with his family.

There is one thing our cultures share. We both leave rocks on the tombstone after visiting. Jacob has added his own interpretation. Wherever he goes, he looks for rocks to bring back to his father's grave.

I always felt that the life Peter and I had carved together for twenty-five years was richer because it was fed from more than one spring. In dealing with his passing, I have buried the idea that death, and the customs that surround it, need be singular as well.

On Not Feeling Sad

JOAN GUSSOW

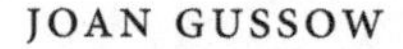

Several years ago, someone once asked me what was the best thing my parents ever did for me. At first, of course, my mind turned to childhood, but none of the memories that arose seemed significant enough to meet the criterion. For it seemed to me essential that the "best thing" be something life changing, something that had carried through the decades until my present advanced age.

And so I asked myself what there was in my life that might express the best thing my parents ever did for me. As it happened, the question arose just as I was experiencing fallout from the publication of a book in which I told a difficult truth about myself. Which is how it occurred to me that undoubtedly the most important thing my parents ever did for me was to teach me to search hard for the truth, and having found it, to be honest enough to speak it. It now seems obvious that most of my major successes in life have been a consequence of my parents' gift.

As I recounted in that book, the spring my husband died, after forty years of what I had viewed as a happy marriage, I found myself, just two weeks after his death, skipping down the street. I was appalled and confused; I believed myself to have had a happy marriage, but—thanks to my commitment to truth—I could not conceal from myself my lack of grief, unacceptable as it seemed.

All that followed began with my inability to fool myself about my real feelings—although I tried, initially, to fool others. "As good as can be expected," I would say, in response to the question "how are you?" indicating that I didn't want to talk about it. I was convinced that my lack of grief was something to avoid talking about or, certainly, writing about. But as I began to be able to show some part of how I was feeling to my closest friends, they urged me to begin to write it down, insisting that other people probably felt that way too and needed to have someone say it. So I set out to try to write the truth.

Nine years later, when I had managed, after much struggle, to tell the story in a way that I hoped was both candid and kind, and when I put it together and found a publisher for a book that told, among other stories, the tale of my failure to mourn, the book was scheduled to be published under the title *Growing, Older: A Chronicle of Death, Life and Vegetables.* As a consequence of its impending publication, I was interviewed by the wonderful Anne Raver, garden writer for the *New York Times.* She had interviewed me nine years earlier when my first memoir came out, shortly after Alan's death, and we had liked each other immensely, but I had not seen her since.

Now a freelancer, and thus no longer constrained by the *Times*'s don't-make-friends-with-interviewees rule, Anne spent two days with me in the garden, stayed overnight, read both my new book and my first one, did all the readings for the class I taught at Columbia University Teachers College, and generally inhaled my thinking. And when she had finished writing the article, it featured prominently the fact that my new book opened with my stunned discovery that I didn't miss the husband whose death I had reported in passing in my earlier volume.

And then, two mornings before her story was to run in the *Times*, Anne called me laughing. "The *New York Times* called this morning," she reported. "They said, 'You're saying Joan didn't mourn her husband. Is she OK with your saying that?' and I said, 'Well I guess so, since she wrote a book about it.'" We laughed together—recognizing the power of the code I was breaking—and I assured Anne that I was happy she had "outed" me. I was scheduled to do a series of book talks in the coming months, and since I believed my grief-free reaction might very well be seriously off-putting, it seemed better to make it public as soon as possible.

The *Times* story ran in late August, and nothing came back to me from the reading world to let me know what the public reaction might have been. My total absence from "social media" might have protected me, since I have no idea what, if anything, was said there! The book was published in early November, and I had a date to talk to an audience about my book later that month when I was slated to speak to the garden clubs of Somerset Hills and Morristown in Bedminster, New Jersey. I arrived as each of the clubs was finishing up its business meeting, after which a hundred or so women assembled in the auditorium of the Fiddler's Elbow Country Club to hear my speech.

I walked up front, explained that I was going to start off by reading from my new book, do a brief talk on how I had gotten committed to eating locally, and end with a slide show of the destruction and "extreme makeover" of my garden. And then I began my talk: I opened by saying that my book called *Growing, Older* had been prompted by the fact that when my husband died, following what I thought was a happy marriage of forty years, I discovered that I didn't miss him.

I don't know what I expected would happen. I think I anticipated that there might be a shifting of chairs in an uncomfortable silence, a whispering behind hands, and some sharply raised eyebrows. What I did not expect was that the entire roomful of women would burst out laughing. I was so taken aback that I took a step backward and began to laugh with them, realizing that I had struck an unexpected chord. Later I found myself thinking how lucky it was that there were no men in the room—although I'm not sure how I knew that would have made a difference. When I got home that night, I emailed a thoughtful male friend:

> Since I just got home from New Jersey doing a reading to a garden club there, I cannot resist telling you of this astonishing thing that happened. As I started my talk and told them I was going to read a bit from my book, I said a little about the book and what it was about and when I said that I discovered after my husband died that I didn't miss him, the entire room (of women) broke into unrestrained laughter.
>
> Make of that what you will. God knows it wasn't what I expected.

I am amused to report that this very thoughtful and sensitive man wrote back attributing the women's behavior to the fact that "people sometimes laugh when they are embarrassed and don't know how to react." These women were *not* embarrassed. And 102 of my books were sold.

Meanwhile, out in the literary world, the apparently more normal anguish of widowhood, which had been brought front and center both in print and on stage several years earlier by the brilliant Joan Didion, had been inflicted on another of our small stable of celebrated female authors. Joyce Carol Oates lost her husband of forty-seven years early in 2008 and in February, 2011, published *A Widow's Story: A Memoir*, presumably to "tap into," in the somewhat snarky words of the *Times*'s Janet Maslin, "the increasingly lucrative loss-of-spouse market that has thus far been dominated by Joan Didion's *The Year of Magical Thinking*." Maslin was referring, presumably, to the fact that the interim between Oates and Didion featured spouse-loss books by at least three other female authors.

However, in the same week that the *Times* reviewed Oates's grief story, they published an opinion piece called "Grief Unedited," that told a very different story about spousal loss. There has been some research, it turns out, on how people react after the death of a spouse. The major research has been done by a clinical psychologist at my own University, Dr. George Bonanno. Making use of data from a long-term study of older couples at the University of Michigan, Dr. Bonanno did follow-up interviews with one thousand of these individuals who had lost a spouse. In as little as six months, about 50 percent of the survivors showed little sign of grief—"contradicting the popular maxim of widowhood," the reporter observes, "that 'the second year is harder.'"

My second garden club reading, scheduled for Connecticut in late January, was canceled by snowy weather and did not take place until late February. And when I began my talk to this new group of women by reporting my discovery that I didn't miss my husband, exactly the same thing happened. The room broke up. It would appear that there are a lot of women out there who can imagine not missing their husbands. And wherever I have gone to speak about my book and acknowledged its surprising opening, women sidle up to me and say, looking me full in the eyes, "I need to read your book," or, having read it, take me aside and say, "I think my husband is a lot like yours." Why then was my story a solitary one in this spouse-loss market? Why is there nothing else out there that tells widows (or widowers as well, presumably) it's OK *not* to fall into profound grief when your mate dies?

There are some clues. The first is that toward the end of my spate of talks to women's garden clubs, I was asked to speak at a library in Connecticut—to what would be a mixed audience. I forecast to a friend who was planning to attend that this audience, which included men, would not laugh when I spoke of not missing my husband. And I was right, they didn't.

The second clue is that when George Bonanno's findings were first published in 2004, he encountered both professional disbelief and serious criticism that his sample was poorly chosen and didn't include the worst cases. People just didn't like his message, although later work confirmed it.

Finally, Joyce Carol Oates, who writes in her grief memoir of feeling "like one who has been slammed over the head with a sledgehammer," does not mention in her book published three years later that she was happily engaged to another man eleven months after her husband's death. So lack of prolonged grief seems to be not so much unusual as just unspeakable—and in a culture deeply devoted to myths, especially touching ones, very few widowed people seem to feel obliged or even able to publicly tell the truth.

I am happy to have done so though. Except for one woman who told her husband (who told me) that she would not read my book because I just didn't love my husband enough, I have not been punished for my honesty. Of course I don't know how many people out there are offended and haven't let me know, but I do know that I continue to get notes from women who thank me for helping them allow themselves to honestly experience their real feelings.

What They Don't Tell You

KATHRYN TEMPLE

In 2006, my husband died of an aggressive, always fatal, cancer, and suddenly in the space between one breath and the next, the one that did not come, he was gone, and I was transformed. I became a widow. But I was not alone. It suddenly seemed that everyone was a widow, as widows' memoirs now stocked the bookstores, and women, mostly in their fifties and older, began to mourn their lost husbands and lost lives by writing memoirs. It was a long time before I could read these memoirs: Joan Didion published her memoir in 2005, and I didn't read it until 2013. Joyce Carol Oates's *A Widow's Story* came out in 2011, and although I had seen bits and pieces of it, it too has been a recent read. When Sheryl Sandberg's account came out last year I read a short section, but her focus on resilience seemed too pat to me, too much like my mother's favorite children's book, *The Little Engine That Could*. Having surfed the web recently looking for other examples, I can see that almost every possible plot has been recounted; we have heard from the widow who discovers later that she was never married, the widow of a serviceman, the widow of a suicide, the widow of the son of an internationally known Ponzi scheme artist—all of these women have written memoirs. Surely husbands have died and widows have mourned throughout history, so why this sudden explosion of memoir writing?

These memoirs often begin with shocked, trembling descriptions of the loved one's death. If other widows are like me, we read those accounts gingerly, aslant, trying not to look too hard, to feel too much. After the shock, comes the adjustment, the chronicling of almost indescribable feelings of loss, of loneliness and despair, eventually of the immense effort it takes to deal with the lost one's affairs, to sort out the old medical bills, still clamoring for payment despite the patient's death, to remember to do the chores that he always used to do. Sometimes there's advice and hope: this too will pass as widows find new lives, find themselves, realize that their marriages were as constraining as they were enlivening. What these memoirs leave implicit though is that they mark widows themselves as memorials to the deceased. In past eras, widows were marked by widows' weeds, wearing black, or in some cultures all white. Now we mark our status, meaning our loss, meaning our lost spouses, not by wearing black, but by writing memoirs.

What memoirs tell us is that widows are survivors, and survivors always represent those they have survived. These widows have left behind deceased husbands, in the hospital bed, the funeral home, the grave, while moving forward, continuing to live, and, in doing so, becoming survivors. They don't call themselves survivors: in common usage, survivors have become today's heroes, while all that widows have survived is the death of someone close to them. For widows, there's nothing heroic about being a survivor. They have not climbed out of a burning plane or "fought" cancer or endured captivity as a prisoner of war. Their survivor status arises instead from the simple fact of continuing to live after their husbands have died. But like all survivors, simply by surviving they have taken on a survivor's responsibility, and with it, survivor's guilt. Few memoirs say much about this: they don't mention that in addition to grief, loss, loneliness, greater workloads, the raising of children who are also suffering a loss, that in addition to all of this, they may feel much like the sole survivor of a plane crash. Why am I here? they'll ask to empty rooms, why him and not me?

After my husband's death, this feeling haunted me, perhaps made worse because we had worked in the same place, done similar tasks, loved our daughter equally, been fortunate to have a beautiful house surrounded by parkland. At least for me, to continue to work at my university, teach my students, raise my daughter, and do so comfortably in the house we had both worked to buy seemed cosmically unfair, a terrible joke played on both of us: on him, because he had loved life so much, and on me, because I had never imagined how devastating the grief could be or how undeserved the good fortune. Over time, I realized that despite grief counseling, widow support groups, online forums, and even this flood of widow's memoirs, there's a lot they tell you about grief, but not much about being a survivor.

One big thing they don't tell you is that for a while at least you might feel as if you don't have a life, not in the popular "get a life" sense, but as if you actually are not alive. This thought used to come to me unbidden, when driving home from the hospital on the day he died, while at the grocery store, while talking to my daughter, while sitting in traffic. "My life is over now, I'm dead," I would think, oddly illogical given that I was a breathing, driving, talking, above all, living human body. I would remind myself that I was lucky. My daughter was and is smart, beautiful, and healthy; my financial resources stable; my job secure; my house a refuge. I was young(ish), in good health, with warm and supportive colleagues and friends. Of course, I had a life! But this thought came over and over again, for years, although less often as time passed. A counselor explained that I was overidentified with my husband, that those years of caregiving had bound my life to his, but that never felt quite right. Instead, I think that for me to have a life would have diminished my value as a memorial. If I could continue on without him, then what was the meaning of his life? As a survivor who felt dead, who repeatedly had to remind myself that I had survived, that I did have a life, I could continue to represent him, to serve as a memorial to his death, to refuse to forget what he had suffered and what his life had meant.

What else don't they tell you? They don't tell you much about the survivor's posttraumatic shock. For me, this took the form of visions I seem to have stolen from old apocalyptic movies. In *Terminator 2*, Sarah Connor dreams of playgrounds where happy children are suddenly reduced to charred corpses. She ends up confined in a mental ward. For me, it wasn't fire, but cancer. After two years in hospitals, on cancer wards, in caregiver chatrooms, cancer dominated my imagination. Everyone I met had a cancer story, no one seemed immune. Walking through Manhattan one day, I could see only walking corpses. I convinced myself that these hardy New Yorkers speed-walking down Broadway on a spring day were riddled with disease. I could see and feel what they couldn't: visible, protruding tumors; open, bleeding sores; weakness; peripheral neuropathy; mental confusion; that metallic taste in the mouth. That they seemed oblivious to their woes made no difference to me: I knew that denial could be very strong. Why, I thought, do they bother to go to work, eat lunch, buy a newspaper, or do anything at all? I felt I should warn them, but there were so many and, in any case, it was hopeless and I was tired. This was not something, by the way, that I shared with my grief counselor.

No, there's a lot they don't tell you. They might say you should rest, but they don't tell you how very, very tired you are going to be. It's hard work being a survivor, always representing the other, one foot on the brake, one weakly reaching for the accelerator since even though you feel dead, life must go on. Sometimes I felt so tired I could hardly move. A few hours at work was the most I could endure. A full day unthinkable. One day at work during a meeting to discuss how to replace my husband as writing director, I was so tired that I put my head down on the conference table. Every evening for over a year I would come home with my daughter and we would lie on the couch and watch TV in a stupor. It was all I could do to go to the grocery store. It was all I could do to fold a load of laundry. Removing that old shovel someone left in the backyard was impossible; it sat there accusingly for over a year. Much, much later, a beloved colleague told me sadly, "you just seemed so tired, so exhausted." I was. It is exhausting to be a survivor.

Do widow's memoirs tell you as much as they should about anger? You're not supposed to be angry really, no matter the "stages of grief." You're supposed to be sad and then supposed to "get over it." If you're angry, you're supposed to be angry at God or fate or cancer, not at the deceased. Forgive me then if at the first back-to-school night in my daughter's high school, I was furious, so angry at my husband that I could hardly hear the teachers or find the rooms I was supposed to go to. How dare he leave me alone to deal with this huge school and these indifferent teachers with their rules and admonitions. Didn't he realize he needed to be there? He was the one who did well in school, he was the one who knew how to bully back when needed, he would have dazzled them with the right questions and the right answers. I was also oddly angry every week when I took the trash out. Week after week I wondered where that anger came from until one day I realized: until he got sick, he always took the trash out. He wasn't sick anymore. When was he going to do his chores?

Another thing they don't tell you is that your husband's death offers no immunity. Others are going to die too, and soon. My parents had made it to my husband's funeral, but they were in their late seventies when he died. They failed quickly, my mother to dementia, my father to Parkinson's. They died in their early eighties, first my father, then a month later, my mother. When my younger brother died of a drug overdose the following month, it seemed less like a coincidence and more like a pattern. My best friend was diagnosed with ovarian cancer. Another close friend's husband died of lung cancer. A third, diagnosed with prostate cancer. A fourth had a heart attack. Most middle-aged people experience this; we turn a page of the calendar over and it starts to seem like everyone's dying. Once widowed though, it feels different, more personal, more pointed. Why did the phone seem to ring almost every day with bad news? Was it something about me? Why had I been spared? Visiting my debilitated father in the nursing home, watching while my mother stopped eating, doing their laundry, making sure they were safe, choosing a hospice, deciding not to tube feed my mother, not to treat my father for pneumonia—I did these tasks even as I came undone, as the work of mourning increased, and the guilt of survivorship grew. Five years after my husband's death, I was more tired than ever, even as everyone else was getting tired—of my sadness, of my excuses, of accommodating me at work. They were as tired of me as I was of myself.

Widows' memoirs also don't tell you that when you're not tired, you will be anxious. For years after my husband's death, I could not leave town without imagining my daughter dead. Yet I desperately needed to leave town because I had to move, do something, go somewhere, do anything other than lie on the couch and rest my head on conference tables. In cabs on the way to the airport, only five minutes from the house, I would begin to cry as I fought the urge to call her. She is fine, she is fine, she is fine, I would tell myself. When I wasn't traveling, I was just as anxious. One day I became convinced that my daughter had died at her middle school. I called the school and persuaded the guidance counselor to check on her. Is she in class? Is she all right? If he thought I was crazy, he was right. Later that night my daughter looked at me and said, "Oh, Mom. Really?" Years go by and she is in college, the college where I teach, so although she lives in the dorms, she's never far from home. Weeks into it, she doesn't respond to a text. I text again, text again, call, call again, no answer. Finally, she calls back, "Mom, I was in the shower. It was a ten-minute shower. How long did you wait before that second text?" This is the problem with being a survivor: I understand the structure of survival; I know that others had to die so I could live; I know that anyone could die, anytime, anywhere.

Maybe one reason I was so tired for so long is that I dreamed about him for years. These dreams were terribly sad: in the dreams, he was alive, precancer. He had not been diagnosed, and still had so much to endure, the hospitalizations, the chemo with its devastating debilitating effects, the daily losses of strength and mentally acuity, then the pain, and the struggle to breathe at the end. In every dream, I already know this because, while he is "precancer" in my dreams, I am always "post" and know how this is going to play out. At last one day I dream that he is "postcancer," still alive, and for some reason residing in an old hotel out near the Eastern Shore. In the dream, I am rather irritated. If he's recovered, why hasn't he come home? "What are you doing?" I ask, "why are you here? You need to be with us." He tells me he's comfortable now, he doesn't plan to leave this new home. Pleasant, but distant, he's unmoved by my pleas. That dream was the last one in which he appeared alive; I do not dream about him anymore.

Maybe I'll be judged because I do not dream about him anymore. Widows' memoirs might tell you you'll be judged, but they don't always explain why. As a survivor, I was the living memorial to my husband and thus was scrutinized for my feelings: was I sad enough, distraught, too distraught? Was I taking too long to "get over it"? Or was I getting over it too soon? The first time this happened was the night of his death when a colleague called me at 3 A.M. to commiserate. I was in a deep sleep: it was the first night in two years that I could sleep without worrying about an emergency: all the emergencies were over now. My colleague could not keep the shock out of his voice: "What? I thought you would be awake and need to talk." When I didn't want a viewing, I was judged. When I chose cremation, I was judged. When I wrote about our experiences with hospice, I was judged ("You sound angry," a friend said). I was judged about what I did say and about what I didn't say. Much later, another "friend" invited me to tea so we could "chat." It turned out she wanted to lecture me about dating. If I was out with someone, I must not be sad enough, I must not have cared enough about my husband, maybe I'm even glad he's dead, maybe I don't even care about my daughter. I was told that I should "think about her and her needs." Of course, I did think about her needs. All the time. I thought she needed a father. I thought we needed people in our lives.

Widows' memoirs don't tell you that every joy will be mixed. When my daughter graduated from high school, I was thrilled. She had done so well! But this came with profound sadness because he should have been there to see her. When she got into the college where I teach, it was also the one he had taught at for over twenty-five years, the one his benefit paid for. And he was not there to be thrilled, to talk with her about it in that calm, measured way he had of taking her seriously. He won't be there either when she graduates, won't be on the stage to see her get her diploma, won't be the first to hear when she gets her first job. And she does want him there. No matter that twelve years have gone by, she wants to see her father standing by me on the graduation stage. We will visit his on-campus memorial that day and thus feel his presence, but that's not enough. That's why the only thing she wants for graduation is a memoir of her father. No checks, no travel abroad, no class ring. She wants to know what he was like, what we were like together as a family, what he would have thought about her now. And it's my job as a survivor to get her what she wants, to dig through boxes of memorabilia, to find the video of the memorial service and finally watch it with her, to help her through this because he cannot. In short, it is my task now, twelve years later, long after "widowed" has disappeared from my Facebook page, years into a new relationship, most of the time quite happy, hardly ever tired anymore, to do what a survivor is supposed to do, and once again serve as that living memorial. I will buy a lovely scrapbook, will visit our storage unit and take out the bins full of memories. I will sort through the photos and diaries and jewelry, through all the remnants of a sixteen-year marriage. I will now—lovingly, painstakingly, and with care—write a widow's memoir.

Nine Things Resilient People Do after Losing a Spouse or Partner

CARRIE L. WEST

Widowhood was one of those challenges I always thought I would deal with when I was old and tastefully gray. By then, of course, I would have accumulated enough life experience and wisdom to handle it gracefully, I would look fabulous in black, and I would have reached most if not all of my life goals. I mean, I expected to live through the loss of older family members, but I was not prepared to become a widow at the end of my twenty-eighth year. And then, on the night before my twenty-ninth birthday, my husband, Shane, died suddenly in a car accident. I spent the next several months trying to come to grips with my new reality and erratically alternating between "I wish everyone would stop telling me what to do!" and "Would somebody please tell me what to do?" I immediately resented the prescriptive and predictable stages described by Elizabeth Kubler-Ross while I was also freaked out by the untethered feeling I got when I was told grief is an individual experience and there was no right or wrong way to grieve. Sometimes no rules are as bad as too many rules.

While I didn't want to be judged by others for how I was grieving, I also did not know how to judge my own progress. I wanted to know if I was on the right track or if I had completely gone off the rails. I know now how important it is to avoid the hang-up of what is "normal" because there is no normal, but I at least wanted some guidelines. The idea of "no right or wrong way" actually felt a lot like "best of luck to you." Eventually, I found good resources and connected with some really smart and caring people who had been here before me. I wanted to know what I could learn from other widows who have been through a similar experience, and what it is that resilient people do after they lose the person they thought they would spend the rest of their life with.

For decades, researchers have investigated why some individuals adapt better than others after a traumatic experience. Resilience is about how individuals bounce back or adapt after encountering major life setbacks like loss. How we grieve is affected by our unique personalities, life experiences, relationships, and expectations as well as a combination of protective factors, such as available social support, and risk factors like financial trouble.*

Regardless of the protective and risk factors each individual possesses, taking an active and process-based approach to resilience is empowering. Recently, research in this area has transitioned from a deficit approach to this process-based approach. Deficit models of resilience focused mostly on children and on existing protective or risk factors, such as having had parents divorce or having had mental health issues, while a process-based approach seeks to identify the behaviors and skills that lead to more resilient responses.

Because resilience has gotten a lot of attention in research and self-help books, one of the more difficult things to deal with as a grieving adult is the overload of advice available. It is not always good advice, and it can be difficult to know what is worthwhile and what is just noise. When my husband died, many well-meaning friends and family brought me books about grief. One problem was that I had two small boys, a one-year-old and a six-year-old, and as a newly single parent and grieving spouse, my scarcest resources were time, and mental and emotional energy. I wasn't even sure which book I should start with, and when I did try to read, the books were full of conflicting advice or useless platitudes instead of practical help. I felt so discouraged because my investment of precious time and energy left me with more questions than answers. Eventually those books just started piling up on the shelf in the office, and as the stack grew taller, so did my feelings of failure.

* O. Friborg, O. Hjemdal, J. H. Rosenvinge, and M. Martinussen, "A New Rating Scale for Adult Resilience: What Are the Central Protective Resources behind Healthy Adjustment?" *International Journal of Methods in Psychiatric Research*, 12, no. 65 (2003). Retrieved from http://onlinelibrary.wiley.com/journal/10.1002/(ISSN)1557-0657.

The strength of a process-based approach, or active approach to resilience, is that it foregrounds the power each person has to change how loss ultimately affects them, regardless of their life circumstances before their loss. In this way resilience is something you do rather than something that you are. When we look at doing resilience rather than being resilient, we can focus on strategies that can be learned through instruction and practice, and see our resilience as a work in progress.

So, what do the most resilient people do after the loss of their spouse or partner? I've spent years reading and studying grief and resilience, and I've asked some of the widows I most admire for their input. Here are nine ways to be resilient.

1. Resilient people find ways to honor their deceased spouse and the life they had.* Honoring my past was one of the most difficult things for me to do as a young widow because so many of the more traditional practices did not feel authentic for me. Even just the identity of widow was difficult to embrace. Should I wear black? For how long? Do I keep my wedding ring on? When do I take it off? What do I call my in-laws now? How often am I supposed to visit the cemetery? If I publicly memorialized my late husband I discovered I was inviting conversation and judgment about my actions and my personal life that I didn't want. Also, I didn't need these big formal rituals to remember my late husband, because there was no way I was going to forget about him. I was surrounded every second by our life, our furniture, his clothes, and our kids. As a widow, it makes people uncomfortable if you're spending too much time thinking about or talking about your late spouse because they would really like you to move on. However, it also makes them really uncomfortable if they don't think you're talking about your late spouse enough. It can be really confusing.

Regardless, decorating his grave or wearing black didn't hold any meaning for me, and as a widow in my twenties, it was really difficult to find any role models. I was at a loss about how I should honor my past without making me or everyone else uncomfortable. It wasn't until more than ten years later that I attended my first Camp Widow and saw there were other ways to honor my past life that felt more natural. Camp Widow is a weekend of peer-based support for widowed people, and one event at each camp is a message release.

* L. E. Bryant, "Ritual (In)activity in Postbereaved Stepfamilies," in *The Family Communication Sourcebook*, ed. L. H. Turner and R. West (Thousand Oaks, CA: Sage Publications, 2006), 281–293.

I asked Michele Neff Hernandez, the founder and executive director of Soaring Spirits International and of Camp Widow, her ideas about honoring the past and here is what she said:

> It is about finding positive ways to stay connected to your loved one, while allowing yourself room in your life and your heart for a different type of life than the one you were living. That is what the message releases are about, staying connected while also allowing space to move forward.

The message releases are always different but include a meaningful and visual way to honor something about one's deceased spouse or partner. Some examples of past message releases are written remembrances sent out into the ocean, set afloat on a pond, or tossed into a fire. There was also a nighttime display of candles with spoken remembrances placed into a whole-group memorial spelling out "Long Live Love," and one where participants wrote a word on a rock describing a type of support they could give to other widows and placing it in a tabletop "river," and then each person also took a rock describing support that they needed. These different types of rituals helped me understand that there are so many ways to honor the past without being defined by it.

2. **In addition to honoring** the past, living fully in the moment is another ability of resilient widowed people. Sadness is naturally a part of life when your spouse dies. However, it is important to be able to take breaks from dealing with the sadness and loss. I remember feeling relief and then guilt after Shane's funeral. I got caught up in the moment and laughed out loud when one of Shane's cousins told a funny story about him as a kid, and I remember looking around to see who noticed. Giving the present too much focus can lead to thinking short term or ignoring consequences; however, one of the lessons of grief is that every day is precious, and that means embracing the moments of joy and happiness of the present without feeling guilty.

3. **Resilient people** are able to have hope for and make plans for a happy future.* They are able to set and work toward big and small goals. Setting and accomplishing small goals can be among the easiest first steps to take toward resilience, and each goal that is checked off the list adds to feelings of accomplishment and self-confidence.

* A. D. Ong, L. M. Edwards, and C. S. Bergman, "Hope as a Source of Resilience in Later Adulthood," *Personality and Individual Differences*, 41 (2006): 1263–1273.

4. In addition to balancing the past, present, and future is the ability to reconcile them all with each other because sometimes the past and present identities and realities overlap, or they don't know where they fit.* I remember going into my first appointment at a therapist's office. I felt I should talk to a professional and do my grief work, and so I dutifully made and showed up for my first appointment. I only made it as far as the waiting room before I met my first challenge. The form I was given asked me to mark my marital status, and among the options were married, single, and widowed. I remember just staring at it and thinking, "so I just choose one? Or is this a 'mark all that apply' situation?" I hadn't even made it in to start the real work and I already felt like a failure.

5. Next, resilient people identify and focus on the positive things in their lives.† Researchers found that 42 percent of bereaved persons reported feelings of positive change in their lives after bereavement.‡ Acknowledging personal growth and positive results from loss does not diminish the grief and sadness, but recognizes that there may be some things that are better about who you are or what your life looks like after loss than before. One positive result of surviving loss might be the confidence you get from surviving one of your worst fears. Old problems may not look so big anymore, and new problems may feel more manageable. After all, you have already been tested, and you passed.

6. Resilient people are proactive about taking care of themselves, mentally and physically.§ One of the things I read and was repeatedly warned about was the increased chances of depression, anxiety, illness, and things like car accidents after bereavement. It is understandable to stress-eat or feel overwhelmed after the loss of a spouse or partner, and, of course, depression and anxiety, at least temporarily, can be expected after losing your spouse. But resilient people are proactive about their health and well-being. This is how self-care looked for one widow:

> I was about six months out. Past some of the acute and disabling grief. I was working full time, trying to figure out what to do with

* N. C. Taylor and W. D. Robinson, "The Lived Experience of Young Widows and Widowers," *American Journal of Family Therapy*, 44, no. 2 (2016): 67–79.

† Y. Dutton and S. Zisook, "Adaptation to Bereavement," *Death Studies*, 29 (2005): 877–903. Retrieved from http://www.tandf.co.uk/journals/tf/07481187.html.

‡ S. R. Shuchter and S. Zisook, "The Course of Normal Grief," in *Handbook of Bereavement: Theory, Research, and Intervention*, ed. M. S. Stroebe, W. Stroebe, R. O. Hansson (New York: Cambridge University Press, 1993), 23–43.

§ J. Cacciatore and M. Flint, "ATTEND: Toward a Mindfulness-Based Bereavement Care Model," *Death Studies*, 36, no. 1 (2012): 61–82.

dead animals under the house, a mouse in the kitchen and finding a solution to "where are my keys!" I decided I needed to get away for a short time and be taken care of and in a place no one knew me and no one asking the dreaded question "really, how are you?"

I chose to go on a five-day cruise where I didn't have to fly—I had my brother take me and pick me up. I spent five days being taken care of, meals, bed made and bathroom cleaned, and a whole ship full of interesting people to talk to and never once telling anyone I was a widow. I painted, walked the decks, watched movies and the sunrise and sunset, swam and had a couple of massages. I never left the ship, just took care of me.

I came back with a skip in my step and a new appreciation for the person I was becoming without my husband, Gary. I just took care of me.—Lynn Campbell

According to Kath McCormack, founder and former executive director of The Healing Center and widow, "I believe self-care is the single most important tool that we have to assist us in building resilience." For example, in addition to eating well and engaging in physical activity, she suggests incorporating a daily ritual into your routine, explaining that these practices have long-lasting benefits. "I have worked with thousands of widowed men and women and I see that the skills they used to survive continue to support them as they emerge from their grief and learn to live fully with passion and purpose." These daily practices can be anything that resonates with you, but might include journaling, choosing an inspirational quote or meditation card, or depositing a daily note about one thing you are grateful for into a gratitude bowl. This last suggestion also incorporates the resilient practice of finding and acknowledging positive things in life.

7. **Practicing good self-care** means resilient people are able to reach out to help others. The next thing resilient widowed people do is to ask for help when they need it and to help others.* Both can create meaning after loss as well as help to establish and maintain important social connections. Usually family and friends genuinely want to help but sometimes fumble their offer or their attempts to be supportive because they just aren't sure how. Helping others is a way of giving support but being able to articulate needs, and giving others the opportunity to help can

* P. M. Buzzanell, "Resilience: Talking, Resisting, and Imagining New Normalcies into Being," *Journal of Communication*, 60 (2010): 1–14. doi:10.1111/j.1460-2466.2009.01469.x.

enhance the benefits of the social support process for both parties. Lynn describes another example of how asking for support played a dual role in her experience:

> I have had a wonderful lifetime of being independent and not asking for much help. So, now I needed to get assistance with the three acres of land my husband had loved. I really didn't want to ask a stranger, although I did find great relief hiring the plumber and the pest control guy! I asked my son-in-law who was busy with his service in the Navy to help and he was so excited to be able to drive the tractor. I actually laughed, who would have thought that in asking for help I was giving someone the chance to do something they thought was fun. Hmmmm.
>
> It was a wonderful time spent together enjoying each other's company and getting to know him better. It turns out that this created some great memories as he died suddenly one year after my husband, leaving my daughter with two children, a very young widow. It was my daughter, Mary, who found Soaring Spirits International, a loving and caring group of widows and widowers from all over the world that we both still find loving and caring after many years.

8. Resilient people don't feel like they need to find a new partner, but are open to the idea of finding love again. Dana explains what that looks like for her:

> I think from my experience in order to be ready and open for new love, I had to be really good with just me. Not being Joe's wife or widow, but just being Dana. I wanted to be able to take care of myself and enjoy life on my own. I didn't see myself for a very long time even thinking of the idea that I would want a new love, so being alone was fine and great and not lonely at all. I enjoyed being able to travel whenever and whereever I wanted. I did a lot of just being good on my own before opening my heart and mind to the idea of love. When I did, it was amazing. I knew all the long and hard work was worth it because I could love wholeheartedly, not feel a pinch of guilt, look towards a future with someone other than my late husband. My new partner adds to my life; he doesn't complete it. It was already completed by me. My words of wisdom are take however long you need to be your best friend and really love your life, and then when new love comes, it's easy to see.

9. A final practice of resilient people is finding or creating meaning because of their loss, and the process of meaning finding and positive reframing can lead to personal growth after loss.* I was frustrated with the resources I found as a young widow. I kept thinking somebody must have a checklist of things I should be doing to help myself and my sons. What I didn't find in support groups and self-help books, I did find in a family communication course at my local university. Even though the course wasn't specific to grieving, I could easily take theories about relationships, support, and effective communication and apply them to my everyday interactions. I realized I could help develop better resources for young widowed people, and one way I have created meaning from my loss is by taking what I've learned and helping widowed people who are just starting to figure out what comes next. These exact practices or examples of resilience might not look the same or work the same for everyone, but finding ways to make them your own can give you a place to start.

* R. G. Tedeschi, C. L. Park, and L. G. Calhoun, *Posttraumatic Growth: Positive Transformations in the Aftermath of Crisis* (Mahwah, NJ: Lawrence Erlbaum Associates Publishers, 1998).

Make Lemonade?!

LISE MENN

Lemon

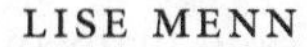

The nastiest, sourest, lemon life ever gave me to suck was losing my husband, Bill. I certainly had no idea of making lemonade of that lemon. If anyone had been such a fool as to tell me to "make lemonade," I would probably have stared at them and burst into tears. How could I possibly want to "do something" with my overpowering misery? I felt like I was the standing half of a tree that had just been ripped in two by lightning, unable to do anything but look down in shock at my fallen half, and wail. I was just trying to make it from one day to the next. It used up all the energy I had, barely holding up my end at work and slowly dealing with the legal and financial stuff I was suddenly supposed to take care of.

When I did start, nine months later, to make a little poetry about how I felt, it was for myself. When I eventually found myself writing poems every couple of days, it was still for myself, and for the psychiatrist who was nursing me through my depression. Having him read my week's poems at the beginning of each session was a compressed and effective way to let him

With many thanks to Bruce Kawin, Jacqueline Lapidus, and Nan Bauer-Maglin for insightful editing and helpful corrections and suggestions, and to Will Van Derveer for recommending journaling to me in the first place.

know where my mind and heart had been since he last saw me. We could get down to work after that.

But after enough time—several years—I showed some of my writing about grief to a few writer friends, and found that they thought it was publishable stuff. My widowed college classmate Jacqueline Lapidus, a professional editor, suggested that we start with the best of the poetry we each had written, and see if we could collect enough poetry and short poetic prose from other widows to make a book. I had no idea how to go about such things, but Jacqueline did. She placed notices in lists and periodicals like *Poets & Writers Magazine*, and, amazingly, we got over four hundred submissions. We accepted about half of them, and requested reprint rights to an additional handful of fine pieces by well-known contemporary widowed authors. We ended up with *The Widows' Handbook*; seven and a half years after my Bill died of a brain tumor, it turned out that the sorrow of almost ninety widows had become lemonade after all.*

Since then, Jacqueline and I and many of the other contributors to *The Widows' Handbook* have been trying to get the word about it out to people we think the book could help: widows, widowers, their families, their friends, and people who work professionally with those of us who have lost beloved partners.

This piece is about how both making that book and having made it turned out to be helpful to the people who made it: Jacqueline, myself, and quite a few of the other contributors. If you are toying with the idea of sharing your own experience of bereavement with someone who might be helped by it, or if you are thinking of encouraging someone else to share her or his story, keep reading. Yes, each person's story is different, just as each person and each marriage is unique; and yes, none of us can really convey the full truth of our emotions with words (or any other form of art). But many of us can still create work that touches our fellow mourners (and their friends, families, and therapists)—work that helps them feel that even though they are unique, and even though they are agonizingly lonely, they are not alone.

You probably know that books by widows about being a widow or losing your life partner have started to appear fairly regularly, starting with Joan Didion's *The Year of Magical Thinking* (2005);† a more recent narrative, by one of our contributors, is Roselee Blooston's *Dying in Dubai* (2016).‡

* Jacqueline Lapidus and Lise Menn, *The Widows' Handbook* (Kent, OH: Kent State University Press, 2014); see also www.widowshandbookanthology.com.

† Joan Didion, *The Year of Magical Thinking* (New York: Vintage International, 2005).

‡ Roselee Blooston, *Dying in Dubai* (Baltimore: Apprentice House Press, Loyola University Maryland, 2016).

But why would you write about being a widow, if other women are already doing it? And how could you hope to bring your writing to the public if you don't have the clout of Joan Didion, Sheryl Sandberg, or Mary Oliver, and can't imagine spending years trying to find a publisher or an agent? Especially if you've never written anything beyond what you had to do for school or work?

And how can writing about grief and loneliness be good for you? Or be worth reading? You have probably run into advice like "Think about something else." "Try to get over it." "Don't dwell on it." If you write about your loss and what it's done to you, aren't you dwelling on it? Isn't that the wrong thing to do? Before we go any further: no, it is the *right* thing to do. Repressing sadness does not make it go away and does not help you heal. If someone tells you otherwise, get away from them.

Mercifully, other people may tell you that keeping a journal of how you are feeling is a good thing to do. If they haven't, you're hearing it here, and it's true. So let's junk that useless "Don't dwell on it" advice right now. When your grief is fresh, you are dwelling *in* it, whether or not you are consciously dwelling *on* it at some moment. Grief will not go away because you are thinking about something else; it's always there, waiting for you to come home to it. Time is indeed your friend, as a bereaved mother told me; unbelievable as it seems, you will feel better some day, although life will never be the same as it was. But when your heart is broken, then regardless of whatever face you may need to wear for the world, it's worse than useless to pretend to yourself that you are not miserable. Of course you're miserable, and you have a right to be. You—and, if possible, the people around you—need to acknowledge that grief and grieving are real. After all, if you could put your grief aside voluntarily, it would feel like denying that you ever really loved your husband, your partner, your wife. Frankly, I think people tell widows and widowers to "get over it" because our grief makes *them* uncomfortable. Well, too bad for them. You will heal, eventually—but not to please others. You will heal (although you will carry a great scar) because, amazingly, it's in the nature of hearts to heal, given enough time.

Journaling—Writing Just for Yourself (Lemon Juice)

So, especially if you're still near drowning in your depression, your apathy, your exhaustion, and your feeling of numbness or of being unable to do anything but grieve, get a modest-sized spiral-bound notebook or some other kind of book with blank lined pages (better than a computer, I think; it's easy to carry, it doesn't need charging, and you don't have to "save" your files). But if you'd rather use your tablet or smart phone, just do it. Spend some time each day writing about anything that comes to mind, and when your grief comes up, don't push it down. If your grief is still the biggest thing in your life, summoning up the energy to write (or to do more than keep putting one foot in front of the other) probably feels impossible. Yet, once you start writing, the words will probably come, at their own pace—sometimes slowly, maybe sometimes even faster than you can get them on paper.

I started journaling because my shrink recommended it. I was dubious, but willing to try almost anything, so I got in bed at night and wrote until I was tired—about how I was feeling, what I was remembering, what I did that day; trivial or deep, it didn't seem to matter. Often, I wrote as if I were talking to Bill. Getting my thoughts out on paper also helped to keep my mind from going in circles; after I wrote for five, ten, even forty-five minutes, I could sleep. And I desperately needed sleep.

Keep your journal private, so that you can write whatever comes into your heart without considering what anyone else might think. What you write in a journal is not lemonade; call it lemon juice. Just get your real feelings onto paper—through drawing, if images come to you more easily than words. If you can't write sentences, just write words and phrases. Rant, rage; repeat a phrase until you're exhausted. It may become unintelligible even to yourself in the future, but don't worry about that. This kind of writing is what the beat writers of the '60s called "first thought, best thought": it may seem random, with the ideas connected (at most) by associations. But don't edit it; think of journaling to heal yourself as pure self-expression, and forget about whether or not it could also function as communication to others. Editing for them may come later.

Your journal is to help you and the people who are trying to help you—your therapist or therapy group, if you have one. But it's not for them to read; it's for you. Keeping a private, uncensored journal will not only release your thoughts and emotions, it will help you understand what your real feelings are. That in turn will make it easier for you to think about them and talk about them to yourself and to helpful others. It's as sour as lemon juice, but making it is worthwhile. And you may come to like the taste.

Crafted Writing—Writing for Others (Making Lemonade)

Crafting poetry and clear prose is very different from writing in a private journal: words that are capable of communicating your thoughts and feelings to other people can't generally be "first thought." Remember the saying "genius is 90 percent perspiration and 10 percent inspiration"? Most writers don't imagine themselves to be geniuses, but we all need to perspire a bit. You'll need to discover a good form for your crafted writing: does it work better as poetry, poetic prose, or plainer expository prose? If it's poetry, can you use a classic form (sonnet, ballad, blank verse, renga, haiku) without sounding strained and strange? Even free verse has rhythm; it's not just prose cut into lines. Prose, too, needs to be crafted with care; paragraphs need to be coherent and in an order that makes sense, sentence lengths need to be comfortable, and your vocabulary needs to be appropriate for your audience. Making your writing clear and graceful takes thinking, editing, and revising, so do it on a computer or tablet if you can. And when you're done with a draft, make sure that it still expresses your ideas accurately, your feelings simply and honestly. Your crafted writing is your lemonade. And it may very well be something that other people will want to read—a bracing drink for strength on a difficult day.

Is creating this sort of crafted writing therapeutic for you? Well, it won't lessen the intensity of your emotions any more than journaling will, but while you are re-creating and polishing, your attention shifts to the work: to being accurate and precise, to crystallizing, ordering, and clarifying. Like any worthwhile art or craft, making writing capable of communicating your ideas, emotions, or memories absorbs you. And as you already know, absorption in a task gives you a respite from pain, even though that respite may be partial and temporary.

Also, your finished writing is likely to become something that you can be pleased with, and pleased with yourself about. These emotions may have become rare since you lost your spouse. After all, if you had a good relationship, your significant other often praised you for things you said or did, as well as for how you looked. Losing that feeling of positive support is something people don't talk about much, even to other bereaved people (it sounds so self-centered, right?). But it can be one of the most devastating problems of being left single, because it subtly and continually undermines you.

The Uses of Lemonade—How Writing, Editing, and Speaking Out Have Helped

First, there was the help from the absorption in crafting my own poems, rewriting and polishing them so that they would really be poetry and make sense to readers instead of being just a jumbled torrent of words. Then I became absorbed in the editorial work for *The Widows' Handbook*, helping Jacqueline select the two hundred-odd poems and prose pieces, making spreadsheets to keep track of everything, corresponding with the authors whose work we accepted, and all the tasks involved in finding a publisher for the book and then working with the one that finally accepted our manuscript.

Second, there was the sense of companionship, even if at a distance, as I recognized in the work of many of the other women feelings much like my own. It was good to feel less alone. Yet no two of us seemed to feel exactly the same; our griefs were as individual as our loves had been. That was consoling too: each of us was still herself; we were not a homogeneous group of just "widows," any more than we had been just "wives" or "lovers."

Third, I realized that other women faced serious real-world problems that I had never thought about. One of our contributors was about nine months pregnant when her husband died, another had two young children, still another found herself running a working farm all on her own. The adult children of another widow moved back in with her, bringing their own problems. And many of the contributors faced sudden social isolation in a world of couples, plus infuriatingly insensitive comments from "friends."

Fourth, I discovered that I had written about a few things that no one else had: about wanting to hide from daylight as the days grew longer; about trying to figure out why my blues would suddenly come back full force long after I had started to feel better; about facing the strange problem, when I started dating the man who has become my partner, of where to put Bill's picture and the other mementos that I treasured. When I started to share my own writing with other widows and with grief counselors, their reactions told me that I'd hit some nails on the head. That gave me a comforting sense of accomplishment.

Finally, I got a very important validation from reading all those pieces by our contributors: seeing that for other people as well as for me, the idea of recovery as going through distinct stages of grief that are supposedly the same for everyone is only a rough approximation of what really happens. My psychotherapist had fortunately already told me that the five "stages" that Kubler-Ross proposed (for the experience of dying, not for mourning) were not reliable, but it was a real help to see the evidence for it in the writings of our widowed contributors. Their work pulsed with many different moods, only some of which corresponded to one of the proposed stages of denial, anger, bargaining, depression, and acceptance. But as sensitive grief professionals know, not everyone feels all of these, or feels them in that order. When I was widowed, I experienced only some of them, and they were often mixed together. I might lurch back and forth among several of them on the same roller coaster day.

Should you speak out about your painful personal experiences or your enduring sadness? Maybe it's not the right thing for you. But before you reject the idea entirely, think about what public honesty can do for people. As we all know, people who have had to suppress their deep beliefs or their very identities because they belong to a stigmatized minority—gays, atheists, Jews and Muslims in Christian-majority countries, Christians and Jews in Muslim-majority countries, people of color in white-dominated societies, and so on—have often felt great encouragement and relief at finally hearing the voices of others who have had similar experiences.

If you live in a social setting where widows seem to be inconvenient "others"—if you have felt invisible or even rejected once the condolences stopped—then writing about it is of potential value to everyone else who finds herself in the same boat. If you have the opposite problem, being besieged by matchmakers or suitors when all you want is to be left to mourn in peace and quiet (as can happen, especially to financially secure widows and widowers), there are people out there who are going through the same bombardment. They might feel understood and validated, and even become brave enough to demand that everyone shut up and back off, if you can write something that resonates with their own experience.

The Practicalities of Starting to Write

If you want to write about the experience of widowhood but didn't keep a journal, start journaling now and see where it takes you. What have you learned about life since the person you loved died? You can write about the ways that the person you loved, still love, and may always love comes up in your thoughts. Are you an expert in something, or did you become one after you were left single? Write about your job, your cats, your children—about anything and everything that has changed since your partner died. How people treat you; the tension between wanting to be faithful to the memory of your partner and wanting to be part of the world of the living; finding out that someone you thought cared for you was only after your money; finding that your partner had a hidden life. Or about what people say that comforts you or infuriates you. Or about what you no longer want to do and how you got stuck with doing it in the first place. Or about what you would like to try if you could pull yourself together—move to another state? travel? study law or theology or automobile repair?

Writing that comes out of your experience of loss doesn't have to be only about your feelings. Are you now in a position to write about widowhood and taxes? Home repairs? Job hunting? Scammers and fortune hunters? Dealing with inheritance, insurance, and government bureaucracy? Adjusting to living on a third of your former income? Life with tenants, cohousing? Getting back into dating? Starting or running a business? Changes in family interactions after the person you loved died?

Writing about such topics from your new vantage point (no matter how unwanted that vantage point was) might be helpful for other people. If you join a widows/widowers group in your town or online, you can get a sense of the dozens of issues that you might be able to address—if not now, then perhaps a year or two from now.

Poetry or prose? Try your hand at whatever seems to be more natural for you. If you have no writing experience that seems relevant, read work by other people for a while. Find out what words, poems, or stories that you read affect your emotions or your desire for action or increase your understanding and compassion, and what words or phrases stay in your head. The stories that stay with you are probably related to important incidents in your own life, and those might well be the ones you can write about. The words or phrases from other writers that stay with you may be the keys that will help you unlock your own story. (Keep notes on who wrote them and where you found them; if you use someone else's phrase in your work, you'll need to use quotation marks and give credit where it's due.) Don't start by planning to write a whole book, unless you're quite sure of yourself—work up to it. You can publish single poems and short prose pieces in online journals, and you can always try submitting them to well-known print magazines. Some people get a lot of support from having a coauthor/coeditor, or from belonging to a writing group. It's like having an exercise buddy—they help you keep at it.

How will you know whether your writing is good enough to submit to a publisher or to a magazine? That dilemma confronts almost every writer, not just the novice. Look for writing support groups, writing workshops, writer friends, or grief support groups that happen to have writers in them. Ask them to read your work and comment on what they liked and what they didn't really get. Also, read other materials published by your target online or hard copy publication, and if you don't like them or don't feel an emotional response to them, look for a different place or a different way to publish. But (like other people, except for established best-selling authors) be prepared for the reality of publication: rejection, rejection, rejection. (*The Widows' Handbook* was finally accepted by the fifteenth or sixteenth publisher that we approached.) If you get to the point where you can't take another form letter or even a polite note explaining why the publisher or editor doesn't want your work, consider "vanity" presses: people who will print your book if you pay them to do it. It may seem degrading to pay for print when you hoped to be paid for it, but a browse through, say, Wikipedia's entries on authors will show you that some major works of literature first appeared as vanity publications or electronic publications because no "real" publishing house wanted them.

Books need to be publicized in order to sell, and most publishers will put forth only the most cursory effort, unless you are already famous. You'll have to do it yourself, through readings, talking to local bookstores, sending free copies to book reviewers at local papers, and whatever else your ingenuity suggests. Whether it's worth that much work depends on what you consider sufficient payback for your labors. Publishing your book is very unlikely to make you rich, and not all that likely to break even. Don't quit your day job. However, if you can afford to work for intangible rewards, the answer is probably yes, publishing and publicizing are worth the effort.

If your work has been written to help other people, and they can't find out that it exists because it's getting little or no publicity, how is it going to help them? Jacqueline and I have been facing this problem since *The Widows' Handbook* came out. We got a few reviews in newspapers (all positive) and a lot on Amazon, but not enough to sell many copies. Fortunately, because our work was an anthology, we were able to organize group as well as solo readings of the poems at bookstores, libraries, senior centers, and so on. And quite a few of the contributors also organized readings on their own in cities around the United States. More recently, I've been collaborating with a widowed friend, a licensed social worker with many years of experience working in hospice settings, to give readings and lead discussions at senior living facilities. I've also reached out to hospice boards, some of which have been welcoming. It takes more energy than one might think, but the experience of sharing intense writing with other widows and widowers and hearing their stories in return has been very, very rewarding.

Writing about grief—what it's like, how one lives with the unbearable—is, despite everything, lemonade: it's doing something potentially useful with that overwhelming bleakness that has sucked the joy out of your life. And in the work of crafting and sharing prose or poetry that someone else can respond to or use for practical purposes, you will almost certainly feel that your own life has more meaning and still has rewards worth living for.

Part V

Epilogue

The Missing Vow

CHRISTINE SILVERSTEIN

I write here for widows like me, who have endured a sudden vanishing, but also for husbands and wives, whose arms can wrap around each other, still.

Yes, he's going to die.

No, these are not the words of some medical professional with downcast eyes and a whispered tone informing you that your husband's illness is no longer treatable. These words you might be able to comprehend on some level. Instead these are my words, my widow's admonition. My broken heart is here to tell you something your heart knows. The man sitting at the kitchen table across from you, the man who snored last night, again, the one you chose to spend your life with, your whole life—this man is going to die. And there is a fifty-fifty chance you will be the one left standing.

I woke up at 6:00 A.M. on a sunny June day an ordinary woman and crawled back onto my bed at midnight an expert on the subject of sudden death. What transpired in those eighteen hours blew the doors off my otherwise unremarkable day. One thing I discovered in the following days and months is the merciless truth that nobody wants to talk about death—not now, not ever. Nobody is ready for death.

Death isn't something we have on our list. We know it exists, but it's more like a third world country with a name we can't pronounce, a climate that seems unfriendly, and a location that is nearly impossible to imagine finding. So we don't give it a second thought. It's off our radar. It doesn't appeal to us. It's not worth the research. It's too hard to pack for. So we don't go there, in so many words. And we never talk about it as a destination either. If it comes up in conversation, we change the subject because we'd rather visit anyplace else on the planet.

There are two kinds of death. One comes at the end of a time continuum. It comes after enduring some named illness or, if you are one of the blessed, at a ripe old age in a quiet diminishment. The other kind of death is the sudden kind. It comes in a fiery crash or at the end of a deadly weapon. It comes in a seizing of the heart, a mysterious sleep apnea, or some aneurysm deep within. At my not-so-ripe age of forty-nine, I was catapulted by the sudden kind, and I am here to tell you that it's time to get packing. When my adorable and healthy husband's heart seized right before my eyes I never saw it coming.

There I was, on a sunny morning in October, standing in the parlor of a country inn on a remote New England island ready to say my "I do's." I took my sweet time to marry at forty-one, and everything about that day was about this man I had chosen to love until "death do us part." Funny I don't remember dwelling on the word "death" that day. I remember the dress, the dancing, glimpses between us across the room, the small cadre of family and close friends. I remember the light, the food, the moody silences, and the uproarious laughter. I remember the word "husband." It gave me a thrill to say it, to think it. This one person would be my intimate, my confidant, my challenge, and my contentment. This husband would hold my hand, hold my heart, hold down the fort and never forsake me until death. "Not until death" we promise.

But do we? Do we hear that word "death" in our repeats after me? Do we give death a second thought? Was there a fleeting image lurking in the back of my mind that day of two fragile souls crawling into bed together, holding hands and never waking up? Surely we'll be the lucky ones.

Of all the promises we make on that day there is one we don't make. We don't promise to make death an honorary member of our family. We don't promise to be ready for death. Why would we?

And there I was seven years later on a sunny morning in June standing alone in the ER, my hands resting on my beautiful husband's collar bones as if to conjure a levitation, surrounded by needles, tubes, ripped clothing, and life-saving paraphernalia—signs of the unspeakable strewn in every corner. He woke up at 8 A.M. that day, healthy and in a happy mood, and was dead by 11. Somewhere in my subconscious were those indecipherable words again, long forgotten, "till death do us part."

People my age are dropping like flies. Husbands and wives are heading off to work, finishing rounds of golf, shoveling driveways, kissing goodnight in dark bedrooms, and never uttering another word to each other again. My story is no different. What is different is my preoccupation with all the other widows in the world—past, present, and future.

It didn't happen right away. In the first days and weeks after I walked out of that emergency room, I dove into the bottomless quarry of my broken heart. Days were surreal, filled with an absurd juxtaposition of life's routines and a parade of well-meaning friends and family.

It was the nights that were real. Night after night I awoke in a cold sweat wondering where he was and when he'd be back. I eventually turned these panic attacks into an archaeological dig. I pulled out anything and everything I could find, any clue that could answer the question, "Where is Robert?" I opened every drawer, searched each coat pocket, paged through the calendar on his desk to see what lay ahead, what appointment was written there for him to keep. I sat for hours in the middle of the night in our basement, opening boxes carefully stored away for some future use. I became the forensic detective meticulously combing through the evidence of this life, our life.

It was during one of these subterranean sessions deep in the night between sobs that I came across the box where my notorious sentimentality was lurking. I think I started this habit as a child, but still, as a grown woman, I had stowed away those cards. You know the ones I mean. Those greeting cards exchanged over the years for birthdays, anniversaries, or just because. Guilty as charged, I kept them for no good reason. Or so I thought. As I held each card between my fingers, rubbing the pen marks he had made there, reading the words that he had written just to me, as I uncovered the artifacts that would soothe and torment me, my obsession with planning for death took hold. As I studied the picture on the front of one card of an older, white-haired couple, dressed to the nines, dancing alone on the bow of a ship, I knew what was coming. I opened it first to see the date and then Robert's handwriting, bold and exuberant on the paper. "My dearest love, this is us in thirty years. Be my Valentine. Love, R." Three months later he was gone.

That's when the yearning hit me. Where is the letter that I need to read? Where is the letter from him that says "Dear wife, life might not be long enough for us so this is the moment of our secret pact"? I rummaged through every other box, every nook and cranny of our home. There was no letter. There was no pact. These words were not in our solemn vows: "for richer, for poorer, in sickness and in health, for now and for after I'm gone, I will leave you a scavenger hunt for the soul. I vow to leave behind a feast for the emotional starvation that will come when I am gone."

I wish I had known to make this vow on that giddy day in that lacy dress. I wish we had made ourselves ready for death, not by writing a will or buying insurance, but by leaving love letters in the underwear drawer. Not by articulating medical directives or burial wishes, but by leaving evidence of our deepest devotion in our own words, our own voice.

These boxes in our basement held relics of our lives, markers of milestones and contingencies. Graduations, promotions, relocations, and vacations, all commemorated. Even the vestige of an argument and reconciliation was there in so many heartfelt words. But what about the big enchilada? What about the mother of all milestones? There is no holiday for death. We only go toe to toe with death when it happens. Where is the letter that I need to read? I can write it now. I can write it to console myself with words meant for his eyes only.

Dear Robert,

I know you are in the next room. I can hear you shuffling papers. I think you are working on our taxes of all things. This is an ordinary day and we are living our lives in our way. If only you knew how extraordinary our simple life is to me. Don't cringe but I am writing this letter to you to tell you what it means to me to hear you there, to have and to hold you, until this moment. You are reading this letter because I am gone. . . .

ACKNOWLEDGMENTS

How do I turn this summer around? Is there still an I and no You
in this problemed space? Can I sort through our shared
moments without your orange pants, your color-blinded
syllogisms, and hull of near-end turbulence?

—**Prageeta Sharma**, excerpt from "Seattle Sun"

Many, many people contributed to the making of this book, especially in suggesting writers or sources for locating widows. Because there are too many people to thank in name, I will mention only a very few: Alice Radosh and Dorothy Rowdy Brewick for leading me to websites, blogs, and books; Stephanie Golden for publicity ideas; several people for recruiting writers: Robert Bence, Priscilla Derven, Jacqueline Lapidus, Ian Marshall, Betsey McGee, Lise Menn, Susan O'Sullivan, Donna Perry, Barbara Rubin, Ashley Schneider, and Florence Tager; Daniel E. Hood, Avis Lang, and Yael Ravin for editing—Yael went over draft after draft of the introduction; and Kimberly Guinta, editorial director, for her critical yet supportive eye; Jasper Chang, editorial assistant, for carefully shepherding the manuscript at each step of the process; and the entire staff at Rutgers University Press for their hard work. My friends and family and bereavement group were crucial for getting me through the first year. Quin's daily text messages kept me smiling.

ARTIST'S STATEMENT

TARA SABHARWAL

In 2011, following my husband's sudden and unexpected death, I found myself in deep shock and unable to paint. Moving color on canvas opened the burning wound, and it was unbearable. However, running away did not work either, so I resolved to blind leap into the work, trusting that I would survive the fire and eventually touch ground. I did. An old set of etchings drew me in, a set I had begun and discarded just before my husband got sick. Here I could enter the past, touch the calm energy of that time, and bring it to merge with the present turbulence. This set led to an opening up and soon I was back at work. A recurrent image in the work of this period is liquids (because I literally felt like a sieve of leaking fluid) and included rain, rivers, tears, and waves. Rain became an apt metaphor for grief—an uncontrollable outpouring, but also a cleansing and rejuvenating catalyst for renewal. Gradually painting led to acceptance and healing.

Editor's note: Tara Sabharwal's artwork, "Eye Triptych," appears at the beginning of Parts II, III, and IV in this book and on the cover.

NOTES ON CONTRIBUTORS

NAN BAUER-MAGLIN worked at City University of New York for almost forty years before she retired. She now volunteers for Girls Write Now and The Whitney Museum. She edited *Cut Loose: (Mostly) Older Women Talk about the End of (Mostly) Long-Term Relationships* and coedited *Women and Stepfamilies: Voices of Anger and Love*; *"Bad Girls/Good Girls": Women, Sex, and Power in the Nineties*; *Women Confronting Retirement: A Nontraditional Guide*; *Final Acts: Death, Dying and the Choices We Make*; and *Staging Women's Lives in Academia: Gendered Life Stages in Language and Literature Workplaces.*

ANNE BERNAYS is the author of ten novels, and a coauthor of two books of nonfiction and has been publishing her work since 1962. She has contributed hundreds of essays, book reviews, and op-ed pieces in national magazines and newspapers and has taught writing for almost fifty years. Bernays was born and raised in New York City, moved to Cambridge, Massachusetts, in 1959, and is the mother of three daughters, six grandchildren, and two great grandchildren.

SUSANNE BRAHAM is presently retired from full-time editing for Columbia University. She earned her BA in comparative literature at Columbia and a master's in theater education from Emerson College. She was an elementary school librarian while her son and daughter (now thirty-seven and thirty-one) attended New York City public schools, and began writing poetry as catharsis following her husband's sudden death in 2002. Writing and sharing her poetry and photography have become addictive antidotes to grief and hearing loss.

EDIE BUTLER was born in Philadelphia and has lived the last four decades in New Hampshire. She attended the University of Pennsylvania and received degrees from the University of New Hampshire. Active in the peace and justice movements, Edie was a health worker at the New Hampshire Feminist Health Center (now the Concord Feminist Health Center) and a writer/editor of *WomenWise*, the Center's quarterly publication. Butler teaches English classes at her local community college, writes, and has two grown daughters and a grandson.

ALICE DERRY has published eight volumes of poetry. Her most recent book, *Hunger*, was released by MoonPath Press in 2018. Derry has written essays on Lisel Mueller and Raymond Carver. "Paying Attention" appeared in *ISLE: Interdisciplinary Studies in Literature and Environment*. She taught English and German for forty years, the majority at Peninsula College in Port Angeles, Washington, where she codirected the Foothills Writers Series. She lives and works on Washington's Olympic Peninsula.

PENELOPE DUGAN recently retired from Stockton University. She has published a number of personal essays and articles. She divides her time between New Jersey and the Adirondack mountains.

KELLI DUNHAM is the author of seven books, including *Freak of Nurture* (2105), a collection of tragic-comic humorous essays, and the best-selling *Boys Body Book*, now in its fourth edition. Dunham is cofounder and producer of Queer Memoir, NYC's longest-running LGBT storytelling event, and the founder of Organ Recital: A Festival of Stories about Bodies, Health & Healthcare. She is currently working on a book tentatively titled *Shit This Hurts: An Irreverent Guide to Grief.*

MELANIE K. FINNEY is a professor and the chair of the Department of Communication and Theatre at DePauw University in Greencastle, Indiana. She earned her PhD at the University of Iowa. Her research has focused on communicating social support, coping with grief and loss, and how individuals and communities create meaning from significant loss. Her most recent project is a photographic narrative about her search for healing after the loss of her husband by discovering the thin places of Ireland.

KATHLEEN FORDYCE is a professional writer living in New York. She has been weaving her love of words and storytelling for fourteen years as a reporter for the *Miami Herald*, as an official writer for the CEO of a public health system, and now as a freelancer writing articles and helping companies communicate to wide-reaching audiences. She is also working on her first novel.

DORIS FRIEDENSOHN was married to the painter Elias Friedensohn for almost twenty-five years. Since his death in 1991, she has often written about his work. Professor emerita of women's studies at New Jersey City University, she was awarded the American Studies Association's Bode Pearson (lifetime achievement) Prize (2003). Among her recent publications are *Eating as I Go: Scenes from America and Abroad* (2006) and *Cooking for Change: Tales from a Food Service Training Academy* (2011).

MERLE FROSCHL has more than thirty-five years of experience in education and publishing, developing innovative programs and materials that foster equality of opportunity for students regardless of gender, race/ethnicity, disability, or level of family income. She is the author and coauthor of numerous articles, chapters, and books, including *Supporting Boys' Learning: Strategies for Teacher Practice, PreK-Grade 3*, published by Teachers College Press. Recently Froschl has "found her voice" as a singer.

ALICE GOODE-ELMAN is a professor emerita at Suffolk County Community College. She is the editor of the *Complete Poems of Richard Elman (1955–1997)* (Junction Press, 2017).

JOAN GUSSOW is the Mary Swartz Rose Professor Emerita and former chair of the Columbia University Teachers College, Nutrition Education Program. She lives, writes, and grows organic vegetables on the west bank of the Hudson River. Long retired, she still coteaches her nutritional ecology course at TC every fall. She is the author, coauthor, or editor of five books, including *The Feeding Web* (1978), *This Organic Life* (2001), and her latest, *Growing, Older: A Chronicle of Death, Life and Vegetables* (2010).

PARVIN HAJIZADEH, an Iranian American, was born in Iran in 1961. All of her education was in Iran, where she majored in Farsi literature. She left Iran in 1985 for Germany and got married the following year. In 1990 they immigrated to the United States; she has been living in Williamstown, Massachusetts, since then. She has two sons and currently works at the Williams College Museum of Art. Her interests include painting, gardening, and traveling.

MICHELE NEFF HERNANDEZ is the founding president and executive director of Soaring Spirits International, a nonprofit organization providing peer support programming for widowed people worldwide, as well as a speaker, writer, and community activist. She has received local, state, and national recognition for her work in founding Soaring Spirits. Michele resides in Simi Valley, California, with her three amazing kids, and one very Australian husband.

ANDREA HIRSHMAN is a collaborative attorney and family mediator in New York City. She owns her boutique law firm, which helps people get married and divorced outside of court. She has two grown sons who are at the center of her heart. Her late husband and best friend for forty years bragged that he shared birthdays (11/20) with Duane Allman, an idol of his. Were he alive, he would brag that he also shared deathdays (10/29) with Duane.

DEBORAH E. KAPLAN has published *Jane Austen among Women* and articles on Restoration comedies, hoarding, professional issues, and, most recently, Anne Frank. She retired from George Mason University's English Department in 2016.

JEAN Y. LEUNG is a native New Yorker. She received her master's degree in journalism from New York University and her bachelor's from State University of New York at Stony Brook. Early in her career she wrote reviews and bios but settled into editing while crafting a family. As life matured, she returned to writing, beginning with memoir pieces and expanding into playwriting. Her latest project, a musical about life with dialysis, was inspired by her husband's travails.

PATRICIA LIFE completed a PhD in English literature at the University of Ottawa in 2014 at the age of sixty. Her academic research has focused on stories of the nursing home in Canadian literature and on the age ideologies that inform them. This work began as a result of having provided support to her mother throughout her experience with dementia.

MAGGIE MADAGAME was born in St. Ignace, Michigan. She graduated from Michigan State University in 1979 and taught elementary school until retirement in 2012. She lives in Ann Arbor and volunteers for the University of Michigan Medicine Comprehensive Gender Services Program. She writes a blog (staingIasseyes@blogspot.com), poetry, and songs. She creates art from found pieces from Great Lakes snorkeling. She is an avid reader and traveler. She sings with Our Own Thing Chorale.

MAXINE MARSHALL was born in Trinidad in 1970 and moved to the United States in 1988 with her parents and brother. She met her husband in 1993, and it is his niece whom she has interviewed for this important work. She is honored to be able to tell Raquel's story. She attended Rutgers University for both undergraduate and graduate studies. She lives in New Jersey with her husband Ian and son Joshua.

BARBARA E. MARWELL is a PhD psychologist and directed several innovative programs in the Madison, Wisconsin, schools as well as maintaining a private practice. Since moving to New York, she has had leadership roles in two volunteer organizations, on the board of The Transition Network and currently as chair of the Curriculum Committee at The New School's Institute for Retired Professionals.

DEBBY MAYER writes the blog 2becomes1: widowhood for the rest of us, at debbymayer.blogspot.com. She is the author of a memoir, *Riptides & Solaces Unforeseen*, and a novel, *Sisters*. Her short stories have been published in the *New Yorker* and numerous literary magazines. She has received two grants from the New York Foundation for the Arts, one in fiction, for a short story, and one in creative nonfiction, for an excerpt from *Riptides*.

MOLLY MCENENY has had a long career in law firm management. She currently serves as chief human resources officer for a large national firm, a broad role providing strategic advice on human resources and business issues as well as talent development and succession planning. A lifelong New Yorker, Molly is a frequent theatergoer and sings with an adult choral group.

LISE MENN is a coeditor of and contributor to the anthology *The Widows' Handbook* and is professor emerita of linguistics at the University of Colorado/Boulder. Born in Philadelphia in 1941, she graduated from Swarthmore College and earned her PhD at the University of Illinois. Her second husband, linguist William Bright, died in 2006; her poems about grief started coming about a year later. Menn has several children and grandchildren. Her partner, writer Bruce F. Kawin, has warmly encouraged her writing.

JOAN MICHELSON's publications include new poetry collections, *The Family Kitchen* (2018), *Landing Stage* (2017), *Bloomvale Home* (2016), and *Toward the Heliopause* (2011). The earlier book is a response to her husband's death. These poems engage with loss and how we live with it. Her writing has been published in British Council and Arts Council "New Writing" anthologies and in books and magazines in the United States and United Kingdom. Originally from New England, Joan lives in London, England.

TRACY MILCENDEAU has enjoyed a career in the pharmaceutical industry since earning her BS at the University of Notre Dame and master of jurisprudence in health law from Widener University School of Law. Widowed in 2014, she became passionate about pursuing, without hesitation, all that makes life happy. Recently remarried, she and her husband are building a home in a Delaware beach town, where they can be found biking, beaching, or spending time with their pets.

P. C. MOOREHEAD, after several years as a widow, remarried and lives now in rural Wisconsin. She appreciates the beauty and quiet of the woods and the inspirational environment that they provide for her writing and reflection. Nature images permeate her poetry and prose, which have been published in many anthologies, journals, and other publications.

ALICE RADOSH is a research psychologist with a doctorate in neuropsychology. Since retiring she has coedited a book on women and retirement and published a series of articles on sexual bereavement and disenfranchised grief. She lives in Woodstock, New York, where she enjoys hiking, canoeing, and splitting wood.

RAQUEL RAMKHELAWAN was born in London, United Kingdom, in 1967. She met her husband and soulmate, David, at University College London Hospitals in 1992, where they both worked in the Information

Management and Technology Department and where she is still employed. She still lives in London with their three wonderful, loving, and supportive children, Alisha, Rekhelan, Kylan, and her fourteen-month-old granddaughter, Faith.

RONI SHERMAN RAMOS graduated from nursing school in 1968 and worked in health care for the next thirty-five years. In 1970 Roni and Paul Ramos founded the Betances Health Center, where she worked in nutrition and reproductive health education. Roni's last health care experience was working for 1199SEIU in nursing education reform. A parallel interest in fine art grew from childhood and continues today. As a member of the Atlantic Gallery, a cooperative art gallery in Chelsea, she exhibits her abstract paintings annually.

SONIA JAFFE ROBBINS is a writer, teacher, activist—and by trade a copy editor. She has been managing editor of *Publishers Weekly* and deputy managing editor of the *Village Voice* and has written for both publications. Publications include chapters in *Red Diapers: Growing Up on the Communist Left* and *The Women's Guide to the Wired World*. She is a cofounder of the Network of East-West Women, which supports women activists in eastern Europe.

TARA SABHARWAL was born in India and is based in the United States. She graduated from Baroda University and Royal College of Art, London. Her career spans thirty-eight years, with forty-four solo shows in the United States, the United Kingdom, Japan, Germany, and India. Her awards include the British Council, Myles Meehan, Durham Cathedral, Joan Mitchell, and Gottlieb, among others. Her work is in the collection of the Victoria and Albert, DLI, British and Peabody Essex Museums; the Library of Congress; and the New York Public library.

ELLEN SCHRECKER is a retired professor of history at Yeshiva University. She has written extensively about the Cold War red scare and American universities. Among her books are *No Ivory Tower: McCarthyism and the Universities* (1986), *Many Are the Crimes: McCarthyism in America* (1998), and *The Lost Soul of Higher Education: Corporatization, the Assault on Academic Freedom, and the End of the University* (2010). She is currently writing about professors and politics in the 1960s and '70s.

MIMI SCHWARTZ is the author of several books, including *Thoughts from a Queen-Sized Bed* (2003); *Good Neighbors, Bad Times: Echoes of My Father's German Village* (2008); *Writing True: The Art and Craft of Creative Nonfiction* (2013); and *When History Is Personal* (2018). Her essays have appeared in *Agni*, *Creative Nonfiction*, *The Writer*, *Calyx*, *Prairie Schooner*, *Tikkun*, the *New York Times*, the *Missouri Review*, among others, and nine were Notables in Best American Essays. She is professor emerita in writing at Richard Stockton University.

NANCY SHAMBAN has worked in the field of mental health for her entire career. She started as a psychiatric nurse and went on to get degrees in psychology and psychoanalysis. Most of her work life was as a psychotherapist and administrator. From 2009 to 2011 she went to Sri Lanka to volunteer as a mental health professional to help improve the mental health systems of the country. Since returning to the United States Nancy has spent her time saying yes!

CHRISTINE SILVERSTEIN spent the first half of her career in diverse entrepreneurial pursuits, including property design and development. Her interests morphed when she married late in life and moved with her new husband, a police sergeant, to Nantucket Island. She became founding executive director of the nonprofit Sustainable Nantucket. Her favorite accomplishments were the establishment of a farmer's market and an affordable housing program. She now lives in Magnolia, Massachusetts, dabbling in political activism and writing.

HEATHER SLAWECKI grew up in Bucks County, Pennsylvania, and graduated from Widener University in 1989 with a BA in English. She worked for ad agencies in the Philadelphia area before advancing as a senior writer and vice president at Bank of America in Wilmington, Delaware. Heather was married to her first husband in 1994 and widowed in 1996. She remarried in 2001 and lives with her husband and fifteen-year-old daughter in North Wilmington, Delaware.

KATHRYN TEMPLE is an associate professor at Georgetown University and the author of *Scandal Nation* and *Loving Justice* (2002). Her work focuses on the intersection between affect and institutional structures. Her next book, about the relationship between narratives of survival and neoliberalism, is entitled *Culture of Survival*.

LAUREN VANETT is on the faculty at UC Berkeley's Osher Life Long Learning Institute, where she teaches courses in positive psychology and the wisdom of grief. She spent thirty years at San Francisco State University designing, directing, and teaching in extended education programs for the community. A dancer, hiker, and artist, Lauren lives with her partner, Rod, in San Rafael, California, where, among many other things, they are quietly creating a cloak of their own.

ELISA CLARKE WADHAM was born in Australia and educated in Canberra, New York, Sydney, and Mexico City. She has had two careers, one in book publishing and the other as an interior designer, which she has run for the past twenty-five years. She has always meant to be a writer, a passion that is now her primary focus, along with an ever-extending family spread around the world. She divides her time between Sydney and New York.

CARRIE L. WEST is an assistant professor of communication studies at Schreiner University and the director of research for the Soaring Spirits Resilience Center at Schreiner University. Dr. West earned her PhD in communication from the University of Denver, with a focus on interpersonal and family communication. Her research and teaching include an emphasis in interpersonal, family, and health communication. Dr. West's research is primarily focused on helping widowed people construct resilience.

NANCY H. WOMACK is a retired educator from the North Carolina Community College System. However, she is anything but "retired." Active in various organizations, she maintains a busy schedule but still finds time to do the things she loves: reading, writing, gardening, entertaining, playing the viola, decorating her home, and, most of all, spending time with family. Her work has appeared in several journals and anthologies, including *The Widows' Handbook* and *Kakalak*.